International Macroeconomics

A.J. Makin

FINANCIAL TIMES
Prentice Hall

An imprint of Pearson Education

Harlow, England · London · New York · Reading, Massachusetts · San Francisco
Toronto · Don Mills, Ontario · Sydney · Tokyo · Singapore · Hong Kong · Seoul
Taipei · Cape Town · Madrid · Mexico City · Amsterdam · Munich · Paris · Milan

Pearson Education Limited
Edinburgh Gate
Harlow
Essex CM20 2JE

and Associated Companies throughout the world

Visit us on the World Wide Web at:
www.pearsoned.co.uk

First published by Pearson Education Australia Pty. Limited under the title
Open Economy Macroeconomics © Pearson Education Australia Ltd, 1996.

First published in the United Kingdom 2002

ISBN-10: 0-582-36992-4
ISBN-13: 978-0-582-36992-4

British Library Cataloguing-in-Publication Data
A catalogue record for this book is available from the British Library

Library of Congress Cataloging-in-Publication Data

10 9 8 7 6 5 4 3 2
09 08 07 06

Typeset in 10/12pt Palatino by 35
Produced by Pearson Education Asia Pte Ltd
Printed in Malaysia

Contents

List of figures

List of tables

Preface

In view of the attention given to macroeconomic issues by national and international policymakers and the world media, it seems that the need for a high level of economic literacy has never been greater. There are now many textbooks which aim to improve that literacy, although I have found that the gap between what students are presently taught and what applied macroeconomists working in the real world actually need to know remains quite wide. This book aims to narrow that gap.

What standard macroeconomics textbooks most obviously under-emphasise is the meaning and significance of the globalisation of goods, services and asset markets, and the role that international factors such as exchange rates, competitiveness, exports, imports, the terms of trade, current account deficits, world interest rates, capital flows, external debt and foreign investment play in influencing the behaviour of individual economies. In contrast, this book stresses international influences on the macroeconomy from start to finish.

Another understated facet of textbook macroeconomics and international finance is the meaning and significance of economic data itself. As many applied macroeconomists working for firms or government will tell you, much of their time is spent poring over the latest statistics to discern trends in economy-wide behaviour. For this reason, this book covers macro-economic measurement issues in some depth.

It then develops the theory using mainly graphical techniques, beginning with basic stand-alone models of exchange rates and the external accounts through to more advanced models of open economy behaviour that examine the interactions between asset markets, interest rates and exchange rates.

At the same time, the book contains what is still considered the core of modern international macroeconomics. This includes for instance, the IS-LM-BP and AD-AS frameworks, which are at the centre of theoretical analysis of the effects of fiscal and monetary policies. Finally, it considers the key determinants of long-run growth in open economies.

This text also introduces new material and methods for understanding important international macroeconomic relationships. For instance, new pedagogic tools are used to examine the linkages between international capital flows and interest rates, the choice of exchange rate versus money growth rules, aggregate production, spending and exchange rate determination, the process of economic growth and the significance of external account imbalances, foreign debt and national wealth.

Acknowledgements

I am grateful to Phil Lewis of the University of Canberra for contributing Chapter 10 'Wages, employment and unemployment', to Barbara Dempsey and Amy Lindley for typing the text and preparing the many figures and tables, and to Brenda Marshall for suggestions on style. Thanks also to Tina Cadle (Managing editor), Laura Prime (Editorial assistant), Jane Kerr (freelance), Caroline Ellerby (freelance) and the team at Pearson Education for their professionalism and patience.

A.J. Makin
May 2001

Abbreviations

AD–AS	aggregate demand–aggregate supply
apc	average propensity to consume
APEC	Asia-Pacific Economic Cooperation
ASEAN	Association of South East Asian Nations
BB	budget balance
BOP	balance of payments
C	consumption
CAB	current account balance
CAD	current account deficit
CPI	consumer price index
e	exchange rate, 'academic' definition
E	exchange rate, 'market' definition
FDI	foreign direct investment
FX	foreign exchange
G	government spending
G7	Group of Seven (USA, Japan, Germany, France, Italy, UK, Canada)
GATT	General Agreement on Tariffs and Trade
GDP	gross domestic product
GNP	gross national product
i, i*	domestic, foreign nominal interest rates
I	investment
X	exports
ILO	International Labour Organization
IMF	International Monetary Fund
IPD	implicit price deflator
IPI	import price index
K	capital stock
KAB	capital account balance
KAS	capital account surplus
L	labour force
LCH	life cycle hypothesis
LRAS	long-run aggregate supply
M	imports
M^s	money supply
Mercosur	Mercado Común del Sur (Southern Cone Common Market)
MFP	multi-factor productivity

MNC	multi-national corporation
MP_K	marginal product of capital
MP_L	marginal product of labour
mpc	marginal propensity to consume
NAFTA	North American Free Trade Agreement
NAIRU	non-accelerating inflation rate of employment
NFI	net foreign investment
NNP	net national product
OECD	Organization for Economic Cooperation and Development
ORA	official reserve assets
P, P*	national, foreign price levels
PDI	public debt interest
PIH	permanent income hypothesis
PPP	purchasing power parity
Q	financial wealth of residents
QTM	Quantity Theory of Money
R	the real exchange rate
RBC	real business cycle
RGDI	real gross domestic income
r, r*	domestic, foreign real interest rate
rp	interest risk premium
S	saving
SDR	Special Drawing Rights (IMF)
SNA	System of National Accounts (UN)
SRAS	short-run aggregate supply
T	multifactor productivity
TOT	terms of trade
TWI	trade weighted index
UIP	uncovered interest parity
UNCTAD	United Nations Conference on Trade and Development
W	nominal wages
WTO	World Trade Organization

1

The global economy

Households and firms in advanced economies are continuously transacting with foreigners, buying and selling goods and services. This could, for instance, mean purchasing Brazilian coffee or German cars, selling coal to Japan or wheat to Egypt, watching Hollywood movies, travelling to France or providing hotel accommodation to visiting Korean tourists. Not only are goods and services freely traded across country borders, but so too are financial and real assets. Citizens may purchase shares issued abroad by foreign companies, domestic companies may borrow foreign currency from foreign banks, and foreigners may purchase domestic real estate. All in all, economies have become far more integrated with the rest of the world, both through goods and services markets and through exchanges of financial assets. The nature of these linkages is depicted in Figure 1.1.

This integration has proceeded on the principle that increased trade in goods, services and assets confers overall income gains, an economic principle as old as economics itself.

Accordingly, it is no longer meaningful to study an economy's behaviour without regard to the strong linkages it has with the rest of the world. As

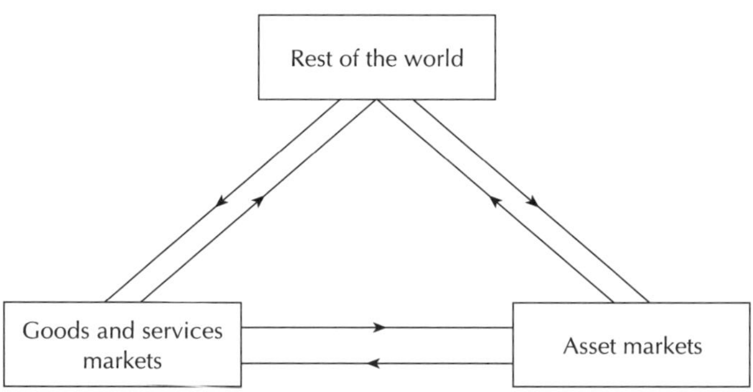

Figure 1.1 Domestic–international linkages.

economies become more integrated through international trade and investment flows, external factors have a larger impact on the economy and influence the transmission of domestic economic policies to the national economy. Because of the closer integration between domestic goods, services and assets markets and those markets in the rest of the world, the domestic business cycle can be strongly influenced by the cycle of economic activity in the nations with which it trades.

By definition, a *closed economy* is an economy which does not exchange goods, services or ownership of assets with other nations. An *open economy*, by contrast, exports and imports goods and services to and from other nations, as well as experiencing international financial inflows and outflows. Unfortunately, much of modern macroeconomics is still founded on the assumption that economies are closed, which is part of the Keynesian legacy to economic theory. Indeed, John Maynard Keynes' very influential work, *The General Theory of Employment, Interest and Money* (1936), often acknowledged as a seminal work which defined macroeconomics as a distinct field of economics, affords no role at all to international influences on the economy.

For instance, there are no exchange rates, exports, imports or international capital flows in the original Keynesian model of an advanced economy which has dominated most textbooks on macroeconomics over recent decades. Clearly, the original closed-economy Keynesian model has limited applicability under present circumstances. This book recognises that it is imperative to treat economies as open to international influences from the outset of any macroeconomic analysis.

International macroeconomics treats the nation as an economic unit within the global economy. This is an important area of study because the overall economic performance of an open economy directly or indirectly affects each and every resident of that economy. The fact that macroeconomic phenomena are usually major headline stories in the media is evidence that the general public is keen to learn about the latest developments in the economy. The rate of inflation, for instance, affects the purchasing power of one's income, whereas growth in employment and unemployment influences individuals' job prospects. So newspaper headlines such as 'Inflation on the rise' or 'Unemployment hits high of seven per cent' are quite common.

This book differs from other books on international macroeconomics, in so far as it maintains an emphasis on the international linkages between domestic and global goods, services and asset markets from start to finish. Only when the significance of an economy's international economic integration is recognised, is it sensible to pursue answers to the major economic questions confronting the nation. Such questions include: What is national competitiveness? What causes inflation? What causes unemployment? Is national saving too low? To what extent is inflation determined abroad? How may the government influence the domestic economy's business cycle using fiscal and monetary policy? What factors determine long-term prosperity? Why do some economies usually import more than they export? When is the level of foreign debt too high? Should foreign investment be allowed?

The main focus of this book is to provide answers (where they exist) to these questions using open-economy analysis. Before beginning such a task, however, it is necessary to gauge the causes and consequences of the globalisation of economies.

GLOBALISATION

Globalisation refers to the dynamic process driving the integration of national markets for goods, services and assets with markets elsewhere in the world. As the very term suggests, globalisation has been far-reaching geographically, affecting lifestyles, production, consumption and work practices in all areas of the world. It means that economies have become far more interdependent as a result of greatly increased flows of exports, imports and foreign investment. With increased international economic interdependence, production, spending and finance are less constrained by political borders.

The arguments for free international trade first espoused by the classical British economists Adam Smith, David Ricardo and John Stuart Mill still provide the strongest intellectual foundation for advocating globalisation. Meanwhile, there has been a long history of outright hostility toward high levels of foreign trade and investment, stretching back to Vladimir Lenin's misplaced view that foreign investment was inherently exploitative of host countries and represented the last stage of global capitalism.

We first gauge the extent of globalisation and its main causes – technological advance and market liberalisation policies implemented worldwide. Then we evaluate key issues in the ongoing debate about globalisation, before placing the phenomenon in historical context.

1. Extent and causes

The value of the sum of exports and imports, a measure of economic openness, has more than doubled over recent decades in advanced economies. In many developing economies, the pace of globalisation as reflected in growth in the volume of international trade in goods and services has been even faster (see Figure 1.2), accompanied by strong growth in foreign investment and cross-border financial flows.

Economists would argue that this rapid internationalisation helps to explain why many developing economies grew so quickly from the 1960s. Economies in South East Asia, for instance, such as Malaysia, Singapore and Thailand, have significantly higher proportions of trade to gross domestic product (GDP) ratios than many Organization for Economic Cooperation and Development (OECD) economies.

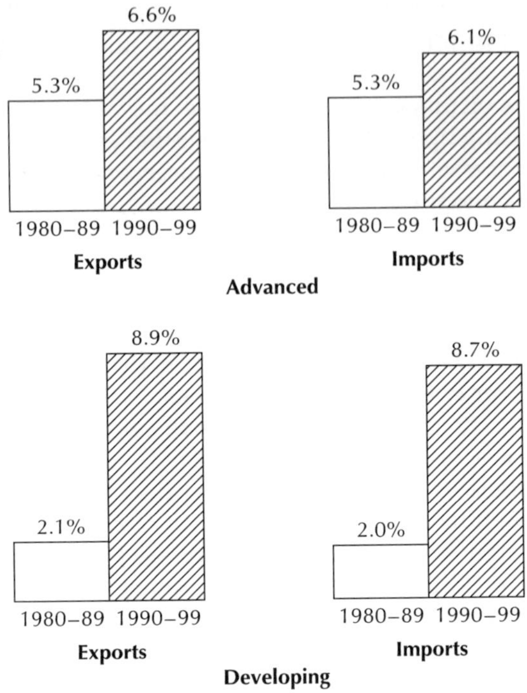

Figure 1.2 Volume of world trade, advanced and developing economies. (**Source** Data calculated from International Monetary Fund, *World Economic Outlook*, May 1999.)

The two fundamental causes of globalisation have been leaps in technology and the liberalisation of markets for goods, services and finance. Technological advance has revolutionised communication via facsimile, email and the internet, shrinking the natural barriers of time and distance. Real computer processing costs have fallen by an average of 30 per cent per annum over recent decades and the cost of communicating has also been dramatically reduced (*The Economist*, 1997). For instance, the real cost of phoning New York from anywhere in Australia is a tiny fraction of what it was decades ago.

In addition, numerous United Nations related institutions established after the Second World War when political internationalism reached its zenith have fostered globalisation. For instance, under the auspices of the World Trade Organization (WTO), and its predecessor body, the General Agreement on Tariffs and Trade (GATT), many governments around the world have actively promoted freer international trade in goods and services over recent decades, though not without serious disagreements along the way. Large regional trading groupings, such as the Association of South East Asian Nations (ASEAN), the North American Free Trade Agreement (NAFTA), the European Union, Mercosur and Asia-Pacific Economic Cooperation Conference (APEC), have also been founded to encourage increased cross-border trade flows by eliminating import quotas, tariffs and export restraints.

Table 1.1 Global foreign direct investment.

Activity	*Annual growth (per cent)*	
	1986–90	*1991–9*
FDI inflows	23.6	20.1
FDI outflows	27.1	15.1
Cross-border mergers and acquisitions	21.0	30.2
Sales of foreign affiliates	16.3	13.4
Gross product of foreign affiliates	16.6	6.2
Total assets of foreign affiliates	18.3	24.4

Source Adapted from UNCTAD, *World Investment Report, 1999*, p. 2.

At the same time, the deregulation of international capital markets has also substantially improved access to the pool of global saving for advanced and emerging economies. Many economies have experienced much larger external account imbalances in the form of current account deficits associated with these capital inflows, with these external imbalances providing a measure of the extent to which foreign funds enable additional economic activity in host countries.

What also characterises this era of globalisation is the role and prevalence of foreign direct investment (FDI) and the multinational company (MNC), many of which have turnovers greater than the national incomes of individual nations. The momentum of growth in FDI, cross-border mergers and acquisitions, and international production since the early 1980s is evident from the annual average growth rates included in Table 1.1.

2. Arguments for and against globalisation

Economists familiar with the principles of international trade theory naturally endorse globalisation on the grounds that increased international integration of markets expands exchange opportunities. By enabling greater international division of labour and more effective allocation of resources, including saving and finance, globalisation allows producers to reap rewards from specialisation and consumers to enjoy a wider range of product choice at the cheapest prices.

However, globalisation continues to provoke dissent from non-economists, who seem as much opposed to market processes and capitalism as a system of production and exchange, as to globalisation *per se*. These opponents generally do not question the economic growth enhancing power of globalisation, but instead are preoccupied with equity considerations, claiming that the very poor in globalising economies are further impoverished through the process.

This is ultimately an empirical issue, however, with the evidence suggesting, to the contrary, that the incomes of the poor in a wide range of countries at various stages of development rise equivalently with incomes overall. While concerns are raised about a widening differential between the earnings of skilled and unskilled labour in many economies as they undergo internationalisation, it should be recognised that the fundamental source of this divergence is technological advance, not globalisation.

In economic policy debate in countries around the world, protectionist sentiment and concern about the impact of foreign investment also remain central to the views of economic nationalists whose policy platforms reflect strong antipathy to globalisation. There are losers from the process of liberalising trade and investment in advanced economies, the worst affected being the owners and employees of previously highly protected firms in industries that find it difficult to compete with more efficient foreign producers. Yet, the fact remains that economies that have adopted free-trade principles and internationally oriented development strategies have prospered more than those economies that have favoured protectionist, inward-looking strategies.

While there is widespread agreement among economists and policymakers about the longer-term benefits of free trade in goods and services, there is relatively less recognition of the benefits of free investment. For instance, many commentators neglect that as a result of foreign investment, many economies have been able to invest more domestically, and hence grow faster than otherwise, while generating higher yields for international investors. On this basis, the process of international capital market integration and the associated rise in international capital mobility has been, in theory, a welcome development.

Furthermore, in the context of heightened financial globalisation, international investors judge domestic fiscal stabilisation measures that boost public spending harshly whenever such spending is deemed unproductive. Accordingly, this has alienated those Keynesians who favour frequent and active use of public spending to smooth out business cycle fluctuations. In a globalised economy, if international investors disapprove of fiscal activism and the associated higher budget deficits, foreign investment, direct and financial, could diminish, resulting in higher long-term domestic interest rates, less real capital accumulation and consequently a lower rate of economic growth.

Foreign investment in the form of subsidiary operations of large multinational companies enables technology to be transferred from advanced economies to emerging and less developed economies. For this reason, governments of all political persuasions around the world are today in constant competition to attract foreign investment of this type, sometimes using specific tax concessions and subsidies for this purpose.

Meanwhile, conservationists tend to oppose globalisation because greater economic activity harms the environment. There is no denying that real environmental problems do arise as a consequence of accelerated economic growth, as indeed they did in advanced economies during the industrial revolution, and this remains the most challenging issue in the debate.

Nonetheless, opponents of globalisation should appreciate that democratically elected governments in many emerging economies perceive environmental problems as a by-product of a development process they choose to prolong in order to raise average income levels.

3. How new?

In light of the extensive discussion of the causes and effects of globalisation over recent years, it would seem that many would have us believe that the world economy is going through a phase like no other before. The process of globalisation is not, however, an economic phenomenon that first began in, or is exclusive to, the late twentieth century. The world economy has previously experienced an era of globalisation during the so-called *belle époque*, which was similar in many respects to the present one.

During this period, there were also substantial movements of people, emigrating mainly from the economies of Britain and Western Europe to colonies and former colonies in North America, South America, Africa and Australasia. In common with the current era of globalisation, the earlier era was spurred by major breakthroughs in technology that greatly improved transport and communications, such as the telegraph, railways and steamships.

At the beginning of the twentieth century, international capital flows between some nations, such as Britain and its former colonies Australia and Canada, as reflected in current account imbalances, actually exceeded levels of today measured in terms of national production. The share of exports in world output, for instance, reached a peak in 1913 that was not surpassed again until 1970. Moreover, in the first globalisation era, migration rates and international labour mobility were also proportionately higher than they are today. Yet geographically, globalisation was actually less global in its reach then. Now more areas of the world, including parts of Asia, Latin America and Eastern Europe are affected, with trade in services also much greater than ever before.

4. The future of globalisation

These days very few economists would dispute the theoretical proposition that free trade in goods and services improves economic growth, national income and hence overall economic welfare. As long as governments worldwide continue to appreciate the economic arguments in its favour, the process of globalisation should intensify into the future, notwithstanding some stalling along the way due to periodic financial crises.

The main difference between the contemporary international economic and political environment and the *belle époque* is that there now exists a well-established supranational institutional framework fostering international economic exchanges. In contrast, in the first globalisation era, all economic institutions were strictly nationally based and no independent authorities existed to oversee the economic conduct of participants in international exchange.

The current framework is comprised of numerous supranational institutions pursuing pro-globalisation objectives, such as the OECD, the WTO, the International Monetary Fund (IMF) and the World Bank. In this regard, although the *raison d'être*, objectives and policies of these taxpayer-funded organisations are by and large economically sound, at the same time it is difficult to disagree with suggestions that their activities should be more transparent and their non-elected officials more accountable.

Considerable potential remains for increased integration of the markets for commodities, manufactures, services and financial assets. The proportion of trade to national income remains relatively small for many advanced and developing economies, both relative to the past and relative to the most open economies in the world. Additionally, most of the domestic investment that occurs in many economies is still financed by locally sourced saving, which implies that much greater scope exists for increasing the scale of international saving and investment flows.

MEASURING OPENNESS

Economic interdependence between all nation states arises mainly through trade flows, international commodity prices and global capital flows. Exchange rates play an important role in transmitting the effects of changes in these variables to the domestic economy. An important function of the IMF is to monitor the behaviour of the important international macroeconomic variables affecting open economies, as well as tracking how the world economy as a whole is behaving. To do this, the IMF groups economies by region and stage of development, as shown in Table 1.2.

The set of *advanced economies* are the most developed and are also members of the OECD. Within this category, the Group of Seven (G7) economies – the United States, Japan, Germany, France, Italy, the United Kingdom and Canada – are considered to be the world's most advanced and influential economies. The *developing countries* greatly outnumber the developed industrial countries and have, by definition, much lower living standards. The *economies in transition* are former Communist countries, mainly in Eastern Europe, which have moved away from centrally planned systems of allocating resources toward market-oriented systems.

One commonly used indicator of the degree of an economy's openness is the percentage value of the sum of exports (X) plus imports (M) as a share of national product, or GDP, i.e.:

$$\frac{X + M}{GDP} \times 100$$

This measure has increased markedly for many economies over recent decades consistent with the trend of relatively rapid internationalisation.

Table 1.2 Overview of the world economy (annual percentage change).

	1997	*1998*	*1999*	*2000*
World output	4.1	2.6	3.4	4.7
Advanced economies	3.4	2.4	3.2	4.2
Major industrial economies (G7)	3.2	2.5	2.9	3.9
United States	4.4	4.4	4.2	5.2
Japan	1.6	−2.5	0.2	1.4
Germany	1.4	2.1	1.6	2.9
France	2.0	3.2	2.9	3.5
Italy	1.8	1.5	1.4	3.1
United Kingdom	3.5	2.6	2.1	3.1
Canada	4.4	3.3	4.5	4.7
Other advanced economies	4.7	1.0	5.5	5.8
Industrial countries	3.2	2.7	3.0	3.9
European Union	2.6	2.7	2.4	3.4
Euro area	2.3	2.7	2.4	3.5
Newly industrialised Asian economies	5.8	−2.3	7.8	7.9
Developing countries	5.7	3.5	3.8	5.6
Africa	2.8	3.1	2.2	3.4
Asia	6.5	4.1	5.9	6.7
Middle East and Europe	5.1	3.1	0.8	4.7
Western hemisphere	5.4	2.2	0.3	4.3
Countries in transition	1.6	−0.8	2.4	4.9
Central and Eastern Europe	2.1	2.0	1.3	3.1
Excluding Belarus and Ukraine	2.5	2.0	1.8	3.8
Russia	0.9	−4.9	3.2	7.0
Transcaucasus and central Asia	2.6	2.5	4.6	5.3
World trade volume	9.8	4.3	5.1	10.0
Industrial country import volume	9.2	5.7	7.6	10.3
Developing country import volume	10.4	0.3	–	10.0
Commodity prices				
Oil (US$ per barrel)	−5.4	−32.1	37.5	47.5
Non-fuel primary commodities	−3.2	−14.7	−7.1	3.2
Consumer prices				
Advanced economies	2.1	1.5	1.4	2.3
Developing countries	9.7	10.1	6.6	6.2
Countries in transition	27.3	21.6	43.8	18.3

Source Adapted from International Monetary Fund, *World Economic Outlook*, October 2000 (tables 1, 2, 8, 22 and 23 in Statistical Appendix).
www.imf.org/external/pubs/ft/weo/2000/02/index.htm

Table 1.3 Index of openness.

Country	*1970 (per cent)*	*1998 (per cent)*
Argentina	10	23
Australia	29	42
Austria	60	85
Belgium	100	141
Brazil	14	18
Canada	43	80
China	4	39
Hong Kong (SAR)	181	250
Denmark	60	69
Finland	53	71
France	31	49
Germany	–	52
India	8	25
Indonesia	28	98
Ireland	79	142
Italy	50	–
Japan	20	21
Korea, Republic of	37	85
Malaysia	80	207
Mexico	17	64
Netherlands	89	105
New Zealand	48	57
Nigeria	20	55
Norway	74	75
Russian Federation	–	58
Saudi Arabia	89	67
Singapore	232	287
South Africa	46	50
Spain	27	56
Sweden	48	81
Switzerland	64	75
Thailand	34	101
United Kingdom	45	58
United States	11	26

Source Adapted from World Bank, *2000 World Development Indicators*, 2000 (table 1.5). www.worldbank.org/data/databytopic/databytopic.html

Table 1.3 provides summary measures of economic openness for select economies.

On this measure, the two largest advanced economies, Japan and the United States, are relatively less open, and the majority of advanced economies are less open than some smaller, fast-growing Asian economies such as Malaysia and Singapore.

Another way of gauging the openness of the real, or goods and services, side of an economy is to identify the relative share of tradable versus nontradable production in GDP. Tradable output here includes goods and services which may not actually be exported or imported, but which could potentially be sold to foreigners, whereas nontradable production includes goods and services, such as garbage collection services and haircuts, which could never enter into world trade. The ratios of tradable economic activity to total output and spending, where available, suggest that economies are more open than is shown by the trade to GDP ratio. What economic factors actually determine whether any particular activity is tradable or nontradable is considered in more depth later in this book.

The measures of openness discussed so far only apply to the markets for goods and services, whereas openness, of course, has other dimensions. For instance, an economy would be relatively more open, the less regulated were its financial and asset markets and hence the more exposed these markets were to international exchange. It would also be more open, the more easily it permitted the entry and exit of foreign residents through international migration or as guest workers (also known as *gastarbeiter* arrangements).

Both domestic and international financial transactions were tightly controlled in many economies up until the early 1980s. For instance, at the domestic level there were quantitative limits on bank lending, deposit and lending rates were controlled, and bank reserves were subject to strict regulatory arrangements, whereby trading banks had to lodge a proportion of their deposits with central banks. Many restrictions also previously impeded international capital inflows and outflows.

Historically, the process of international financial market integration began gathering pace worldwide from the mid-1970s with the relaxation of capital controls in North America. By the end of the 1970s, the United Kingdom had abolished all exchange controls and throughout the 1980s Japan gradually relaxed restrictions on foreign outward investment by institutional investors. Liberalisation of financial markets in many advanced economies was virtually complete by the mid-1990s, and institutional barriers impeding the movement of financial capital within the entire developed world have now largely disappeared.

Deregulation proceeded essentially because there was widespread acceptance that microeconomic efficiency gains could be realised by removing domestic interest rate distortions and by fostering increased competition between financial intermediaries. Deregulation was also expected to improve the effectiveness of monetary policy as a macroeconomic stabilisation instrument. Accompanying the deregulatory changes were strengthened prudential supervisory arrangements. Capital backing of banks was the basis of prudential regulation, and guidelines consistent with international banking practice have been adopted by central banks. These set out the appropriate ratio of capital reserves which banks were obliged to hold against risk-weighted assets, and were intended to strengthen the capitalisation of banks and hence the security of the financial system.

In an overall sense, the abolition of official restrictions on financial transactions transformed financial systems from being heavily regulated and segmented, into ones that were lightly regulated and internationally integrated. Access to international financial capital and services increased greatly, due in particular to the abolition of exchange controls and the entry of foreign banks into domestic financial markets. Combined with the removal of capital controls abroad and the development of the Eurodollar market, this boosted borrowing opportunities of open economies and implied that international capital movements increased significantly.

With enhanced international mobility of funds, in reality there is now a very close correspondence between domestic and world interest rates consistent with the small country assumption (see Chapter 4). Funds flow virtually instantaneously across country borders to maximise returns and eliminate interest differentials, after allowing for expected exchange rate movements.

The institutional environment in which macroeconomic policy is conducted has therefore changed markedly over recent decades. In terms of the actual operation of monetary policy by central banks, the most significant change has been a shift away from credit rationing approaches, previously implemented via techniques to decrease or increase the amount of funds which the commercial banks could lend, to market-oriented approaches.

FACTS, THEORY AND POLICY

This book examines the macroeconomic behaviour of open economies. To describe how well economies actually perform, it is necessary to rely on official statistics which measure the key macroeconomic variables. These provide an up-to-date picture of the *facts* describing the behaviour of any economy, both in relation to its behaviour in the recent past and in relation to the macroeconomic performance of major trading partners.

To instil conceptual understanding of how the major variables are linked together in *theory* – in other words, what causes what – various analytical models are put forward. These models are best seen not as rival means of explaining macroeconomic behaviour, but as complementary in an overall sense. Indeed, taken together, the theoretical models in this book provide an overall framework for analysing the major factors influencing an economy's international macroeconomic performance.

One of the enduring issues of macroeconomics is the role that governments may play in managing overall economic behaviour. In the new era of globalised markets, decisions made by policymakers to influence domestic

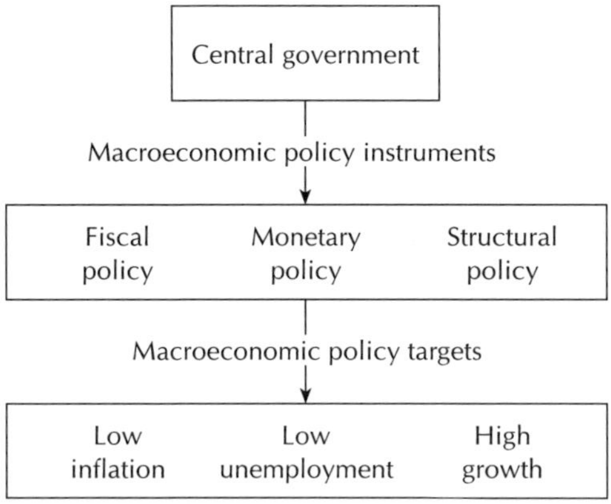

Figure 1.3 Macroeconomic policy instruments and targets.

economic behaviour are now always made with international implications in mind.

Macroeconomic policy is the use by the national government of policy *instruments* to explicitly manage changes in those macroeconomic variables which are considered to be appropriate targets of policy. The Nobel prize-winning Dutch economist Jan Tinbergen formally established that any government in managing its economy could not achieve its macroeconomic policy targets, unless it could control at least as many quantitative policy instruments as it had policy targets. This proposition is known as the 'Tinbergen rule'.

In advanced economies, the main instruments and targets of macroeconomic policy are those shown in Figure 1.3. The instruments at the disposal of the governments are fiscal, monetary and structural policies. These policies are used to influence the targets or goals of low inflation, low unemployment, high growth and, under certain circumstances, the exchange rate and the balance of payments with the rest of the world.

An economy achieves *internal balance* when it attains the objectives of low inflation and low unemployment. The term *external balance* refers to the exchange rate and balance of payments objectives. Just what external balance means depends very much on the nature of the exchange rate regime, however. Indeed, as we will see, the notion of external balance is not straightforward under a floating exchange rate regime.

Economists of all persuasions have rarely questioned the desirability of achieving the macroeconomic policy objectives of low inflation and low unemployment. However, some of the greatest debates in macroeconomics in the past, such as that between the Keynesians and the Monetarists in the 1970s, have centred on the best policy means of attaining them. For instance, differences of view still exist among academic economists and policymakers about the benefits of structural policy and whether fiscal policy, monetary policy or some other alternative such as prices and incomes policies is the best way to accomplish low inflation and low unemployment.

SEQUENCE OF THE BOOK

This book examines economy-wide behaviour within a global context by first introducing the main macroeconomic variables. Applied economists these days spend much of their time poring over the latest data releases, such as the national accounts, the balance of payments accounts and employment numbers, as well as monitoring Reuters screens to keep up to date on daily movements in the exchange rate and interest rates both at home and abroad. For this reason, the meaning and significance of macroeconomic data is treated in some depth.

For instance, Chapter 2 goes further than other textbooks in presenting a detailed framework for understanding how the main domestic and international macroeconomic variables are defined. Chapter 3 then introduces the exchange rate, which, according to many economists, should be considered the single most important price for an open economy. This chapter first explains the main differences between alternative exchange rate systems, before introducing some basic approaches to explaining the short-run and long-run behaviour of floating exchange rates.

Chapter 4 addresses important linkages between local and foreign markets for goods and services. It outlines approaches to understanding such issues as the determination of the trade balance, and the international transmission of inflation based on the distinction between tradables and nontradables. It also highlights the macroeconomic significance of the terms of trade, the relative price of exports and imports.

Chapter 5 explains the flow of funds in an open economy, by relating domestic saving, domestic investment, international capital flows and interest rates. In so doing, this chapter expounds the essential theory of domestic saving and investment behaviour and the role of foreign borrowing.

Chapter 6 then introduces the key concepts and features of fiscal policy and monetary policy management, including an examination of the linkage between budget deficits and the external accounts and the functions of the central bank. It outlines the major techniques available for implementing monetary policy in a deregulated financial system.

Chapter 7 presents the Mundell–Fleming model of the open economy, which implies that the effectiveness of fiscal and monetary policy as an influence on national income and employment depends on whether exchange rates are fixed or floating. A variation of the standard model shows that the nature of the exchange rate system can also affect the size of GDP fluctuations.

Chapter 8 examines key linkages between asset markets, interest rates, investor expectations and exchange rate behaviour. It also further develops the analysis of the short-term effects of monetary policy on interest rates and the exchange rate.

Attention then shifts to longer-run issues in Chapter 9. This chapter reconciles the standard short-run analysis of Chapter 7 with aggregate demand–aggregate supply (AD-AS) analysis, which allows the overall price level to vary. It also outlines the monetary approach to explaining domestic inflation and exchange rate behaviour in the long run.

Chapter 10 analyses the macroeconomic implications of labour market arrangements in more depth by contrasting alternative theoretical perspectives on wage setting, employment and unemployment.

Chapter 11 addresses the fundamental causes of long-run growth in aggregate output. It examines the contributions of technology, capital and labour, the dynamics of the growth process and policies that enhance growth.

Finally, Chapter 12 examines the macroeconomic implications of international capital and labour flows. It also discusses the policy significance of current account imbalances and foreign debt levels.

Further reading

Burtless, G., Lawrence, R., Litan, R. and Shapiro, R. (eds) (1998) *Globaphobia: Confronting Fears About Open Trade*, Washington, DC: Brookings Institution.

Eichengreen, B. (1996) *Globalising Capital: History of the International Monetary System*, Princeton, NJ: Princeton University Press.

The Economist (1997) 'One world?', 18 October, p. 99.

Keynes, J.M. (1936) *The General Theory of Employment, Interest and Money*, London: Macmillan.

Tinbergen, J. (1952) *On the Theory of Economic Policy*, Amsterdam: North-Holland.

2

Open economy measurement issues

Ever since the work of Sir William Petty in England in the mid-1600s, economists have been refining techniques for measuring how an economy performs. What has evolved for this purpose is the system of national accounting relating aggregate spending, production and income. It is important to understand the fundamental concepts of national accounting because they allow us to monitor overall economic activity, which influences economic growth, employment, unemployment and the rate of inflation.

A nation's central statistical authority is responsibility for publishing its macroeconomic data in an objective and reliable way and in line with internationally agreed conventions about macroeconomic data collection and presentation. The quality of statistics is judged on the basis of criteria such as statistical methodology, coverage and reliability. The national accounts gauge an economy's performance over time, especially through the measure of GDP, which is at the heart of national accounting.

In addition to national accounting measures, an open economy's performance is also usually gauged with reference to the behaviour of its balance of payments or external accounts, as well as movements in key financial variables such as money, interest rates and exchange rates. To evaluate the behaviour of any open economy, it is necessary to understand thoroughly the established concepts, definitions and measurement of the main macroeconomic variables in Table 2.1. This chapter aims to do this by explaining the main conceptual relations between the key macroeconomic aggregates. These relations underlie the theory of later chapters.

The emphasis in what follows is mainly on the *flows* of expenditure, production, income, investment and saving recorded in the national accounts. A flow is a measure of some quantity per period of time, such as per quarter (three months) or per financial year (say from 1 July to 30 June). These aggregates are, by dimension, quantities. Not all the quantity variables of macroeconomics are flows, however. The other quantity magnitudes are *stocks*, which are measured at a point in time, such as at the end of the financial year. Flow changes usually imply corresponding changes in stock

Table 2.1 United Kingdom: selected economic indicators (annual percentage change unless otherwise noted).

Economic indicator	*1997*	*1998*	*1999*	*2000*
Domestic economy				
Household consumption	4.0	4.0	4.5	3.7
Business investment	7.5	10.1	5.4	2.6
Real GDP	3.5	2.6	2.3	3.0
Employment growth	1.9	1.2	1.2	1.3
Unemployment rate (ILO unemployment)	7.2	6.3	6.1	5.6
Annual inflation (retail price index)	3.1	3.4	1.5	3.0
External accounts				
Export volume (visibles)	8.2	1.2	3.5	10.4
Import volume (visibles)	9.1	8.5	7.4	10.5
Current account balance (per cent of GDP)	0.8	−0.1	−1.4	−1.5
Exchange rate index (1990 = 100)	100.5	103.9	103.8	107.5
Monetary variables				
Budget balance (year ending 30 June in per cent of GDP)	−3.0	−0.2	1.0	2.1
Broad money (per cent change)	11.2	9.8	5.4	6.6
Interest rates (annual average)				
Three-month UK interbank rate	6.84	7.34	5.44	6.11
Long-term rates (gilt yield)	7.05	5.52	5.08	5.31

Source Adapted from HM Treasury, *HM Treasury Pocket Databank*, 10 April 2001 (various tables). www.hm-treasury.gov.uk/e info/overview/index.html

values. For instance, investment as a flow increases the capital stock, the budget deficit as a flow increases the stock of public debt, and the current account deficit as a flow increases the stock of foreign debt.

The following material also examines macroeconomic variables which have a price dimension. Such measures include the overall price level itself, which conveys in a single number movements in millions of individual goods and services prices throughout the economy. The other key economy-wide prices are the exchange rate and the interest rate, which are set on the monetary side of the economy.

EXPENDITURE, PRODUCT AND INCOME ACCOUNTS

An economy's national and international accounts are based on the guidelines set out in the United Nations' *System of National Accounts* (SNA). The

SNA unifies related sets of macroeconomic accounts, such as national income and expenditure, intersectoral flows of funds and the external accounts. Taken as a whole, the SNA group of accounts is designed to provide a detailed picture of macroeconomic activity as well as a framework for applying economic theory.

Economic production is the most basic idea in the national accounting system. Production involves the combination of labour, natural resources, physical capital and technology to generate goods and services, the bulk of which is immediately made available for sale on markets. Definitionally, *gross domestic product* (GDP) is the aggregate value of the output of farms, mines and factories and the value of services produced over a given time period. It is derived after subtracting goods and services used up in final production of all goods and services. Production generates a flow of income for those factors which are combined in the process. Hence, as income, GDP is broadly classified as being paid either to labour as a factor of production (as *wages and salaries*) or to capital and land (known as the *gross operating surplus*).

In principle, GDP can therefore equivalently be measured as the dollar value of total output, as the dollar value of total income received by all factors of production or as the dollar value of aggregate spending on final goods and services.

In practice, therefore, there are three possible ways of measuring GDP. These are:

1. the production, or *value-added*, approach, which sums the market value of goods and services produced by industries, net of goods and services used up in the process;
2. the *income* approach, which adds the incomes which accrue from all domestic sources of production;
3. the *expenditure* approach, which sums all final expenditures on goods and services.

Most goods and services are provided through private markets and accordingly are included at values determined in the markets themselves. However, some goods and services are not explicitly offered for sale on private markets, yet still increase households' incomes. In such cases, as when goods are both produced and consumed on farms, when employees obtain extra fringe benefits from employers (such as the use of company cars for private purposes) or when home owners save income because they pay no rent, *imputed values* are recorded in the national income and expenditure accounts for consistency.

Public services provided by governments, such as education, defence, health, and law and order, also have their values imputed because such services are not priced through trading in private markets. As a rule, public services are valued at the cost of providing them. This cost is generally the wages actually paid to employees delivering public services. Some 'underground' activities such as illegal drug trafficking and unpaid housework are omitted from the national accounts altogether because there are problems of data collection or other practical reasons. Such exclusion therefore tends to understate the true value of national expenditure and income. As the relative size of the underground economy differs from country to country, problems can arise in making consistent international comparisons of GDP levels.

The most basic equation of national income accounting states that spending by households and firms on *private consumption* (C_p) and *private investment* (I_p), as well as *government consumption* (C_g) and *government investment* (I_g), must absorb the total value of GDP. That is, $(C_p + I_p) + (C_g + I_g) = GDP$. Often, government consumption and investment are simply grouped as total government spending and denoted as G, that is, $(C_g + I_g = G)$.

Private consumption mostly includes spending on ordinary goods and services such as groceries, tobacco, alcohol, clothing, tuition fees, haircuts, dry cleaning, public transport, entertainment and accommodation. Some consumption spending is on *consumer durables*, however, which includes cars, furniture and household appliances. Private consumption, the largest component of GDP, averages around 60 per cent or more of GDP in advanced economies. In contrast, private investment spending is smaller and much more volatile. Government consumption includes wages paid to all government employees who provide public services, such as health, education, defence, and law and order.

Investment expenditure by the private and government sectors covers spending on machinery, equipment, houses, home units, hotels, factories, roads, bridges, harbours, railways and amusement parks. Increases in the inventories of goods not yet sold by private and public enterprises also form part of the economy's gross investment.

In the closed economy, the relation that total domestic spending equals total domestic output is an identity because it shows that *ex post* all of the output produced in the economy in a given period must have been allocated in one way or another. If total planned spending did not equate with planned production, then any excess demand or supply would have caused either a run-down or build-up of inventories, which, as already mentioned above, are measured as part of gross domestic investment.

In an open economy, the key difference on the national expenditure side is that part of total spending by domestic households, firms and government falls on foreign-produced goods and services. This is recorded as *imports* (M). On the other hand, part of total production is purchased by the rest of the world and is recorded as *exports* (X). Therefore, the basic national accounting identity is:

$$C_p + I_p + G + X - M = Y$$

Another way of looking at this identity is:

Domestic demand for goods and services	+	Foreign demand for domestic output	=	Total supply of goods and services
$C_p + I_p + G$	+	X	=	Y + M

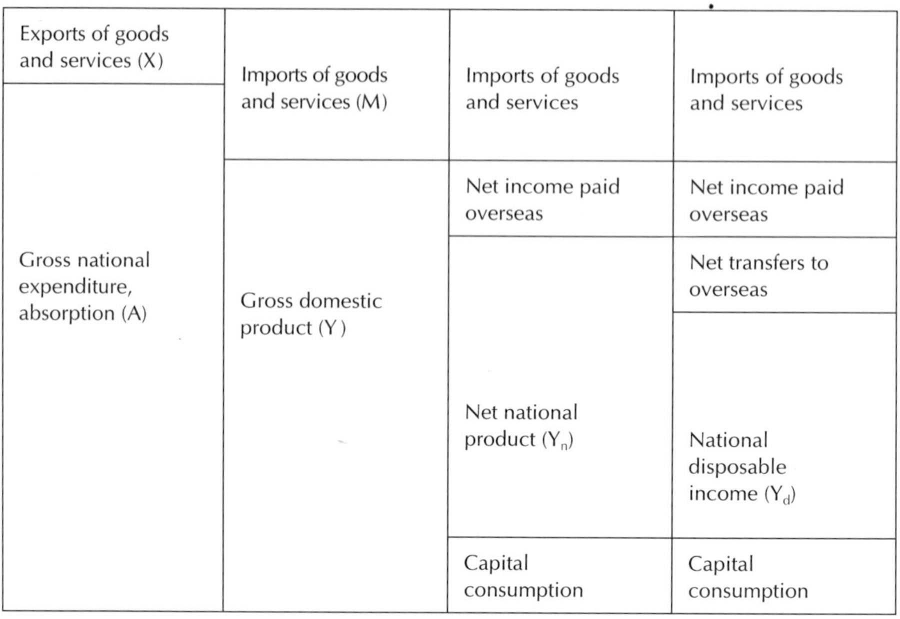

Figure 2.1 Expenditure, product and income relations for an open economy.

Total spending by residents in an open economy is sometimes termed *absorption* (A), which can be greater or less than the total output of the economy. Using this distinction between output and absorption, it is therefore possible to write:

$$Y - A = X - M$$

This states that the difference between what is produced and what is spent by domestic residents is equivalent to the trade imbalance, or simply the difference between exports and imports of goods and services.

Gross national product (GNP) differs from GDP to the extent of net income paid by residents to non-residents. GDP will exceed GNP if income paid to foreigners in the form of interest, dividends and profit remittances exceeds income received from foreigners. The gradual depletion of the value of the economy's productive assets is recorded in the accounts by including the entry *capital consumption,* also known as depreciation of fixed capital. *Net national product* (NNP) is GNP less capital consumption. *National disposable income* is NNP less net transfers overseas such as foreign aid, pensions and gifts to non-residents.

Figure 2.1 provides a summary statement of how the main expenditure, income and product aggregates are related in an open economy.

An economy's national accounts data are usually produced on a quarterly and annual basis. Over the course of any financial year, some types of economic activity exhibit a regular pattern due to seasonal influences. For instance, more foreign tourists may travel during summer or more grain exports may be shipped abroad immediately after the harvest season. To eliminate these regular seasonal factors, many macroeconomic statistics (especially in the national accounts but also in the external accounts) are *seasonally adjusted*. This allows economists to better see what underlying factors are affecting the data.

Official data from the nation's *income and outlay account* distinguish between labour income (*wages, salaries, supplements*) and the return to all other factors, notably capital and land, involved in the production process (*net operating surplus*).

The wages share of GDP has typically been the largest component of the GDP measure in advanced economies, usually ranging between 50 and 60 per cent of national income. Wages play a dual role in the economy, as they represent both income to workers and costs to firms. The behaviour of wages and the nature of the labour market itself have very important implications for economic performance, as we will see in later chapters. We will also see that the return on capital, which can be measured using the ratio of gross operating surplus to the size of the capital stock itself, is relevant to understanding foreign investment flows and long-run growth in the open economy.

The *statistical discrepancy* item appears as a separate entry in the national accounts of many economies. This entry is necessary because there is usually a measured difference between the independent statistical estimates made by national statistics bureaux of national production and national expenditure. The statistical discrepancy (sd) is included in the accounts to ensure that, in practice, measured aggregate expenditure equals measured aggregate output. That is:

$$Y = C_p + C_g + I_p + I_g + (X - M) + sd$$

THE BUSINESS CYCLE

The size of GDP in advanced economies has grown enormously over recent centuries. This has enabled average income levels per head of population to multiply many-fold. The main factors which have caused this long-run phenomenon of economic growth will be covered in depth in a later chapter. Throughout history, however, economic growth has frequently been interrupted by relatively short periods of falling national output, spending and income. Such falls in GDP are usually accompanied by higher levels of unemployment of workers throughout the economy. GDP fluctuations are inevitably followed by a return to the path of economic growth, although it is difficult to predict how long this will take for any economy. For this reason, governments often try to stabilise macroeconomic behaviour.

Any pattern of peaks and troughs in macroeconomic activity is called a *business cycle*. The relationship between the business cycle and the *trend* rate of growth in GDP is depicted in Figure 2.2.

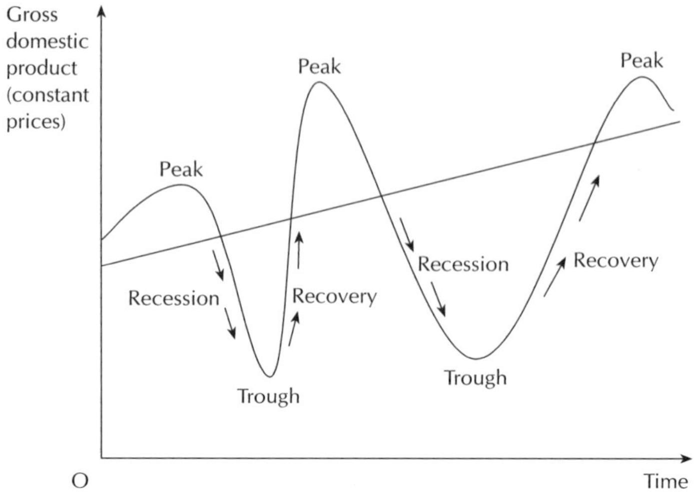

Figure 2.2 The business cycle and growth.

When GDP is falling, that is when GDP moves from peak to trough, the economy experiences *recession* or *contraction*. In practical terms, an economy is in recession if measured GDP falls over two consecutive quarters, or three-month intervals. When GDP is moving from trough to peak, it is in *recovery* phase or in a period of *expansion*. Often, if the economy is considered to be recovering too strongly by economists and policymakers, it is said to be *overheating*. A full cycle of aggregate economic activity is measured either from one trough to another or from one peak to another.

No two business cycles are exactly the same, nor do they happen at constant or predictable intervals. Yet all business cycles do have a few common features. For instance, consumption, investment and employment all tend to move in the same direction and at roughly the same time as changes in GDP. Hence these variables are termed *procyclical* variables. The most volatile of these aggregates over the cycle is usually private investment. Government budget deficits and unemployment levels move in the opposite direction to GDP and are therefore termed *countercyclical* variables.

EMPLOYMENT AND UNEMPLOYMENT

A major reason to be interested in the behaviour of the national accounts is because fluctuations in GDP have implications for employment and unemployment levels. Over time, output and total employment growth empirically tend to move together quite closely. It is because upturns in the business cycle lead to higher employment of people in the economy and because downturns in the business cycle lead to higher levels of unemployment that the national accounts are so closely monitored by economists and policymakers.

In data series on the number of employed and unemployed persons aged 15 and over in the civilian population, individuals are classified as being either employed, unemployed or not in the labour force. Full-time employees are defined as people working a full working week, whereas part-time employees work less than, say, 35 hours per week. The *unemployment rate* is the number of people in the labour force out of work, yet actively seeking it (U), as a percentage of the total number of people in the workforce (W). That is, the unemployment rate is:

$$\frac{U}{W} \times 100$$

The *participation rate* measures the number of people either in work or looking for work (W) as a percentage of the civilian population of working age (POP_w). That is, the participation rate is:

$$\frac{W}{POP_w} \times 100$$

THE PRICE LEVEL AND INFLATION

A general rise in the prices of all goods and services is the macroeconomic phenomenon of *inflation*, defined as the percentage change over a given time in the overall price level. Inflation impacts in one way or another on everyone in the economy. It affects the buying power of household income, influences business contracts, wage negotiations and social security payments, as well as having implications for financial variables, such as interest rates and exchange rates.

In practice, the overall price level is measured in two main ways, through either the *consumer price index* (CPI) or the *implicit price deflator* (IPD) for GDP. Sometimes, the change in the CPI measure is referred to as the *headline* rate of inflation because it always attracts the most attention, whereas change in the IPD measure is referred to as the *underlying* rate.

The CPI aims to capture the broad trend in the prices of literally millions of retail transactions over a given quarter or year. Hence it provides a measure of change in the domestic purchasing power of the currency. The higher is the CPI, the fewer goods and services a given quantity of dollars can command over time. As a single index, the CPI measures the overall level of prices facing consumers. It uses a fixed 'basket' of goods and services which represents the spending pattern of ordinary consumers. To ensure that a CPI represents the typical purchases of households, the basket is updated every five years or so. In advanced economies, the range of goods and services in the CPI basket includes such diverse items as telephone calls, dental fillings and takeaway meals. Typical expenditure classes and hypothetical weightings for an advanced economy are included in Table 2.2.

Table 2.2 Consumer price index.

Expenditure type	*Weighting*
Food	19.0
Clothing	6.9
Housing	14.1
Household equipment	18.4
Transportation	17.0
Tobacco and alcohol	8.2
Health and personal care	5.6
Recreation and education	10.8
	100.0

The actual inflation rate (π) between two periods is calculated as a simple percentage change. For example, if the CPI was 110 in December 2002 and 114 in March 2003, then the 2003 March quarter inflation rate was 3.6 per cent:

$$\pi = \frac{114 - 110}{110} \times 100 = 3.6\%$$

The other main measure of the national price level, the IPD, is simply the ratio of:

$$\frac{\text{Current price GDP}}{\text{Constant price GDP}}$$

Current price or nominal GDP is just the quantity of total output valued at market prices, whereas constant price or 'real' GDP is the quantity of total output valued at the prices which prevailed in a specified base year. The IPD of expenditure on GDP is broader in scope than the CPI. Whereas the CPI reflects movements in select consumption goods, the IPD measure of inflation reflects movements in the prices of all goods and services produced in the economy, irrespective of whether those goods are used for consumption or investment. Percentage changes in constant price values signify real, or inflation-adjusted, growth.

The IPD measure of inflation is simply estimated as the percentage change in the ratio of current- to constant-price GDP. For instance, if the IPD was 1.067 for 2002/3 and 1.094 for 2003/4, then the so-called 'underlying' rate of inflation for 2003/4 would be 2.5 per cent:

$$\frac{1.094 - 1.067}{1.067} \times 100$$

The CPI with its fixed basket is an example of a Laspeyres index, the general formula for which is:

$$\frac{\Sigma P_t Q_0}{\Sigma P_0 Q_0} \times 100$$

where P_t = prices in period t, P_0 = prices in base period and Q_0 = quantities in base period.

The IPD with its variable weights is an example of a Paasche index, the general formula of which is:

$$\frac{\Sigma P_t Q_t}{\Sigma P_0 Q_t} \times 100$$

where Q_t = quantities in period t.

In theory, one type of price-level index cannot be judged superior to another.

Quarterly changes in the CPI are the most frequently reported measures of domestic inflation, even though the IPD for GDP is a more wide-ranging indicator of overall price-level changes. Alternative inflation series based on these respective price-level measures tend to move together quite closely, suggesting that the actual choice of inflation measure is not especially significant.

THE EXCHANGE RATE AND COMPETITIVENESS

The next price variable to consider is the exchange rate, which is literally the relative price of different currencies. Many economists would argue that the exchange rate is the single most important price for an economy which is highly integrated with goods, services and financial markets in the rest of the world. Bilateral nominal exchange rates can be defined as:

the price of a unit of foreign currency per domestic currency unit

$$\frac{\text{Foreign currency}}{\text{Domestic currency}}$$

(the 'market' definition), or as:

the price of domestic currency per unit of foreign currency

$$\frac{\text{Domestic currency}}{\text{Foreign currency}}$$

(the 'academic' definition). In the analysis of later chapters, the symbol E will be used whenever the market definition is used and the symbol e will be used whenever the academic definition is used. Note, however, that

$$E = \frac{1}{e}$$

as one definition is always just the reciprocal of the other.

The value of the economy's exchange rate is important for many reasons. For example, the exchange rate influences the relative price of locally made to foreign made goods and services. The American dollar price of imported Japanese cars, for instance, depends not only on the price of the cars expressed in terms of yen, but also on the value of the American dollar/yen exchange rate which converts the Japanese yen price of cars to a domestic currency price. Exchange rates are also important because they affect the servicing cost of foreign loans. If the American dollar loses value against the yen, American borrowers of yen will have to find more American dollars to meet their loan repayments, which are calculated in terms of yen.

The multilateral measure of an economy's exchange rate is its *nominal effective exchange rate*. The nominal effective exchange is usually known as the trade weighted index (TWI). The TWI gives a fairly complete picture of the 'average' movement of market-defined nominal exchange rates. It measures the value of the currency relative to the currencies of the economy's major trading partners and is another example of a Laspeyres index. Ideally, a TWI includes the currencies of countries which account for the bulk of international trade, with the individual currency weights in the index reflecting the relative importance of each-way trade. The TWI is calculated using a base period when its value equals 100.0.

A country's effective exchange rate, adjusted for domestic inflation and for inflation in its major trading partners, is called the *real effective exchange rate*. The real effective exchange rate is also used as an index of *competitiveness* and is constructed as follows:

$$\text{Real effective exchange rate (competitiveness)} = \frac{\text{Nominal effective exchange rate (TWI)} \times P}{P^*}$$

where P is the domestic price level (measured using the CPI or IPD) and P* is the composite price level of the economy's major trading partners (measured using either corresponding CPIs or IPDs). Sometimes, measures of domestic labour costs, relative to those abroad, are used instead of composite foreign price levels to express competitiveness in terms of relative production costs.

In essence, an economy's real effective exchange rate reflects two sources of change in its overall competitiveness. Competitiveness either improves or worsens because of nominal exchange rate movements or because of changes in domestic prices or costs in relation to prices or costs in its major trading partners. For instance, if the nominal effective exchange rate remained steady, but the UK price level increased 6 per cent while the price level abroad increased only 1 per cent over the same period, then UK competitiveness would have worsened by 5 per cent. Had the TWI itself depreciated by 5 per cent over this time, competitiveness would have remained constant. This is because the loss of competitiveness due to relatively higher inflation would have been offset by a gain in the attractiveness of UK products to foreigners arising from a depreciation of the nominal effective exchange rate.

In practice, nominal exchange rates are far more variable than price levels, inflation rates or labour costs. Hence swings in nominal exchange rates account for most real exchange rate movements over shorter periods. Real exchange rate movements or changes in competitiveness are important over short periods because they impact on real activity, particularly export and import volumes, as we will see in later chapters.

THE BALANCE OF PAYMENTS ACCOUNTS

Next, consider the statistical record of economic transactions between domestic households, firms and governments, and foreigners. This record is the balance of payments or external accounts. The external accounts are effectively a subset of the national accounts, yet provide a more detailed record of the nation's economic transactions with the rest of the world. Often referred to as the *balance of payments* accounts, the external accounts are primarily concerned with monetary settlements between residents and foreigners. However, they also include entries for which financial transactions may not take place, as with goods donated to other countries as foreign aid, or goods transferred between domestic and overseas branches of transnational corporations.

There are two sides to the external accounts – the *current account balance* (CAB) and the *capital account balance* (KAB). In principle, the sum of these balances under a floating exchange rate must be zero; that is, CAB + KAB = 0. This follows from the standard double-entry convention of balance of payments accounting, whereby transactions between domestic residents and foreigners are in pairs of equivalent credit and debit entries. Exports, income receivable, reductions in foreign financial assets and increases in foreign liabilities usually add to the supply of foreign exchange available to domestic residents and are credited. Imports, income payable, increases in foreign financial assets and decreases in foreign liabilities usually subtract from the supply of foreign exchange available to domestic residents and are debited.

The economic, as opposed to accounting, mechanism that ensures the equality between the current and capital accounts is the exchange rate under a floating exchange rate system. Under a managed exchange rate system, in which the nation's central bank is mainly responsible for setting the exchange rate, the *overall balance of payments* (BOP) is measured by changes in the value of *official reserve assets* (ORA), which are the central bank's holdings of financial assets denominated in foreign currency. Under a managed exchange rate system, CAB + KAB = BOP.

The current account includes transactions in goods, services and income between domestic residents and foreigners, and is divided into several sub-accounts. Trade flows are identified as either merchandise (or goods) trade flows, or services trade flows (such as freight and international tourism). Entries in the income sub-account of the current account are shown as either *property income* (interest, dividends, royalties) or *labour and other income* (wages, insurance claims). Lastly, *unrequited transfers* are recorded whenever goods, services or financial assets (foreign aid, pensions, taxes, migrants' transfers) are transferred between residents and foreigners without anything of value being received by domestic residents in return.

The capital or financial account of the balance of payments accounts shows transactions in the economy's foreign financial assets and liabilities. In the capital account, flows are also classified according to whether the *official* sector (general government and central bank) or *non-official* sector (financial intermediaries, private firms and commercial public enterprises) is undertaking the international transactions. Changes in the stock of the central bank's international reserve assets (gold and foreign exchange holdings) are also included under the official category.

If the current account balance is persistently in deficit the deficits are matched by surpluses on the capital account. The capital account data reveals official borrowing activity by the general government sector, including by the central bank as well as net borrowing and investment by the private sector.

The *balancing item*, shown outside the capital account balance of the external accounts, represents the statistical difference between measures of current account components and measures of asset purchases and sales which determine the capital account. In practice, the balancing item forces a numerical equivalence between the current and capital accounts because the two sides must be the same in principle. This entry is often large and arises because data from a range of sources differs in scope, accuracy and timing.

All entries in an economy's external accounts are recorded officially in local currency terms. However, movements in the exchange rate can distort values of some entries, particularly of trade flows and foreign debt servicing payments. Such valuation effects suggest that a foreign currency measure of the imbalance may for some purposes provide a more meaningful measure of trends, particularly if we are interested in the size of the trade balance or the extent of capital flows from a foreign perspective.

For instance, if a reason for concern about an increasing current account deficit, as officially measured, is its effect on the sentiment of foreign investors themselves, or if it is necessary to gauge the extent of foreign currency saving being exchanged for domestic assets, it seems logical to present the current account deficit in terms of foreign currency. This way it is possible to largely abstract from exchange rate valuation effects.

THE INTERNATIONAL INVESTMENT POSITION

The detailed flow transactions in assets and liabilities recorded on the capital account are also reproduced separately in the *foreign investment* statistics. In the foreign investment statistics, transactions in foreign assets and liabilities are reconciled with stock levels of the economy's external liabilities and foreign assets. The difference between the value of the economy's external liabilities and the foreign asset holdings of residents is shown in the foreign investment statistics as the nation's *international investment position*.

A basic distinction in the foreign investment data is that between inward and outward investment. Inward investment entails foreign acquisition of domestic assets, such as equities or interest-bearing financial instruments issued by domestic entities. Alternatively, outward investment is a measure of residents' purchase of equities or interest-bearing assets issued by foreign entities. If inward investment exceeds outward investment there is *net capital inflow*.

Another important distinction here is that between *direct* and *portfolio* foreign investment. Direct foreign investment suggests that foreigners can exert significant influence over the management of a domestic enterprise in which their foreign funds have been invested. Portfolio foreign investment, on the other hand, usually involves purchases of local shares by foreign entities which are not sufficiently large as to entail loss of management control of domestic firms to foreigners.

However, the net international investment position is only part of the story about an open economy's assets and liabilities, even though it usually attracts considerable attention from economic commentators. We will see later in Chapter 12 that a more comprehensive approach to macroeconomic stock measurement would account for all the domestic, as well as foreign, assets of the economy, as presented in national wealth statements.

The main components of the external accounts and the relationships between them, as outlined above, are summarised in Figure 2.3.

<table>
<tr><td>Merchandise trade balance</td><td rowspan="5">Current account balance (CAB)</td><td rowspan="5">Capital account balance (KAB)</td><td rowspan="5">Net foreign investment (NFI)</td><td rowspan="4">Net portfolio foreign investment</td><td rowspan="5">Change in international investment position</td></tr>
<tr><td>Services trade balance</td></tr>
<tr><td>Property income</td></tr>
<tr><td>Labour and other income</td></tr>
<tr><td>Unrequited transfers</td><td>Net direct foreign investment</td></tr>
</table>

Figure 2.3 External accounting relations.

THE NATIONAL CAPITAL ACCOUNT

The earlier discussion of national accounting relations presented the links between spending, production and income in a real, as opposed to financial, sense. Yet behind these aggregates there is also a flow of funds between the various institutional sectors of the open economy. National accounting relations can in fact be used to show that the flow of goods and services on the real side of the economy is closely related to saving activity and to the flow of funds which finance the accumulation of capital.

The term 'capital account' actually has two distinct meanings in the macroeconomic accounts. In the preceding discussion, it has been used in the context of the balance of payments accounts. In the context of the national accounts, however, the *national capital account* is used to show how the nation actually finances its total accumulation of real capital. The capital account measure from the balance of payments accounts and the capital account of the national accounts are actually related in the following way.

Over a given time, the rate of real capital accumulation is the same as the flow of gross domestic investment, which essentially depends on the requirements of private and public enterprises throughout the economy for plant, equipment and buildings. Total investment spending must, however, ultimately be financed out of available saving. National, or domestic, saving is the difference between national income and total consumption ($Y_n - C_p - C_g$) and is largely generated by the household sector of the economy. In an open economy, foreign saving may also be used to finance domestic investment, however, and the extent of the foreign saving used for this purpose is equal to the capital account surplus from the external accounts.

Schematically, the components of the national capital account and the link to the capital account of the balance of payments accounts are shown in Figure 2.4.

In practice, *capital consumption* is also a major item in the national capital account. This item is sometimes hard to measure accurately on a large scale because each type of equipment in use in the economy has a different working life. For example, buildings last longer than vehicles. Also, because capital equipment can quickly become obsolescent, the economic use of that equipment may therefore depreciate more rapidly than implied by actual physical wear and tear. For instance, rapid quality advances in com-

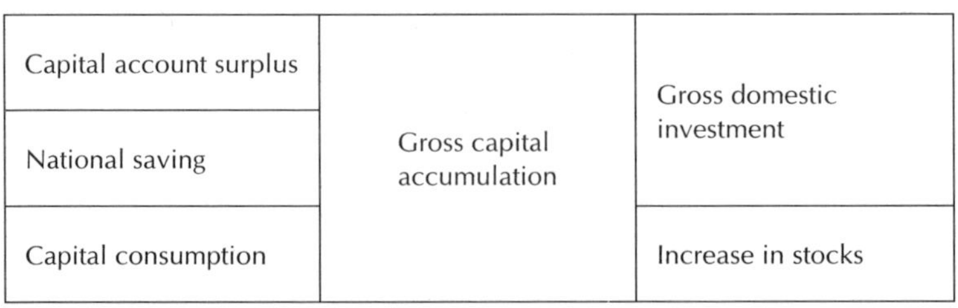

Figure 2.4 National capital account relations.

puter technology have quickly made many earlier computer programs and models redundant, even though they could still work well.

Gross private sector saving is the sum of *household saving* and *business saving*. Business saving is also called corporate retained earnings, and includes provisions for depreciation of the capital stock. At the disaggregated level, the household saving component of private saving has varied considerably over recent decades. Interestingly, however, rises and falls in business saving can over time be offset by opposite changes in household saving. This is referred to as households 'seeing through the corporate veil' and may be explained by the fact that domestic households are ultimately the owners of domestic private firms. In other words, households at large think about private saving in a total sense. They take into account not only how much they will save for themselves but how much firms are also saving on their behalf.

The main feature of the behaviour of *private investment expenditure* is that it can be very volatile from year to year. Moreover, the type of investment undertaken transforms over longer periods. For instance, in the 1990s private investment expenditure in many advanced economies was concentrated in acquiring information technology. The public sector also saves and invests. Its saving is the difference between *public consumption* and *revenue*, whereas *public investment* is expenditure on infrastructure such as roads, dams and bridges.

Some economists argue that investment should include not only investment in physical capital but also in human capital, which is acquired through education and training. However, this is difficult to measure in reality and is not standard national accounting practice. We return to the issue of human capital and its significance in a later chapter on economic growth.

THE FLOW OF FUNDS AND THE MONETARY AGGREGATES

The *flow of funds* accounts show how saving is allocated in the economy in terms of borrowing and lending by sector, and reconcile with the saving aggregates in national capital account data. The flow of funds or financial accounts are also part of the full set of national accounts derived directly from the national capital account. The financial accounts provide greater statistical detail on borrowing and lending between domestic firms, households, government and the rest of the world. They can show, for instance, whether firms and governments are usually net borrowers of funds or whether households are usually net lenders of funds. They also show if the economy as a whole is a net borrower or lender of funds to the rest of the world.

The flow of funds accounts also itemise the different types of financial instruments available to transfer funds between borrowing and lending sectors, and highlight the role of financial institutions as intermediaries

Table 2.3 Sectoral financial positions.

Financial instrument	*Institutional sector*					
	Households	*Firms*	*Government*	*Financial intermediaries*	*Central bank*	*Rest of world*
Currency	+	+	−	+	−	
Bank deposits	+	+	+	−		+
Bank loans	−	−		+		−
Government bonds	+	+	−	+	+	+
Equities	+	−				+
Debentures	+	−				
Foreign securities	+	+				−
Foreign exchange				+	+	−
Net financial position (+ Asset; − Liability)	+	−	−	0	0	+ or −

between savers and investors in the economy. Financial institutions, mainly banks, play a role here by facilitating the movement of funds throughout the economy. For instance, they can accept saving or surplus funds from households, firms, governments and foreigners in the form of deposits and then can lend these funds to domestic firms for investment purposes. Not all lending and borrowing is 'intermediated' through financial institutions, however, as some funds are directly lent without banks or similar institutions being involved.

In addition, the flow of funds accounts measure the changes between two points in time in the net financial positions of the household, firm and government sectors, and those of financial intermediaries, the central bank and the rest of the world. The typical asset/liability structure at any point in time for these sectors is shown in Table 2.3. The main institutional sectors are shown in the columns, whereas the rows reveal the major financial instruments through which domestic and foreign saving is channelled throughout the economy.

An important component within the overall flow of funds is the amount of currency (notes and coin) in circulation. The domestic money supply is mainly determined by the economy's central bank, which has direct responsibility for money supply control. The most commonly discussed monetary aggregates in advanced economies are the *money base* (MB), M1, M3 and *credit*, which are defined as follows:

- MB: private sector holdings of notes and coin plus deposits of banks with the central bank.
- M1: currency plus deposits of the non-bank private sector in cheque accounts with banks.
- M3: M1 plus all other deposits of the non-bank private sector with banks.
- Credit: outstanding loans and advances from financial intermediaries to the private non-financial sector, plus bank bills outstanding.

NOMINAL AND REAL INTEREST RATES

The flow of funds accounts measure intersectoral flows of saving over a given time period. But how are these quantities of funds allocated? As in other areas of economics, the quantities of saving flowing to and from sectors are allocated through adjustments in a price, the interest rate. The interest rate represents the price borrowers must pay for the right to 'rent' money from savers or lenders, for whom the interest earned can be an additional source of income. Interest income may in fact be perceived as the compensation paid to savers for forgoing the consumption that they could have enjoyed instead of actually saving. Interest is also a cost to borrowers, who need the funds of savers to finance investment spending.

The interest rate is a macroeconomic variable and, as with the earlier macroeconomic variables, it is important to distinguish between nominal and real magnitudes. With interest rates, there is the *nominal interest rate* (i) and the inflation adjusted, or *real interest rate* (r).

Interest rates are usually quoted in nominal terms. However, during periods of inflation and deflation, the true cost of borrowing is not properly measured by nominal rates. For instance, consider the case of a farmer who borrows at a nominal interest rate of 10 per cent per year to buy a new tractor, and the inflation rate over the first year of the loan is 5 per cent. Although the farmer must pay 10 per cent of the borrowed amount in actual dollars, these dollars have lost half their value because of the inflation. Therefore, the real interest rate is approximately only 5 per cent, the difference between the nominal interest rate and the rate of inflation.

This distinction between nominal and real interest rates was emphasised by the American economist Irving Fisher, who argued that observed interest rates would incorporate a premium for anticipated or expected inflation (π^e). The so-called Fisher interest rate effect can therefore be summarised as $i = r + \pi^e$.

NATIONAL BALANCE SHEETS

At the level of the individual household or firm, the value of the entity's assets (real and financial) less its financial liabilities is defined as its *net worth*, a stock variable measured at a point in time. National net worth, or national wealth, for a closed economy is therefore simply the total value of all real assets in the economy because residents' financial assets are matched somewhere else in the economy by other residents' liabilities. Real assets include the capital stock (plant and equipment), dwellings and consumer durables (cars, household goods).

However, in an open economy, national wealth is the sum of all real assets, less financial liabilities to foreigners. As a stock measure, national wealth is the conceptual equivalent of the net worth of all of the nation's

Assets		Liabilities
Consumer durables		Foreign claims
Capital stock		– External debt
– Official		– Equities
– Non-official		National wealth
Total assets	=	Total claims

Figure 2.5 National balance sheet.

residents; that is, the sum of the value of residents' tangible and foreign assets less foreigners' claims to those assets.

The items in a simplified national balance sheet are shown in Figure 2.5.

Changes in national balance sheet values should be consistent with aggregate flows recorded in the national capital account and flow of funds accounts. At present, national balance sheets are not published regularly for most advanced economies, although details of the components (like foreign debt and the capital stock) are. Quarterly publication of a national balance sheet would complete the full system of national accounts, as recommended by the United Nations' national accounting guidelines. We will return to national balance sheets later in the book when considering the significance of an economy's foreign debt.

Summary

1. This chapter has introduced the main macroeconomic variables which, taken together, describe the overall performance of an open economy.
2. The national accounts include measures of national output, income and expenditure and their components. The main components of expenditure are consumption and investment, whereas the main components of income are wages and the gross operating surplus.
3. The business cycle reveals short-run movements in GDP around trend, from recession to full recovery. The business cycle is a major influence on the levels of employment and unemployment in the economy.
4. The unemployment rate is simply measured as the proportion of the workforce seeking employment. The participation rate is the proportion of the working age population who want to work.
5. The price level is measured by the CPI or IPD and their percentage rates of change are measures of domestic inflation. The CPI is a fixed-basket measure of the price level and is an example of a Laspeyres index. The IPD has variable weights and is an example of a Paasche index.
6. The TWI is an economy's nominal effective exchange rate. It measures the external value of the currency against the currencies of its major trading

partners. The real effective exchange rate is a measure of competitiveness. In essence, the real exchange rate captures changes in the relative prices of the goods and services a nation buys and sells to its major trading partners, after allowing for relative inflation rates.

7. There are two sides to the balance of payments accounts – the current account and the capital account. The current account includes exports and imports of goods and services and net income paid abroad. The capital account records transactions in assets and also measures the net inflows of foreign investment funds.

8. Foreign investment is also measured as the use of foreign saving in the national capital account, as well as in the flow of funds accounts, which reveal intersectoral borrowing and lending patterns. If an economy's external accounts are persistently characterised by a deficit on the current account and a surplus on the capital account, that economy is a net borrower from the rest of the world.

9. The main money supply aggregates, such as the money base, M1, M3 and credit, are also related to the flow of funds accounts and are controlled by the economy's central bank.

10. Interest rates represent the cost of financing investment but also compensate savers for forgoing consumption. Nominal interest rates differ from real interest rates by the extent of expected inflation.

11. The flow of funds accounts record the pattern of lending and borrowing between the main institutional sectors of the economy – households, firms, government, and the rest of the world. The flow of funds accounts reconcile with the capital account of the national accounts and the capital account of the external accounts.

12. National balance sheets are the stock counterpart to the flow of funds. They can provide estimates of an open economy's net worth or wealth after allowing for foreign claims on domestic assets.

Further reading

International Monetary Fund (1993) *Balance of Payments Manual*, 5th edn, Washington, DC: IMF.

United Nations (1993) *A System of National Accounts*, prepared under the auspices of the Inter-Secretariat Working Group on National Accounts, Brussels: Office for Official Publications of the European Communities.

3

The exchange rate and competitiveness

Before developing theoretical models for analysing the open economy, it is necessary to understand the role of the exchange rate, which is arguably the single most important price in international macroeconomics. The main aim of this chapter is to outline the fundamental influences on the exchange rate and the different systems under which it is set.

Over a century and a half ago, the classical British economist and political philosopher John Stuart Mill (1848) observed that:

> So much barbarism, however, still remains in the transactions of most civilized nations, that almost all independent countries choose to assert their nationality by having, to their own inconvenience and their neighbour's, a peculiar currency of their own.

In other words, exchange rates exist quite simply because each nation produces its own kind of money. Some examples are dollars, euros, rupees, yen, pounds, baht, won, pesos, yuan and dong. Not only, as Mill implies, does the existence of so many monies make cross-border economic transactions for individual traders more complicated, it also adds a further dimension to macroeconomic analysis.

Sudden movements in the external value of the currency are always a key item of any nation's economic 'news' and are often headlined in the financial press. Since the exchange rate is a price – the price of one currency in terms of another – just like other price changes, exchange rate movements can alter economic welfare.

The widespread interest in sharp exchange rate movements is not hard to understand since those affected by such fluctuations include all consumers and producers of internationally traded goods and services, producers who compete with internationally traded goods and services and those domestic enterprises which have assets and liabilities denominated in foreign currencies.

EXCHANGE RATE SYSTEMS

The choice of exchange rate regime is one of the most significant macroeconomic policy decisions any national government must make. The international monetary system is presently characterised by many types of exchange rate arrangements, as indicated in Table 3.1. This obviously suggests that the type of exchange rate regime which is right for one particular economy might not be appropriate for another.

Governments can choose to have the economy's exchange rate determined in one of the following ways. At one extreme, under an *independently floating* exchange rate system, the value of the exchange rate can be established purely by the forces of demand and supply for a given currency in the foreign exchange market where currencies are traded. The foreign exchange market itself is truly a global market on which the sun literally never sets, with currencies traded continually all around the world. Australian dollars can, for instance, be exchanged for other currencies at various times through the day in the markets in Hong Kong, Tokyo, London, New York, Frankfurt or Sydney.

The opposite extreme to an independently floating rate system is a *pegged rate* system in which one nation's currency is officially tied to one or more other currencies. It can either be irrevocably fixed against other currencies or can be set at a certain rate, but periodically manipulated – sometimes called adjustable peg arrangements. In essence, a pegged exchange rate differs from a floating exchange rate because the former is directly managed by a country's central bank.

Interestingly, those countries which presently have independently floating exchange rates are clearly in the minority in the world as a whole. The vast majority of countries therefore prefer some form of exchange rate management. This is evident from Table 3.1 produced by the IMF, which shows the full range of exchange rate systems, including those in between the polar extremes of free floating and pegged.

HISTORICAL DEVELOPMENTS

1. The gold standard

As discussed in Chapter 1, the world economy previously experienced an era of globalisation similar in many respects to the present one which began in the second half of the nineteenth century, but which was interrupted by the First World War (1914–18) and its aftermath. This first era of financial globalisation coincided with the gold standard system that then governed all international economic transactions. The gold standard is usually dated from the later part of the nineteenth century, when the main industrial economies of Western Europe and North America, along with their colonies, defined their currencies in terms of gold. However, some of these and other

Table 3.1 Global exchange rate arrangements.

Currency pegged to				Flexibility limited in terms of a single currency or group of currencies			More flexible	
US dollar	*French franc*	*Other currency*	*SDR*	*Other composite*	*Single currency*	*Cooperative arrangements*	*Other managed floating*	*Independently floating*
Angola	Benin	Bhutan (Indian rupee)	Libya	Bangladesh	Bahrain	Austria	Algeria	Afghanistan, Islamic State
Antigua & Barbuda	Burkina Faso	Bosnia and Herzegovina (euro)	Myanmar	Botswana	Qatar	Belgium	Belarus	Albania
Argentina	Cameroon	Brunei Darussalam (Singapore dollar)		Burundi	Saudi Arabia	Denmark	Brazil	Armenia
Bahamas, The	C. African Rep.	Bulgaria (euro)		Cape Verde	United Arab Emirates	Finland	Cambodia	Australia
Barbados	Chad	Estonia (euro)		Cyprus		France	Chile	Azerbaijan
Belize	Comoros	Kiribati (Australian dollar)		Fiji		Germany	China, P.R.	Bolivia
Djibouti	Congo, Rep.	Lesotho (South African rand)		Iceland		Ireland	Colombia	Canada
Dominica	Côte d'Ivoire			Jordan		Italy	Costa Rica	Congo, Dem. Rep
Grenada	Equatorial Guinea			Kuwait		Luxembourg	Croatia	Ethiopia
Iraq	Guinea-Bissau			Malta		Netherlands	Czech Rep.	Gambia, The
Liberia	Mali			Morocco		Portugal	Dominican Rep.	Ghana
Lithuania	Niger			Samoa		Spain	Ecuador	Guatemala
Marshall Islands	Senegal			Seychelles			Egypt	Guinea
Micronesia, Fed. States	Togo			Slovak Rep.			El Salvador	Guyana
Nigeria				Solomon Islands			Eritrea	Haiti
Oman				Tonga			Georgia	India
Panama				Vanuatu			Greece	Indonesia
St. Kitts & Nevis							Honduras	Jamaica
							Hungary	Japan
							Iran, I.R. of	Kazakhstan
							Israel	Kenya
							Korea	Lebanon
							Kyrgyz Rep.	

St. Lucia	Namibia (South African rand)	Laos P.D. Rep.	Madagascar
St. Vincent & the Grenadines	Nepal (Indian rupee)	Latvia	Malawi
Syrian Arab Rep.	San Marino (Italian lira)	Macedonia, FYR of	Mauritania
	Swaziland (South African rand)	Malaysia	Mexico
		Maldives	Moldova
		Nicaragua	Mongolia
		Norway	Mozambique
		Pakistan	New Zealand
		Poland	Papua New Guinea
		Russia	Paraguay
		Singapore	Peru
		Slovenia	Philippines
		Sri Lanka	Romania
		Sudan	São Tomé & Principe
		Suriname	Sierra Leone
		Thailand	Somalia
		Tunisia	South Africa
		Turkmenistan	Sweden
		Turkey	Switzerland
		Ukraine	Tajikistan, Rep.
		Uruguay	Tanzania
		Uzbekistan	Trinidad and Tobago
		Venezuela	Uganda
		Vietnam	United Kingdom
			United States
			Yemen, Rep. of
			Zambia
			Zimbabwe

Source Adapted from International Monetary Fund (1998) *International Financial Statistics* **51** (1), p. 8.

countries in the world had used gold for international settlements from much earlier times. In the gold standard era, many economies were increasingly internationalised by large trade and investment flows, which were in turn stimulated by the emergence of additional markets in the so-called New World.

The gold standard was suspended during the First World War; afterwards, the currencies of the United Kingdom, France and many other imperial powers floated quite freely until the gold standard was partially restored in the mid-1920s. However, international goods markets generally disintegrated throughout the 1920s, and this reversal of globalisation continued during the 1930s and 1940s as a result of escalating tariffs on internationally traded goods, unstable exchange rates, the Great Depression and the outbreak of the Second World War (1939–45).

2. Bretton Woods

During the 1930s and 1940s, the international economy also witnessed frequent competitive exchange rate devaluations. Near the end of the Second World War, a new international institution, the International Monetary Fund (IMF), with its headquarters in Washington, DC, was established to oversee the so-called Bretton Woods system, which lasted from 1945 until the early 1970s (see Box 3.1). This earlier system was named after a small town in New Hampshire in the United States, where, in 1944, an international conference agreed to establish a global system of fixed exchange rates to prevent the disorderly international monetary arrangements that the world experienced in the 1930s. The General Agreement on Tariffs and Trade (GATT), the precursor to the World Trade Organization (WTO), was also founded at this time for the purpose of scaling back tariffs and other protective measures that had restricted growth in international trade.

Under the former Bretton Woods system, exchange rates were officially managed, although currencies were allowed to fluctuate by a few percentage points either side of the formally established rates. Rates were usually fixed in terms of the United States dollar, which in turn had its value set against gold. A wide range of *exchange controls*, designed to impede international financial flows, accompanied the Bretton Woods system. These restrictions prohibited certain forms of international borrowing and lending and thereby made it easier for central banks to control their exchange rates.

Official intervention in the foreign exchange market, which entails either net purchases or sales of foreign exchange by a central bank, is largely determined by the nature of a country's exchange rate regime. Under the Bretton Woods system of pegged exchange rates, all the major industrialised countries were supposed to have currencies that were convertible into foreign currency at a fixed exchange rate. Under such conditions, official intervention was a passive act because the monetary authorities had little choice but

Box 3.1 Purposes of the IMF

(i) To promote international monetary cooperation through a permanent institution which provides the machinery for consultation and collaboration on international monetary problems.
(ii) To facilitate the expansion and balanced growth of international trade, and to contribute thereby to the promotion and maintenance of high levels of employment and real income and to the development of the productive resources of all members as primary objectives of economic policy.
(iii) To promote exchange stability, to maintain orderly exchange arrangements among members, and to avoid competitive exchange depreciation.
(iv) To assist in the establishment of a multilateral system of payments in respect of current transactions between members and in the elimination of foreign exchange restrictions which hamper the growth of world trade.
(v) To give confidence to members by making the general resources of the Fund temporarily available to them under adequate safeguards, thus providing them with opportunity to correct maladjustments in their balance of payments without resorting to measures destructive of national or international prosperity.
(vi) In accordance with the above, to shorten the duration and lessen the degree of disequilibrium in the international balances of payments of members.

The Fund shall be guided in all its policies and decisions by the purposes set forth in this Article.

Source *IMF, Articles of Agreement of the International Monetary Fund, Article I – Purposes.*
www.imf.org/external/pubs/ft/aa/aa01.htm

to ensure that their exchange rates did not vary beyond the predetermined rates. The Bretton Woods system aimed to restore the exchange rate stability of the gold standard era, although as a point of difference international capital flows were heavily controlled in order to assist central banks maintain exchange rates at their pegged levels. A major reason why nations agreed to fix exchange rates was that this was seen as a way of minimising exchange rate uncertainty, which was thought to deter international trade flows.

3. The generalised float

The Bretton Woods system eventually collapsed in the early 1970s, however, because the pegged exchange rates it promoted could not be sustained in a global financial environment where international capital flows were continually growing, at times circumventing official investment barriers erected by national governments. The irony here was that this strong growth in international capital flows was in part attributable to a re-emergence of increased volumes of exports and imports of goods and services that often had to be financed.

Before the generalised float that followed the breakdown of the Bretton Woods system, domestic monetary authorities treated their respective economy's exchange rate as a macroeconomic constraint or policy instrument to be varied as necessary for balance of payments or inflation control reasons. With the floating of exchange rates, the nature and size of the global foreign exchange market changed dramatically, partly because the many exchange controls, which had impeded international financial transactions, were simultaneously abolished. The most noteworthy exchange controls abolished were those that limited outflows of funds abroad and those that prevented foreign borrowing by resident financial institutions and enterprises.

International capital movements grew markedly in the 1960s and 1970s as national goods and financial markets became more globally integrated. As a result, national monetary authorities found it increasingly difficult to manage exchange rates when confronted with huge flows of international funds. The Bretton Woods system collapsed in the early 1970s as central banks gave up trying to fix exchange rates.

Many nations also wanted more freedom to design and implement their own macroeconomic policy, and it was thought that floating exchange rates would make that easier. Furthermore, under the Bretton Woods arrangements some governments had attempted to maintain fixed exchange rates by imposing severe restrictions on trade in goods, particularly imports. Such policy was also at odds with the global impetus for liberalising international trade.

FIXED VERSUS FLOATING EXCHANGE RATES

A perennial question which arises in exchange rate economics is whether it is better for economies to adopt a floating exchange rate or some form of fixed exchange rate system instead. One argument commonly put forward in favour of fixed exchange rates is that they minimise the price uncertainty which floating exchange rates can generate for a nation's exporters and importers. Uncertainty stemming from volatile and unpredictable exchange rate movements is thought to harm the overall size of an economy's international trade and hence the growth of that economy's GDP. Such thinking actually provided the main rationale for the Bretton Woods system but is still prevalent today.

Interestingly, however, international trade data shows that export and import volumes have not shrunk over the period since the Bretton Woods system collapsed, even though exchange rates have become much more volatile. In fact, under the generalised floating exchange rate system in operation since the early 1970s, international trade volumes have grown markedly, one reason being that exporters and importers are now able to insure against the risks of currency movements through the use of various financial instruments.

The main academic arguments against fixed exchange rates and in favour of floating were first clearly espoused by Nobel prize-winning economist Milton Friedman (1953). Friedman suggested that floating exchange rates would insulate economies from foreign disturbances and allow governments to directly control their money supplies, which could keep inflation low. Firmer control of money supplies also implies that domestic interest rates are less volatile under floating exchange rates.

Another argument in favour of floating exchange rates is that with a floating regime, the exchange rate itself, not the central bank, bears the pressure of adjustment to ensure equality between the demand for and supply of currency on the foreign exchange market. Under a fixed exchange rate system with stringent exchange controls, a higher current account deficit must be financed through a run-down of the central bank's official reserve assets. In contrast, under a floating exchange rate, without central bank intervention, there must be a currency depreciation if the nation is running a higher current account deficit which is not matched by additional private capital inflow from abroad. Through an improvement in competitiveness, this would automatically work to reduce the deficit on the current account by raising exports and lowering imports.

Critics of floating exchange rates stress, however, that if exchange rates are free to float and international funds are allowed to move quickly in and out of countries, then currency speculators may frequently drive market-determined rates away from their fundamental economic values. Such financial market behaviour is called destabilising speculation. In practice, destabilising speculation means that currency speculators will magnify exchange rate fluctuations by creating periodic speculative 'bubbles', increase currency volatility and further raise uncertainty for exporters and importers of goods and services.

Friedman, in his advocacy of floating exchange rates, dismissed the notion of destabilising speculation, instead proposing an alternative view of how speculators actually behave. He argued that speculative behaviour in the foreign exchange market should in effect be stabilising, not destabilising, because destabilising speculative behaviour could not last indefinitely. The argument is that under destabilising speculation, the speculators themselves would continually make financial losses.

Such losses would occur because the speculators would persistently and mistakenly sell a particular currency, driving it even lower when it was losing value, yet buy that currency whenever it became more expensive. Speculators who behaved this way would eventually go out of business. The opposite to destabilising speculation is stabilising speculation, which happens when speculators buy a currency when it loses value and sell that currency when it gains value against other currencies. In the process, speculators would be making profits and surviving. Also, as a result, exchange rate fluctuations would be smoother than otherwise.

Another argument often used to justify central bank management of exchange rates is closely related to the notion that foreign exchange markets are prone to speculative excesses. This argument is based on the assumption of information asymmetry. That is, the central bank is supposed to possess superior economic information than that held by all other agents in the foreign exchange market, on the grounds that the authorities know things about the economy that market traders do not.

Again, decades ago Friedman challenged this presumption by arguing that it was undesirable for central banks to intervene in the foreign exchange market to influence the exchange rate because there was:

> no reason to expect that government officials will be better judges than private speculators of the likely movements in underlying conditions of trade and, hence, no reason to expect that government speculation will be more successful than private speculation in promoting a desirable pace and timing of adjustment. (Friedman, 1953, p. 188)

The pegged exchange rate system essentially reflected a view that the exchange rate was too important a macroeconomic variable to be left to market forces. When any exchange rate is officially managed, it is still likely that exceptionally large revaluations and devaluations can occur from time to time. Moreover, under such a system, foreign exchange flows directly influence domestic monetary conditions. For instance, whenever interest rates rise there are strong foreign capital inflows, and central banks have to buy foreign currency each day in exchange for local currency, thereby adding local currency to the financial system. This makes it difficult for central banks to control the domestic money supply under pegged rates.

With the floating of many currencies from the early 1970s, the nature and size of the foreign exchange market changed dramatically, partly because the many exchange controls, which had impeded international financial transactions, were also simultaneously abolished. The most noteworthy exchange controls were those which limited portfolio investment by domestic residents abroad and those which prevented foreign borrowing by locally based companies. The accompanying liberalisation of financial markets also extended the integration of domestic capital markets with overseas markets. The implications of this integration will be further discussed in later chapters. In short, floating exchange rates marked a major turning point for macroeconomic policy in many advanced economies.

At present, the five most actively traded currencies in the world are the United States dollar, the yen, the euro, the pound sterling and the Swiss franc. Table 3.2 shows the data for the most actively traded pre-euro currencies.

Trading in the foreign exchange markets mainly involves transactions in the local currency against other currencies. However, local trading also includes what is called 'third currency' trading not actually involving the local currency (such as when United States dollars are traded in the United Kingdom market against yen).

Table 3.2 Average daily turnover of currencies in world markets (April 1998).

Currency	*Turnover (US$ billion)*
US dollar	1260
Japanese yen	300
Pound sterling	158
Swiss franc	101
Canadian dollar	52
Australian dollar	44

Source Adapted from Bank for International Settlements, *BIS Triennial Central Bank Survey of Foreign Exchange and Derivatives Market Activity* (Statistical Annex, Table E-1). www.bis.org/publ/r_fx98.htm

BASIC MODELS OF THE EXCHANGE RATE

Obviously, when the exchange rate is fixed, the monetary authorities themselves set the value of the domestic currency in terms of foreign currencies. So there is therefore no need for any formal economic theory to explain the behaviour of fixed exchange rates. But what macroeconomic factors cause movements in the exchange rate when it floats? To answer that question, we consider two basic approaches to exchange rate determination. The first of these, based on flows, shows how short-run external account disturbances may affect the exchange rate. It can also demonstrate what the overall balance of payments means under a managed exchange rate regime. The second approach, called purchasing power parity (PPP), helps us understand what influences the nominal exchange rate over longer periods.

4. The traditional flow model of the exchange rate

Many theoretical models have emerged over the years to explain how the nominal exchange rate is determined in the foreign currency market. The most basic of these applies the standard tools of demand and supply analysis to the foreign exchange market. In its simplest version, this model focuses on the flows of currency which arise from exports and imports of goods and services, as well as international capital flows. Recall from Chapter 2 the distinction that was made between the academic (e) and market (E) definitions of the nominal exchange rate. Here, e, the number of domestic currency units per foreign currency unit, is used.

Consider the bilateral exchange rate between the Canadian and United States currencies. As the Canadian dollar appreciates against the United States dollar ($US), this leads to a greater demand for imports of goods and services from the United States. This is because imports have become relatively cheaper when valued in terms of Canadian dollars. Canadian residents

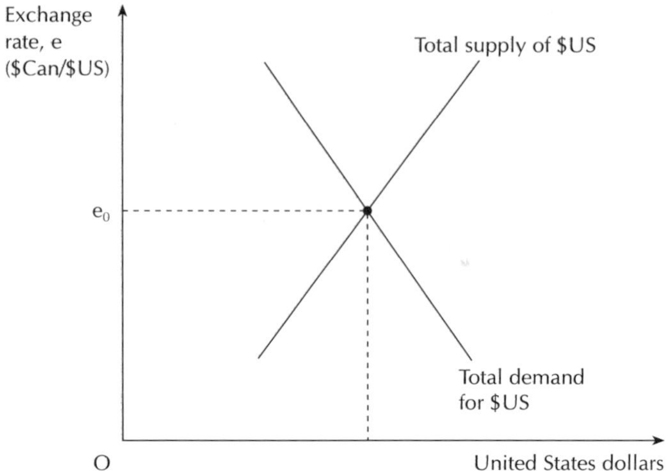

Figure 3.1 The flow approach to the exchange rate.

therefore simply demand more foreign products when their currency is worth more in terms of other currencies. The Canadian demand for $US is a derived demand because residents need $US to settle their accounts with the American sellers of goods and services. Therefore, the demand for $US increases as the exchange rate appreciates (e↓). This is reflected in the downward sloping schedule of Figure 3.1.

We can now add to the flow demand for foreign currency to pay for imports, Canadian residents' demand for $US to purchase American assets. For instance, Canadians may wish to purchase shares in an American company or invest in US Treasury bonds. This demand for $US is recorded as net capital outflow to the United States. It is not directly influenced by the prevailing exchange rate and so can be added to the derived demand for $US to pay for imports.

On the supply side of this market, a depreciation of the $Can leads to increased earnings of $US by Canadian exporters. This is because more Canadian-produced goods and services are likely to be sold if they become cheaper from the perspective of American buyers. Therefore, the weaker is the exchange rate (e↑), the greater is the supply of $US to Canadian residents.

There is also the supply of $US stemming from American purchases of Canadian financial assets, such as domestically issued bonds or shares in local companies. These additional $US arising from American foreign investment in Canada supplement residents' $US earnings from exports of goods and services to the United States. This gives us the upward sloping schedule of Figure 3.1. Together the flow demand and supply schedules of $US establish an equilibrium exchange rate of e_0.

As discussed earlier, under an independently floating exchange rate regime, a central bank is not supposed to use its stock of official reserve

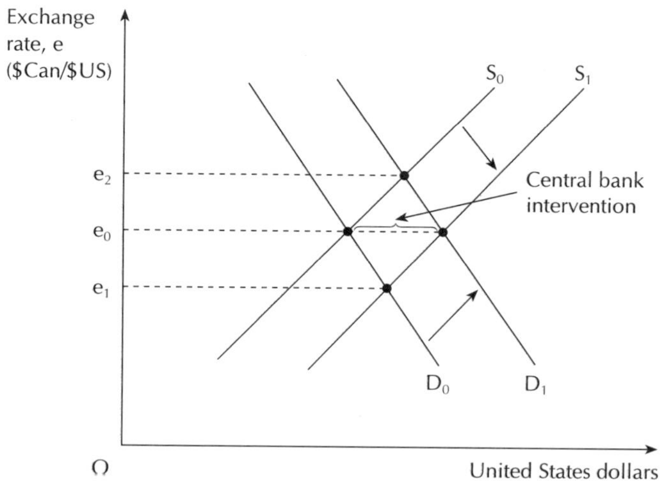

Figure 3.2 Official intervention and the exchange rate.

assets to intervene in the foreign exchange market for the purpose of influencing the exchange rate. All of the international adjustment should be reflected in changes in the exchange rate itself. In practice, however, most industrialised countries have flexible exchange rate regimes which allow for some mix at times of free foreign exchange market adjustment and official intervention.

Under a fixed or pegged exchange rate system, the central bank is continually intervening in the foreign exchange market to set the exchange rate. The change in the central bank's official reserve assets over any time indicates the actual extent of its foreign exchange market intervention. If, for example, an economy experiences a shortfall of foreign currency on combined current and capital account transactions, the monetary authority would have to intervene in the foreign exchange market to finance the overall imbalance at the given exchange rate. In this case it would have to buy the home currency and sell foreign exchange from its own reserves to make up for the shortage of foreign currency from abroad. On the other hand, if there was an overall balance of payments surplus on combined current and capital accounts at the fixed exchange rate, the central bank would be accumulating foreign currency reserves in exchange for local currency.

To further appreciate what official intervention means, refer to Figure 3.2. When the central bank sells part of its official $US reserves, it supplies additional $US in exchange for $Can. As shown, this shifts the supply schedule to the right (to S_1) by the extent of the intervention. As a result, the Canadian dollar appreciates to e_1 ($e\downarrow$).

Alternatively, if the central bank buys $US to add to its official reserve assets, it adds to market demand, shifting the demand curve (to D_1). This would depreciate the exchange rate to e_2 ($e\uparrow$). By augmenting the market demand for $US in exchange for $Can, the central bank's intervention depreciates the value of the local currency, at the same time as its purchases of $US enlarge its stock of official reserve assets.

'News' and the exchange rate

Short-run exchange rate movements are often explained in terms of the reactions of participants in the foreign exchange markets to new economic information, such as the release of the latest consumer price index (CPI) or balance of payments (BOP) data. According to modern views about financial market behaviour, the prices of financial assets and exchange rates quickly reflect all new information, including previously unanticipated economic events.

Additional information about the behaviour of the economy which is unanticipated is called economic 'news'. Examples are unexpectedly bad CPI or BOP statistics. On release of such data, all financial prices adjust instantaneously to absorb the latest information. Therefore, over short periods such as days or weeks, exchange rates exhibit similar degrees of volatility as other financial prices, such as those of equities and long-term bonds, which also adjust rapidly as expectations about their prospects change. By way of contrast, the prices of many consumable goods (like fresh bread) are not affected at all by 'news'.

Economic 'news' and changed market expectations about the future course of economic events have an impact on the exchange rate through short-term international capital flows. In terms of the basic flow model of the exchange rate, if foreign investors are suddenly alarmed by an unexpectedly high CPI figure, there would be a sudden drop in supply of foreign exchange to purchase domestic financial assets. A leftward shift of the supply schedule in Figure 3.3 would therefore immediately depreciate the currency. A similar reaction could occur during periods of great political uncertainty. In general, bad economic news tends to instantly depreciate the currency over the short term, whereas good news tends to appreciate it.

Over longer periods, however, more fundamental economic influences on the exchange rate come into play, and it is to these we now turn.

5. Purchasing power parity

The most durable long-run theory of the exchange rate is called *purchasing power parity* (PPP), which links exchange rate movements to changes in national price levels and inflation rates. PPP has a long history, dating back to the writings of the classical British economists David Hume and David Ricardo. Ricardo, in 1810, for instance, sought to explain why the British pound continued to lose its foreign exchange value in terms of gold. The value of the pound in terms of gold, in those days, defined the exchange rate. In essence, Ricardo argued that a rising British price level eroded the domestic purchasing power of the British pound, which in turn diminished

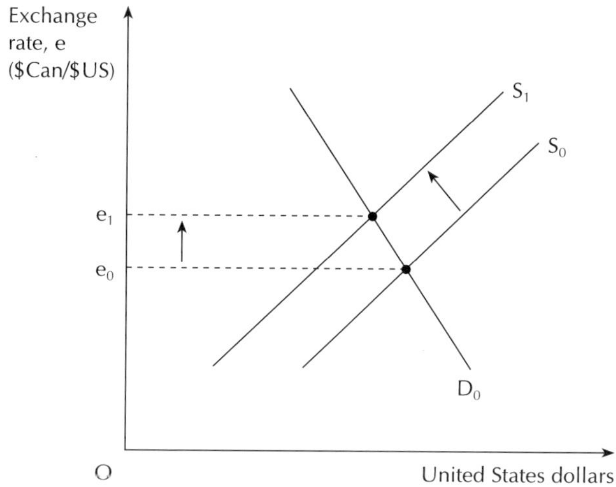

Figure 3.3 'News' and the exchange rate.

the external purchasing power of the currency through a depreciating exchange rate.

The modern form of PPP is usually attributed to the Swedish economist Gustav Cassel, who argued that in resetting fixed exchange rates after the First World War, allowance should be made for changes in national price levels which had occurred during the war. Cassel proposed that those nations which had experienced relatively high inflation should have their currencies devalued in relation to the currencies of nations which had experienced much lower inflation.

In more recent decades, there has been a revival of interest in PPP which has generated a large theoretical and empirical literature in the field of exchange rate economics.

Absolute PPP

There are two versions of PPP – *absolute* and *relative* PPP. The absolute PPP relation can be developed from the *law of one price,* which applies at the single commodity level.

In essence, the law of one price depends on commodity price arbitrage. Arbitrage is the process of buying and selling goods, services or assets to exploit price differences in different locations. In this context, such a process ensures that the prices of homogeneous products are eventually equalised across country borders. For instance, if a tonne of coal sells in Australia for $A100 and the exchange rate against the $US, again defined as e, is 2.00, then, ignoring transport costs, arbitrage should ensure that coal will sell for $US50 in the United States.

Consider what would happen if this was not the case. If the price of coal in the United States was greater than $US50, say $US80, Australian coal producers could make extra profits by diverting sales of their coal from the Australian market to the United States market. This diversion of sales would of itself act to equalise prices. Coal prices would rise in Australia as supply fell and fall in the United States as supply increased. Alternatively, if the price of coal in Australia was \$A110, extra profits could be made by producers in the United States diverting coal for sale in Australia to make extra profits. Again, in equilibrium when extra profit-making opportunities are exhausted, only one price would prevail in common currency terms.

Now to put things in macroeconomic as opposed to microeconomic terms, it is necessary to use national price levels, instead of the price of a single commodity like coal. Consider the case where there are two broad classes of goods in two economies. Call these broadly defined classes of goods commodities (C) and manufactures (M). Using the same two economies as before, Australia and the United States, let us denote the prices of these goods p_C^A and p_M^A for Australia and p_C^{US} and p_M^{US} for the United States.

The national price level for Australia, P^A, can then be expressed as:

$$P^A = \alpha p_C^A + (1 - \alpha)p_M^A \tag{3.1}$$

where α is the weight for commodities and $(1 - \alpha)$ is the weight for manufactures in the Australian CPI basket of goods. For the United States, assuming the same weights in the CPI, the price level, P^{US}, can be expressed as:

$$P^{US} = \alpha p_C^{US} + (1 - \alpha)p_M^{US} \tag{3.2}$$

Multiplying Equation (3.2) by the exchange rate, e, yields:

$$e \cdot P^{US} = \alpha \cdot e \cdot p_C^{US} + (1 - \alpha)e \cdot p_M^{US} \tag{3.3}$$

Assuming that commodity price arbitrage equalises the price of commodities and manufactures, it follows that $p_C^A = e \cdot p_C^{US}$ and $p_M^{US} = e \cdot p_M^{US}$.

Hence, by substitution in Equation (3.3):

$$P^A = \alpha p_C^A + (1 - \alpha)p_M^A = e \cdot P^{US} \tag{3.4}$$

Equation (3.4) thereby establishes absolute PPP in a multicommodity world. It is simply the condition $P^A = e \cdot P^{US}$ and can be rearranged as:

$$e = P^A/P^{US} \tag{3.5}$$

This implies that the higher is the Australian price level relative to the United States price level, the weaker is the purchasing power of the Australian dollar relative to the United States dollar. In other words and in general terms, if Australia's price level rises faster than another economy's price level, the exchange rate of the Australian dollar depreciates against that other economy's currency.

Although this straightforward analysis provides an important insight about long-run exchange rate behaviour, there are some qualifications which should be borne in mind. In practice, there are several reasons why in a multicommodity world, absolute PPP may fail to hold. These are as follows:

1. The weights used in national price indexes are likely to differ across countries as consumption patterns often differ. For instance, the quantity of rice consumed in Japan is much higher per head than in the United Kingdom.
2. Most goods and services are not fully homogeneous across borders. An imported Mercedes Benz is not the same as a locally made Ford limousine, though both are luxury cars.
3. International trade restrictions, such as tariffs and import quotas, impede the free movement of goods and services.
4. Transport costs can be significant.
5. Not all goods and services are internationally tradable.

Relative PPP

Relative PPP is an alternative specification of this approach to exchange rates which restates the relationship between exchange rates and price levels in percentage change terms.

As the percentage change in the price level, $\hat{P}$, is just the same as the domestic inflation rate, π, it follows that the percentage depreciation of the nominal exchange rate over a given period of time should be equal to the inflation differential between the home economy, say New Zealand, and the foreign economy, say the United Kingdom.

$$\hat{e} = \pi^{NZ} - \pi^{UK}$$

For instance, if New Zealand's inflation rate was consistently 5 per cent higher than the inflation rate of the United Kingdom, then the value of the $NZ would depreciate against the £UK at a constant rate of 5 per cent, equal to the inflation differential. Intuitively, what the above expression means is that currencies which lose their domestic purchasing power because of domestic inflation also lose their external purchasing power through a depreciating exchange rate. In other words, exchange rates move over time in line with the relative purchasing power of monies.

The empirical evidence about the validity of PPP holding on a strict one-for-one sense is quite mixed. What may presently be regarded as the conventional empirical wisdom about PPP, as confirmed by a weighty body of econometric evidence to date, is that:

1. PPP does not hold over short periods, although
2. PPP tends to hold over longer periods, especially when differences in inflation rates are large and persistent.

The eminent American economist Ronald McKinnon has nicely summed up views on this approach to the exchange rate in stating that:

> Until a more robust theory replaces it, we should assume that purchasing power parity among tradable goods tends to hold in the long run in the absence of overt impediments to trade among countries with convertible currencies. (McKinnon, 1979, p. 136)

COMPETITIVENESS AND THE EQUILIBRIUM EXCHANGE RATE

The absolute PPP condition can also be understood as a long-run equilibrium condition for the exchange rate. Hence frequent observed departures from this condition may be interpreted as short-run deviations from PPP. Such deviations are equivalent to movements in the real exchange rate and the level of the economy's competitiveness. These deviations may arise for many reasons, one of which is the effects of unanticipated 'news', as discussed earlier.

To understand how deviations from PPP and the real exchange rate are related, recall from Chapter 2 that the real exchange rate or competitiveness, R, is the nominal effective exchange rate, multiplied by the ratio of the domestic to foreign price levels. Returning to the New Zealand–United Kingdom example, on a bilateral basis:

$$R = \frac{e \cdot P^{UK}}{P^{NZ}}$$

If absolute PPP held at all times, P^{NZ} would always equal $e \cdot P^{UK}$. Therefore, the numerator and denominator of the above expression for competitiveness would cancel each other out, ensuring that the real exchange rate of the \$NZ, R, would always be constant and equal to unity. That is:

$$R = \frac{e \cdot P^{UK}}{P^{NZ}} = 1$$

With instantaneous PPP, any rise (fall) in P^{UK} would be fully offset by an appreciation (depreciation) of e. Similarly, any rise (fall) in P^{NZ} would be fully offset by a depreciation (appreciation) of the \$NZ.

In actuality, deviations from PPP, or real exchange rate movements, are common over shorter periods such as weeks, months or quarters. This happens mainly because the nominal exchange rate varies more frequently and by much larger magnitudes than national price levels in the short run.

Economic commentators often suggest that particular exchange rates are *overvalued* or *undervalued*. But if the exchange rate is determined by the forces of demand and supply in foreign exchange markets, in what sense can it be away from an equilibrium value? The PPP approach can be used to answer such a question, since we know that PPP provides a long-run equilibrium condition for the exchange rate. For instance, if the real exchange rate suddenly appreciated, that is

$$R = \frac{e \cdot P^{UK}}{P^{NZ}} < 1$$

this implies a short-term deviation from PPP which worsens competitiveness. This loss of competitiveness could, however, be eliminated by an offsetting nominal depreciation, ($e\uparrow$), suggesting that the nominal exchange rate is currently too strong and is therefore overvalued. On the contrary, if

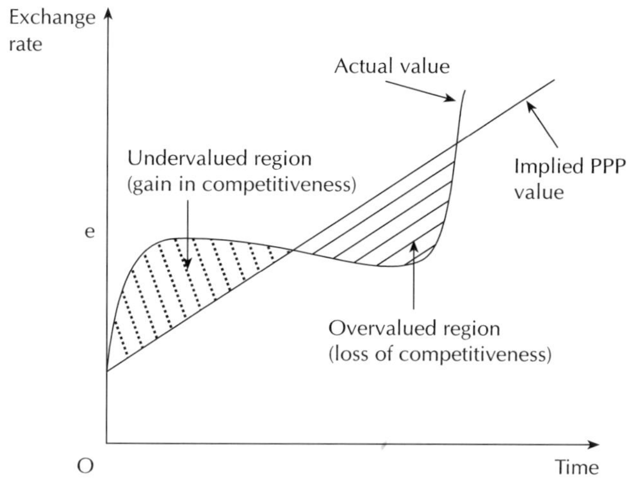

Figure 3.4 Currency undervaluation and overvaluation.

$$\frac{e \cdot P^{UK}}{P^{NZ}} > 1$$

the nominal exchange rate needs to appreciate to restore the PPP equilibrium. Hence, it is presently too weak relative to its long-run equilibrium value, and is therefore undervalued.

The notions of undervaluation and overvaluation of the nominal exchange rate relative to implied equilibrium exchange rate values are illustrated in Figure 3.4. Note that when the local currency is undervalued, competitiveness improves, whereas competitiveness worsens when the local currency is overvalued.

Exchange rate changes alter the prices of domestically produced goods and services relative to goods and services produced in other countries. Hence, they affect the profitability of exporting and the cost of importing from abroad. Competitiveness either improves or worsens over the short term because of nominal exchange rate movements or because domestic prices or costs change in relation to prices or costs of major trading partners. Since nominal exchange rates are far more variable than relative national price levels or labour costs, sharp nominal exchange rate swings account for most real exchange rate movements.

Summary

1. The exchange rate affects the prices at which a country trades with the rest of the world and is integral to open-economy analysis and policy formulation.
2. In the Bretton Woods era, exchange rates were fixed in terms of the United States dollar. These days, however, national governments can choose from a number of alternative exchange rate arrangements, ranging from independently floating to fixed.

3. The ongoing debate about fixed versus floating exchange rates covers issues such as whether currency speculation is stabilising or destabilising and whether central banks possess superior economic knowledge.

4. The decision to float exchange rates and abolish exchange controls can be seen as an inevitable development in light of increased capital market integration.

5. The short-run flow approach to the exchange rate is based on relative movements in the supply and demand for currencies arising from external account transactions such as imports, exports and foreign investment flows.

6. Over longer periods, the most fundamental theory of exchange rate determination is PPP, which links relative price levels and inflation rates to movements in the nominal exchange rate. Countries with higher inflation rates tend to have depreciating currencies relative to countries with low inflation rates.

7. PPP, as a long-run equilibrium condition, can be used to judge whether nominal exchange rates at any time are overvalued or undervalued.

Further reading

Corden, M. (1994) *Economic Policy, Exchange Rates and the International System*, Oxford: Oxford University Press, chapter 12.

Eichengreen, B. (1994) 'History of the international monetary system', in F. Van Der Ploeg, *The Handbook of International Macroeconomics*, Oxford: Basil Blackwell.

Friedman, M. (1953) 'The case for flexible exchange rates', in M. Friedman, *Essays in Positive Economics*, Chicago, IL: University of Chicago Press.

Krugman, P. (1989) *Exchange Rate Instability*, Cambridge, MA: MIT Press.

4

Tradables, nontradables and the terms of trade

If all the economies in the world were ranked in descending order in terms of the value of respective GDPs, the vast majority of nearly two hundred would be grouped at the bottom, with the United States, the world's largest economy, at the top, followed by Japan in second place. Figure 4.1 shows the relative size of the ten largest economies in the world, ranked by the size of GDP. The remaining economies in the world have comparatively small national incomes.

If economies are relatively small, it means the industries of those economies are usually 'dependent' on the prices set in world markets for their products. Small economies are therefore unable to significantly influence the international prices of goods and services they trade with the rest of the world. Just how much of total production and spending, as measured in

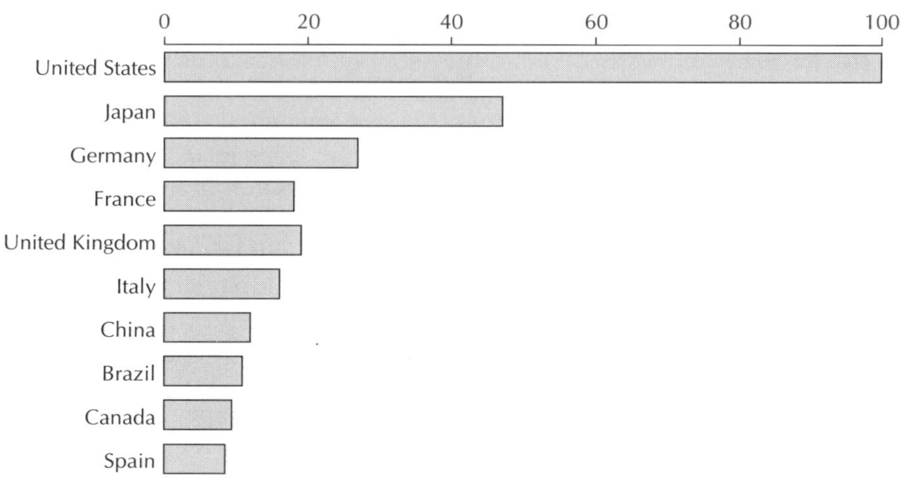

Figure 4.1 The ten largest economies.
Source Adapted from World Bank, *World Development Indicators*, 2001 (table 1.1)

the national accounts, is actually subject to international influences and how much is not has important implications for such things as the effectiveness of domestic macroeconomic policy initiatives to influence the trade balance and the international transmission of inflation.

TRADABLES VERSUS NONTRADABLES

To understand these issues, it is first important to distinguish more formally between goods and services which can be termed *tradable* and those which can be termed *nontradable*. In essence, *tradables* are goods and services which can potentially be bought and sold on world markets. The share of tradable output in GDP is another measure of an economy's openness.

Tradables consist of exports, imports, close substitutes for exports (such as maple syrup consumed domestically by Canadian residents) and import competing goods (such as locally made televisions). In other words, tradables include domestic production which is not necessarily shipped abroad, but which is nonetheless subject to international competition.

The nominal exchange rate translates foreign currency prices of tradables into domestic currency values. For example, if the world price of oil is $US20 per barrel and the exchange rate against the pound is 0.75, then British oil producers can export as much oil as possible, at the given exchange rate, and continue receiving £15 per barrel. Similarly, under the small-country assumption, domestic residents can import as much as possible of any particular commodity at the given exchange rate, without affecting the price paid.

Nontradables, on the other hand, are defined as those domestically produced goods and services which are effectively isolated from the effects of international competition and whose prices are therefore determined by the forces of domestic demand and supply. Nontradables are usually imagined as services, such as public administration, health services, legal advice, school education, construction and entertainment services, all of which are included as part of total GDP. What characterises nontradables, however, is that they are provided exclusively to domestic residents and cannot be bought or sold by foreigners.

Apart from services, many commodities are also nontradable, especially if international transport costs are too high, making shipment unprofitable, or if the goods are perishable in some sense. Ready-mixed concrete is a good example of a nontradable good. Artificial trade barriers, such as tariffs and quotas, or cultural norms which prohibit consumption (like eating pork in the Middle East) can also make certain goods and services nontradable in practice.

Having outlined the distinction between tradables and nontradables, let us now consider some theoretical models of the open economy which apply the tradables/nontradables dichotomy.

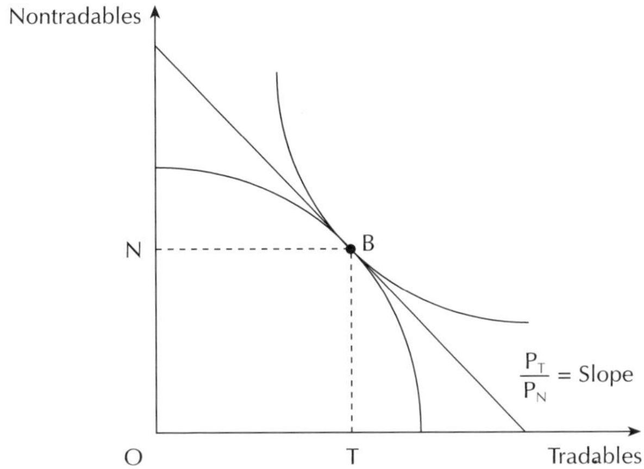

Figure 4.2 The dependent economy model.

THE DEPENDENT ECONOMY MODEL

The tradables/nontradables dichotomy can first be used to examine some important macroeconomic issues through the so-called 'dependent economy' or Swan–Salter model, named after Australian economists Trevor Swan and Wilfred Salter. This approach abstracts from the influence of international capital flows on the open economy, in order to highlight the linkages between competitiveness and expenditure and production of tradables and nontradables. In the variant of the model to follow, the exchange rate is set by the forces of supply and demand for currencies in the foreign exchange market.

In a fully employed economy, the production of tradables and nontradables can be depicted using a production possibility frontier, or transformation curve, as in Figure 4.2. Any point on the curve shows that if more tradables are produced using given technology and factor inputs (the labour force, land and capital) then the supply of nontradable output must be reduced. This is because factor inputs would have to be shifted out of nontradable production and into expanding industries in the tradable sector. Thus the concave frontier reveals possible production combinations between tradables and nontradables on the aggregate supply side of the open economy.

There is also the aggregate expenditure or demand side, which in this model is represented by a community indifference curve. This indifference curve captures the spending preferences of all domestic residents on tradables and nontradables.

The point of tangency of the production possibility frontier and the community indifference curve, shown at B in Figure 4.2, represents simultaneous *internal balance* and *external balance* for the economy. Only at B does desired national expenditure equal desired national output. Internal balance here means that all resources are fully utilised, so that there is no unemployment of labour. External balance in this context means that the balance of trade, exports less imports, is zero.

At B, ON nontradables are produced and consumed, and OT tradables are produced and consumed. The economy is at full employment as it is on the transformation curve and the balance of trade is zero because the value of exports equals the value of imports. Any other point apart from B would represent an imbalance, implying either an excess demand or supply of either tradables or nontradables.

Now the slope of the line tangential to the transformation or production possibility curve is given by the ratio P_T/P_N where P_T is the price of tradables and P_N is the price of nontradables. The relative price ratio P_T/P_N has also been called the real exchange rate or competitiveness, for reasons which should become apparent. Note, however, that this definition of the real exchange rate differs from the more common definition of earlier chapters, where no distinction was made between tradables and nontradables. Implicitly, it was earlier assumed in discussing deviations from PPP and competitiveness that all goods and services were internationally tradable. This new concept of the real exchange rate, based on the tradable/nontradable dichotomy, will be distinguished from the earlier measure by calling it the *alternative real exchange rate* (R^A). More formally:

$$R^A = \frac{P_T}{P_N} = \frac{eP_T^*}{P_N}$$

In essence, real influences affect this alternative measure of competitiveness and hence the slope of the relative price line in Figure 4.2. For example, if the community's tastes change, such that more nontradables are demanded by residents, then the slope of the relative price line (P_T/P_N) must eventually fall to restore equilibrium. Because a small country cannot affect the world price of its tradables, whose foreign currency prices are determined abroad, equilibrium can only be achieved by a rise in the price of nontradables or a fall in the domestic currency price of tradables. If the price of nontradables is for institutional reasons rigid, then the necessary adjustment in the relative price of tradables to nontradables can only come about through an appreciation of the nominal exchange rate. In other words, the price of foreign currency falls as a means of lowering the domestic price of tradables relative to nontradables.

The dependent economy approach can now be generalised to demonstrate the comparative static effects of various real disturbances for a small open economy. To do this, it is necessary to derive supply and demand curves for the tradables sector of the economy from Figure 4.2 in alternative real exchange rate–tradables space. Figure 4.3 shows that on the production side of the economy, the domestic supply of tradables is positively related to a depreciation of the alternative real exchange rate (a rise in R^A). One way of understanding this is to think of a rise in e raising the domestic currency price of tradables, other things being equal, thereby inducing more

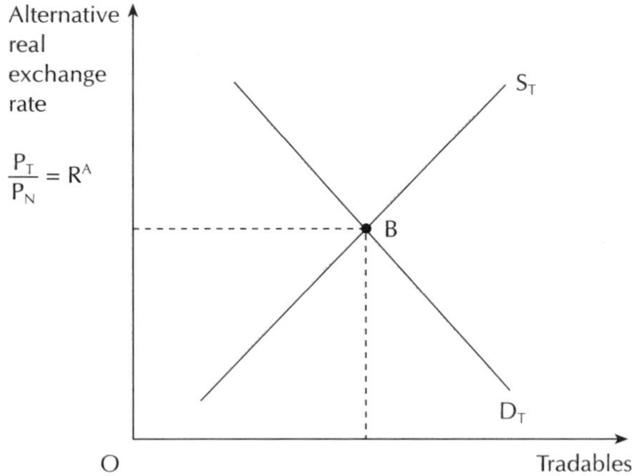

Figure 4.3 The demand and supply of tradables.

local production of tradables. On the demand side, for a given level of national income the demand for tradables is negatively related to a depreciation of the alternative real exchange rate. This is because a real depreciation makes tradables relatively more expensive and hence less attractive to residents than nontradables. In microeconomic parlance, the derived aggregate demand curve for tradables in Figure 4.3 is actually an example of a compensated demand curve which abstracts from income effects.

Equilibrium at B in Figure 4.3 corresponds to the point of internal and external balance shown earlier at B in Figure 4.2. It is also possible to derive similar demand and supply schedules for the nontradables sector of the small open economy. However, this is not necessary for our purposes because if there is equilibrium in one sector (tradables), there must be simultaneous equilibrium in the other (nontradables) in accordance with an important tenet of general equilibrium theory known as Walras' law.

EFFECTS OF INDUSTRY ASSISTANCE AND NATURAL RESOURCE DISCOVERIES

The framework of Figure 4.3 can now be used to analyse the comparative static effects of certain exogenous shocks. For instance, consider what would happen if the government was worried about the trade balance and decided to implement a policy programme of widespread industry assistance to boost the production of tradables for the purpose of achieving a trade surplus. Perhaps this could be done through tax concessions or subsidies to firms in specific tradable industries which the government judged had the potential to increase exports.

Figure 4.4 predicts the following effects. An increase in the supply of tradables will cause a temporary trade surplus in the first instance, as shown

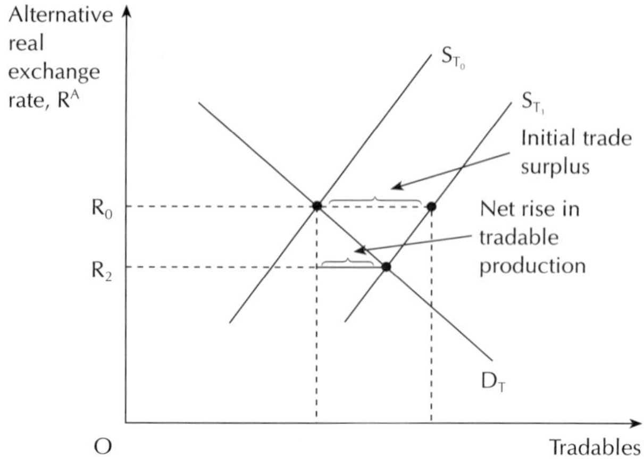

Figure 4.4 Increased production of tradables.

in Figure 4.4. However, the attendant excess supply of foreign exchange would appreciate e and change the relative price of tradables to nontradables. At the same time, the real appreciation stimulates domestic demand for tradables, thereby raising imports. In final equilibrium, the trade account is again balanced with the initial increase in production fully matched by the displacement of earlier exportable production and a rise in demand for importables.

In short, what this application of the dependent economy approach shows is that government attempts to encourage production in selected tradable industries may well raise the overall production of tradables in the short run, but ultimately have no effect on the trade balance as such.

In much the same way as just outlined above, the discovery of previously unknown natural resources such as oil, coal or iron ore can boost the total output of tradables in the economy, with profound implications for existing industries, both tradable and nontradable. As shown in Figure 4.4, the supply of tradables schedule would first shift rightward. This would thereby appreciate the alternative real exchange rate and subsequently increase the quantity of tradables demanded. However, there would also eventually be a 'squeezing out' of some of the tradable production of existing manufacturing industries as a consequence of the real exchange rate appreciation caused by the natural resource discovery.

This phenomenon is also known as the 'Dutch disease' because it was originally observed for the Netherlands following major discoveries and export of natural gas in the 1960s. After these resource discoveries, there was a strong appreciation of the Dutch guilder, which in turn reduced the profitability of other export industries, particularly manufacturing industries.

In other countries, the same consequences have been predicted after the discovery and exploitation of new minerals such as iron ore, bauxite, coal and crude oil, implying an inevitable shrinkage of the manufacturing and agricultural sectors as a result of the growth in tradable output from the mining sector. Consistent with the above theory, Australia's agricultural sector, for instance, actually shrunk in relation to the mining sector following the discovery of new mineral reserves from 1980 onwards.

THE J CURVE

The above discussion has presumed that adjustment on the trade account in response to a change in the real exchange rate is relatively quick and quite smooth. However, in practice, this may not always be so. If there is a significant improvement in competitiveness following a sharp depreciation of the nominal exchange rate, then the adjustment of trade volumes may in fact be quite slow. In reality, there is unlikely to be any immediate impact on the volumes of trade because trade contracts between resident exporters and importers are agreed with foreign buyers or sellers well before the actual delivery of goods.

Import volumes are set by contracts between residents and foreign suppliers. These contracts are often denominated in foreign currency. Following a depreciation the domestic currency price of contracted imports therefore rises on actual delivery. This means the total value of imports in domestic currency terms will initially rise after a sudden depreciation. Yet, after contracts expire the total value of imports should begin falling as volumes drop in response to the relative price change.

The value of exports may, on the other hand, not rise as much as the value of imports immediately after a depreciation as some export contracts could be denominated in local currency. Furthermore, export production is slower to adjust than import demand because it takes time for domestic firms to hire new employees and raise tradable output levels. The net result of import values rising more than export values would be an initial rise in the trade deficit. Yet the trade balance would eventually move toward surplus as import demand falls and export supply rises. The pattern of trade account adjustment under these circumstances would then trace out what has popularly been termed a 'J' curve. This is shown in Figure 4.5.

At time t_0, there is a depreciation. Because import values rise due to contractual arrangements, the trade account initially goes further into deficit between times t_0 and t_1. As import and export volumes begin to respond to the relative price change, the value of imports falls and exports rise, until the trade balance tends to surplus beyond time t_2. The actual extent of the response of the trade balance to the change in competitiveness depends on the export and import demand and supply elasticities. Note also that if the trade flows were measured in foreign currency (as discussed earlier in Chapter 2), the J pattern would not be evident over the adjustment period. In foreign currency terms, there should just be a gradual move towards a trade surplus from the time of the depreciation.

In practice, there has been some evidence of the J curve phenomena affecting economies' trade accounts, particularly following large currency

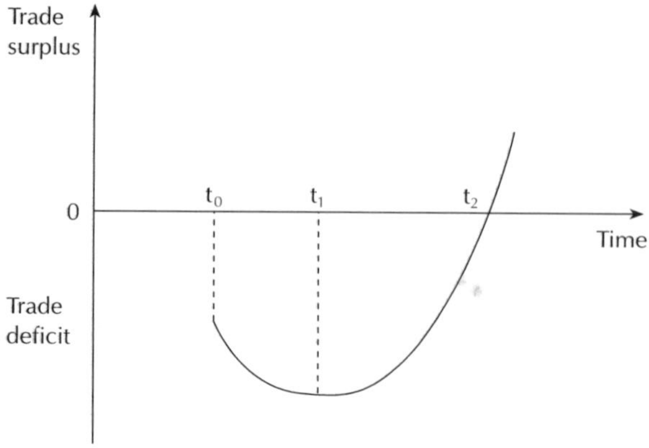

Figure 4.5 The J curve.

depreciations. Nonetheless, it is difficult to disentangle the movements in the trade account due to strictly relative price effects from those due to other influences. It should also be noted that the demand response of importers and the supply response of exporters presume that any sudden exchange rate change will be sustained. If, for instance, exporters do not believe a sharp improvement in competitiveness will be sustained, then the volume response may be negligible.

THE INTERNATIONAL TRANSMISSION OF INFLATION

Another important application of the tradables/nontradables dichotomy is the international transmission of inflation under fixed exchange rates. The model to be outlined in this context is sometimes referred to as the Scandinavian model of inflation, because it was first pioneered by economists in Norway and Sweden. This approach aims to explain how a small open economy's inflation performance is influenced by world inflation levels. At the same time, it reveals an important source of divergence between a small economy's domestic inflation rate and inflation rates abroad.

The main assumption of the approach is that the small economy's monetary authority fixes the exchange rate against other currencies. Also central to the model is the notion that wages in the domestic economy grow in line with changes in the price level, as well as productivity improvements, where productivity is understood as the value of output produced per worker. Wages can grow in this fashion if one imagines a highly unionised labour force, or an economy where wages are indexed to movements in the CPI.

In the tradable sector of the economy, it is possible to express the main sources of wage growth as follows. Domestic firms can afford to pay higher wages if either the world prices of tradables rise or if worker productivity has grown in the domestic tradables industries. Productivity may improve, for instance, if work practices have become more efficient, such that more output is being produced by domestic firms with the same sized workforce. The sources of wage growth in the tradable sector can be summarised as:

$$\hat{W}_T = \hat{P}_T + \hat{\mu}_T \tag{4.1}$$

where $\hat{W}_T$ is the percentage increase in nominal wages in the tradables sector, $\hat{P}_T$ is the percentage increase in the world price of tradables and $\hat{\mu}_T$ is productivity improvement in the tradables sector. Note that if the exchange rate is fixed the only way the domestic currency price of tradables can rise is through foreign price rises.

In the nontradable sector, wages also rise in line with nontradable prices and worker productivity gains in that sector so that:

$$\hat{W}_N = \hat{P}_N + \hat{\mu}_N \tag{4.2}$$

with the variables defined as in Equation (4.1), but in terms of nontradables.

With a centralised wage indexation system in place, growth in wages will be equalised across all industries (that is, irrespective of whether industries are tradable or nontradable). Then it follows algebraically from Equations (4.1) and (4.2) that:

$$\hat{W}_T = \hat{P}_T + \hat{\mu}_T = \hat{W}_N = \hat{P}_N + \hat{\mu}_N$$

$$\therefore\ \hat{P}_N = \hat{P}_T + \hat{\mu}_T - \hat{\mu}_N \tag{4.3}$$

The next step involves using an overall price index such as the CPI which is specifically weighted for tradable and nontradable items in the 'basket' of the index. Domestic inflation, π, defined as the percentage rate of change in the overall price level, would then be measured as:

$$\pi = \hat{P} = (1 - \delta)\hat{P}_T + \alpha\hat{P}_N \tag{4.4}$$

where $\hat{P}$ is the percentage change in the price level and δ is the weight given to nontradables in the price index. Since the weights used for any index should sum to unity, the weight for tradables is $(1 - \delta)$.

By substituting Equation (4.3) into (4.4), it follows that:

$$\pi = (1 - \delta)\hat{P}_T + \delta(\hat{P}_T + \hat{\mu}_T - \hat{\mu}_N)$$

$$= \hat{P}_T + \delta(\hat{\mu}_T - \hat{\mu}_N) \tag{4.5}$$

The term $\hat{P}_T$ conveys the percentage rise in the world price of tradables. However, if we think of this term as being synonymous with 'world' inflation, then Equation (4.5) provides two striking and interesting results about inflation generation in small open economies with fixed exchange rates. These are as follows:

1. Under fixed exchange rates, inflation is largely 'imported' from the rest of the world. That is, domestic inflation (π) is mainly determined by world inflation because the first term on the right-hand side of Equation (4.5) usually exceeds the second.

2. The actual difference between a small country's inflation rate and the world inflation rate arises solely because of differential productivity growth in the tradable and nontradable sectors.

For example, when productivity growth in nontradable industries (such as government services) badly lags productivity growth in tradable industries (such as agricultural and mining industries) yet wages across all sectors rise equivalently, then the domestic inflation rate will be higher than the world inflation rate under a fixed exchange rate system. The intuition behind this result is that if the sector of the small open economy which is sheltered from international competition (the nontradable sector) is relatively less efficient than the sector which is fully exposed to world competition (the tradable sector), then the economy will experience worse inflation than in the world as a whole.

THE TERMS OF TRADE

1. Exportables, importables and the terms of trade

The common feature of the models of the small open economy outlined above is that there are just two classes of goods and services – tradables and nontradables. However, tradables can be split again into *exportables* and *importables*. This further distinction helps us understand a major source of external disturbance for small open economies – changes in the *terms of trade* (TOT), where TOT is defined as the ratio of the price of exportables to the price of importables.

If the composition of an economy's exports exactly mirrored that of its imports the TOT would not matter in a macroeconomic sense. However, many small open economies, particularly among developing economies, tend to export substantially different goods from those they import in terms of value added. Large external macroeconomic shocks are therefore frequently transmitted because the international factors influencing the prices of a small economy's exportables differ from those influencing its importables.

At the industry level, whether a particular product is an exportable or importable depends among other things on that industry's comparative cost structure, and total domestic expenditure on the good. Domestic firms supply tradable goods and services, while residents, other domestic firms and the government sector demand them. If the output of a particular industry is produced beyond that required to satisfy domestic demand, the industry's output becomes exportable. On the other hand, the industry is an importable industry if domestic demand exceeds domestic production.

A fundamental determinant of relative costs is the concentration of factor endowments. For instance, in relative terms, Canada has an abundance of productive land and natural resources relative to working population. These

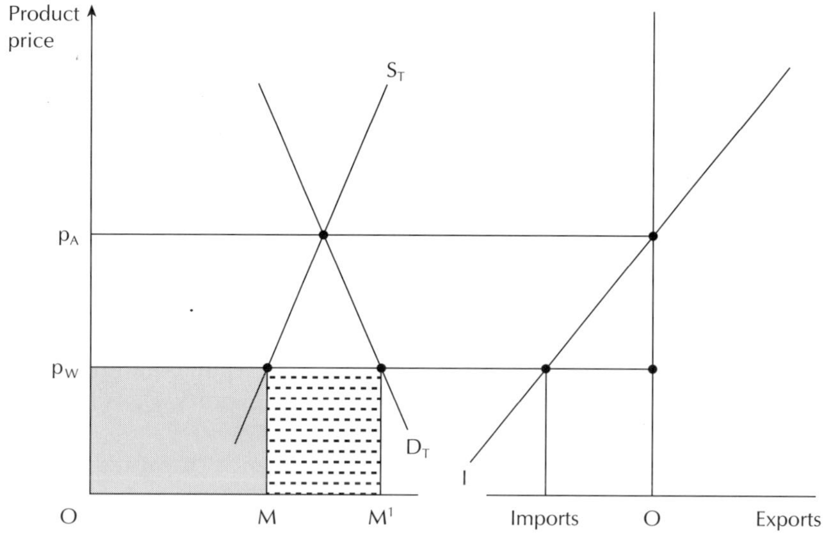

Figure 4.6 Exportables and importables.

resources can be extracted, harvested, or, in the case of visiting foreign tourists, simply observed for pleasure.

In contrast, the economies of the major trading partners of many developing economies, such as Japan and South Korea, have an abundance of labour and capital relative to natural exploitable resources. Those countries find it advantageous to employ the relatively abundant factor in adding value to imported primary products through manufacturing activity. So relatively natural resource-intensive economies and relatively capital-intensive ones like Japan are complementary to one another.

In Figure 4.6, the world price (p^*) of any particular tradable good expressed in domestic currency is $p_W = e \cdot p^*$ where again e is the exchange rate defined according to the academic definition of Chapter 2. At p_W, the industry produces the shaded area, while the dashed area is the value of net imports in domestic currency and is the difference between total spending on the good (the two areas) and the industry's production. At price p_W, therefore, the good is an importable. The good may be tradable at p_A, but is not traded internationally at that price. With a rise in p_W above p_A it becomes exportable.

For a dependent economy, import/export (IE) schedules as shown in Figure 4.6 can be imagined for every internationally tradable good or service for which markets exist. What determines their slope is the responsiveness of both domestic output and expenditure to changes in the domestic currency price. A particular tradable industry's IE schedule would be flatter the more price elastic are both demand and supply, and the higher these elasticities, the greater the industry's contribution to net exports following a rise in the world price of the good.

In contrast, nontradables are completely insensitive to movements in the corresponding prices of similar goods and services set in other economies. For any strictly nontradable category of national product, the IE schedule would lie along the price axis. Hence, a dependent economy's GDP at any point in time is partly exportable, partly importable with the remainder nontradable. The value of the total domestic output of exportables, importables and nontradables less domestic expenditure is the nation's trade imbalance, an accounting relationship established in Chapter 2. In symbols:

$$(\Sigma P_X O_X + \Sigma P_M O_M + \Sigma P_N O_N) - (\Sigma P_X A_X + \Sigma P_M A_M + \Sigma P_N A_N) = \Sigma P_X Q_X - \Sigma P_X Q_M$$

where $P_{X,M,N}$ are prices of individual exportables, importables and nontradables, $O_{X,M,N}$ are the production of exportables, importables and nontradable industries, $A_{X,M,N}$ is absorption, Q_X is the volume of exports, Q_M is the volume of imports and Σ is the summation symbol.

Under a floating exchange rate and in the absence of capital flows, the exchange rate itself will always move to ensure that the value of exports equals the value of imports. However, once capital flows are introduced, this condition no longer holds. External account imbalances are then best understood with reference to national investment and saving behaviour, which is examined in the next chapter.

Using the *input–output* tables which also form part of the full set of national accounts of some economies, it is possible to categorise all intermediate and final production by industry as either exportable, importable or nontradable. In line with the theoretical analysis of the previous section, an exportable industry is classified as one whose domestic production exceeds domestic expenditure, an importable industry as one where domestic expenditure exceeds production, and a nontradable industry as one immune from international influences.

2. The terms of trade and national income

The TOT are measured as the ratio of the prices received for exports to prices paid for imports. In practice, this means calculating the ratio of an economy's export price index (EPI) to its import price index (IPI). That is,

$$TOT = \frac{EPI}{IPI}$$

Both indexes are further examples of Laspeyres indexes constructed along similar lines to the CPI (as discussed in Chapter 2).

Many developing economies are highly susceptible to TOT shocks. To appreciate the economic significance of the TOT, it is useful to imagine a highly simplified production pattern where, say, wool is the only exportable and machinery the only importable. TOT slumps worsen national economic welfare because in the absence of capital inflows, more wool must actually be produced with given resource inputs to generate the foreign exchange necessary for purchasing additional units of machinery. Putting this another way, falling TOT suggest that, for a given volume of exports produced, less imports can be bought from the rest of the world, as earnings of foreign exchange have been reduced. That is, exports and hence national income lose their international purchasing power.

A measure of GDP adjusted for the terms of trade is called *real gross domestic income* (RGDI). This further measure of national income can be calculated as GDP at constant prices – X (at constant prices) + X (at current prices deflated by the IPD for imports).

The method of adjusting GDP for changes in the international purchasing power of exports works by revaluing exports in terms of the import price deflator. When the terms of trade decline because import prices increase more rapidly than export prices, exports contribute less to the purchasing power of GDP.

3. The terms of trade and the exchange rate

Movements in the TOT also have an impact on the nominal exchange rate over shorter periods as they influence the actual currency flows in the foreign exchange market. Recall the flow market approach to short-run exchange rate determination outlined in the previous chapter. In this model, a sudden fall in the world prices received for an economy's exportable commodities would shift the supply of foreign exchange schedule leftward, as shown in Figure 4.7.

From the diagram, it is apparent that the exchange rate would depreciate following a slump in export prices. For this reason, world commodity price movements are regarded as another major influence on many economies' nominal exchange rate over the short term. Accordingly, such currencies are sometimes referred to as *commodity currencies*, meaning that their value is significantly affected by world commodity prices.

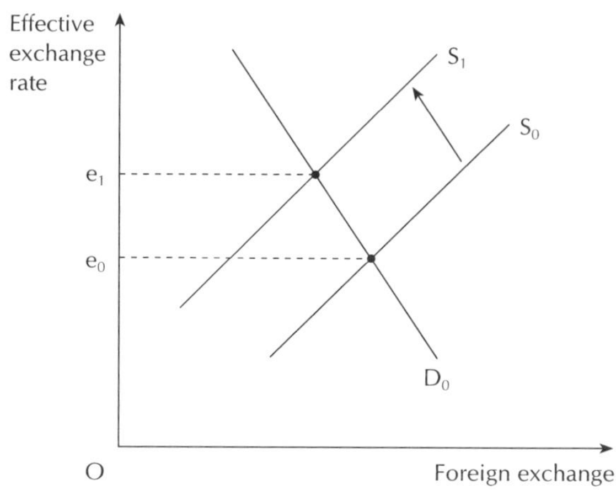

Figure 4.7 Terms of trade and the exchange rate.

Note that depreciations which follow world price falls would help preserve the domestic currency value of exports. That is, the earnings of exporters in domestic currency terms would to some extent be protected by the offsetting exchange rate movements caused by world commodity price falls. This is an example of the *insulation* property of floating exchange rates.

Some argue that increasing manufacturing output in relation to agricultural and mining production in developing economies is the solution to minimising TOT shocks. However, if government policy initiatives successfully raised the output of tradable manufactures at the expense of traditional agricultural and mining activity, where developing economies have long held a distinct comparative advantage, there is the risk that such a strategy would worsen their long-run growth performance.

Summary

1. This chapter has examined the nature of the markets for goods and services in a small open economy. If economies are small, exporters and importers are dependent on the world prices of goods and services.

2. In small open economies, it is important to distinguish between tradable and nontradable products. Tradables are goods and services which can potentially be exchanged on world markets, whereas nontradables are only exchanged between domestic residents.

3. The Swan–Salter model highlights the importance of the relative price of tradables to nontradables as an alternative measure of the real exchange rate. According to this approach, neither widespread industry assistance nor natural resource discoveries yields a lasting trade surplus, but can change the make-up of tradable production.

4. The J curve illustrates that the trade account may not immediately tend toward surplus following an improvement in competitiveness. Because of contracts and adjustment lags, a trade deficit may actually widen before narrowing.

5. The Scandinavian model of inflation suggests that under fixed exchange rates, a small open economy's inflation rate depends on the world inflation rate and the difference between labour productivity in the tradable and nontradable sectors.

6. Tradables can be further split into exportables and importables. The output of exportable industries is greater than domestic demand while that of importable industries is less than domestic demand.

7. Changes in the terms of trade, the ratio of export prices to import prices, affect the purchasing power of exports and hence national income as measured by real gross domestic income.

8. The terms of trade can also influence the nominal exchange rate of some economies over the short term. For this reason, their currencies are referred to as commodity currencies, which can insulate domestic producers from world commodity price movements.

Further reading

Corden, W. (1994) *Economic Policy, Exchange Rates and the International System*, Oxford: Oxford University Press, chapter 2.

Dornbusch, R. (1980) *Open Economy Macroeconomics*, New York: Basic Books, chapter 6.

Prachowny, M. (1984) *Macroeconomic Analysis for Small Open Economies*, Oxford: Oxford University Press.

Salter, W. (1959) 'Internal and external balance: the role of expenditure and price effects', *Economic Record*, **35** (71), 226–38.

Swan, T. (1960) 'Economic control in a dependent economy', *Economic Record*, **36** (73), 51–66.

5

Saving, investment and the external accounts

In the previous chapter, the main focus was the foreign exchange rate and the prices at which an open economy trades goods and services in domestic and world markets. In this chapter, attention shifts to the flow of funds in an open economy and the factors influencing domestic saving, investment and international investment. In this context, the interest rate plays a major role. Like the exchange rate, the interest rate is a macroeconomic variable because of its economy-wide dimension, but also a financial variable because its value is established in a financial market – the market for loanable funds.

The key questions to be resolved are: What factors influence domestic saving and investment? How does the interest rate balance flows of saving and investment? How do domestic and foreign saving combine to finance domestic investment for a small open economy? Where does the exchange rate fit in to the analysis of saving, investment and the current account?

DETERMINANTS OF PRIVATE CONSUMPTION AND SAVING

This section outlines key aspects of the theory of private consumption behaviour. However, this theory also doubles as a theory of private saving because from the national accounting relations, private saving is simply what is left of national income after households' consumption plans have been satisfied. The impact of government consumption and saving on the open economy is taken up in the next chapter.

1. The Keynesian consumption function

The most basic, yet highly influential, approach to modelling consumption is the Keynesian consumption function, first espoused by John Maynard Keynes in his *General Theory of Employment, Interest and Money* (1936). Keynes proposed that:

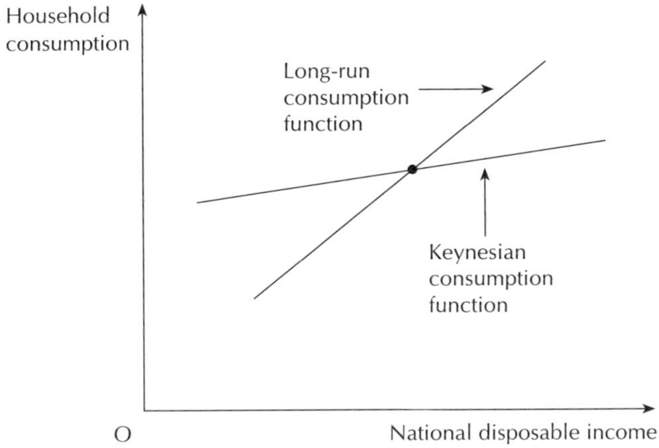

Figure 5.1 Keynesian and long-run consumption functions.

> the fundamental psychological law, upon which we are entitled to depend with great confidence . . . is that men are disposed as a rule and on the average to increase their consumption as their income increases, but not by as much as the increase in their income. (Keynes, 1936)

The Keynesian consumption function is usually expressed as

$$C = \bar{C} + cY \qquad \bar{C} > 0,\ 0 < c < 1$$

where $\bar{C}$ is autonomous consumption (that is, consumption which is unrelated to income) and c is the marginal propensity to consume (mpc). The mpc indicates how much extra consumption there will be from an incremental change in income. It is a fraction lying somewhere between zero and unity.

Graphically, the Keynesian consumption function (see Figure 5.1) shows that current period consumption is determined by current period income. The slope of the Keynesian consumption function is the mpc.

Consistent with this specification, early empirical evidence revealed that there was an apparently strong short-run relationship between current national income and current consumption. However, Nobel prize-winning economist Simon Kuznets demonstrated that over longer periods, such as from decade to decade, the ratio between consumption and income (called the average propensity to consume, apc) was constant. This finding initially appeared inconsistent with the Keynesian consumption function, which implied a falling apc. This inconsistency became known as the 'consumption puzzle'.

Eventually, however, economists realised that it was possible to have both a short-run and long-run consumption function, as shown in Figure 5.2. The short-run function can capture consumption behaviour over periods of

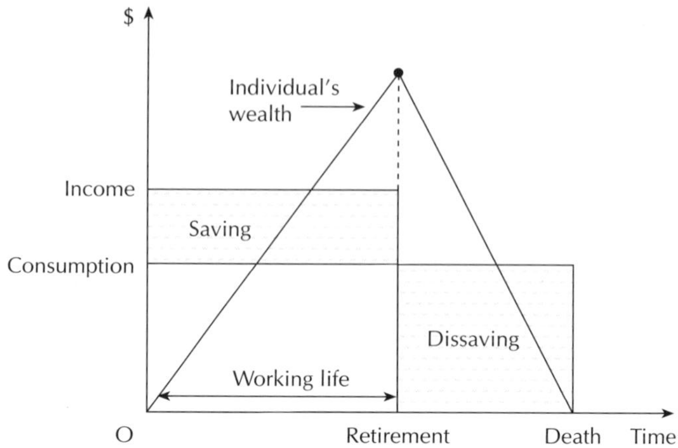

Figure 5.2 Income, consumption and saving over the life cycle.

up to a year, whereas the long-run function relates to periods as long as a decade.

2. The life cycle hypothesis

What the consumption puzzle did was to prompt economists to think more about patterns of consumer behaviour over longer periods of time. In the 1950s another Nobel prize-winner, Franco Modigliani, and others devised the *life cycle hypothesis* (LCH). According to this approach, individuals were not solely concerned about what was happening today but were forward looking and also thought about what could happen in the future.

The LCH proposed that saving allowed individuals to transfer income over the course of their entire lives. In turn, this permitted consumption levels, and hence living standards, to be maintained at a consistent level through life. Maintaining a consistent pattern of lifetime consumption is often referred to as *consumption smoothing*.

Consider the case of people who save through their working lives for retirement. As shown in Figure 5.2, if the individual saves during the working years, wealth (the stock value of accumulated saving) continues to rise until retirement begins. Thereafter, in retirement, the individual lives off (decumulates) lifetime saving by running down wealth or lifetime saving. Running down past saving is also known as *dissaving*.

Another important implication of the LCH approach is that, unlike the simple Keynesian approach, consumption depends on household wealth levels. Therefore, if the ratio of wealth to income remains fairly constant over longer periods, it follows that, as wealth rises along with long-run income, the Keynesian consumption function would continually drift upward. Such an explanation helps reconcile the two different consumption functions of the earlier Figure 5.1.

3. The permanent income hypothesis

The *permanent income hypothesis* (PIH) is another theory of consumption and saving which is closely related to the LCH. It was first proposed by Milton Friedman and also rejects the Keynesian notion that current period consumption only depends on current period income. The PIH stresses that individuals or households may suffer temporary and unpredictable fluctuations in incomes from one year to the next.

Because individuals are forward looking in their decision making, income earned in a given year in the face of temporary fluctuations is best considered as either *permanent* (Y^P) or *transitory*, (Y^T). Hence:

$$Y = Y^P + Y^T$$

Permanent income is that component of income which households expect to remain relatively constant into the foreseeable future. Transitory income is income which is short lived due to a random or unexpected event. A good example may be the behaviour of Australian farmers' income following an upset in global weather conditions. For instance, if a drought in North America this year forces up world wheat prices, the higher income earned by Australian wheatgrowers from a good harvest at home should be perceived by the local farmers as transitory income, as conditions are likely to return to normal next year.

According to the PIH, consumption mainly depends on, and is proportional to, the permanent income component of income, not on random deviations from permanent income. Therefore, transitory increases in income are mainly saved and these savings are subsequently run down to smooth consumption at later times when household income temporarily falls.

Although there are some differences between the LCH and PIH approaches to understanding consumption and saving, they both argue that an economy's consumption behaviour does not depend simply on current income as Keynes had argued, but just as importantly on the expected future stream of income as well.

DETERMINANTS OF INVESTMENT

Investment is the most variable component of aggregate expenditure. Even though it accounts for a much smaller share of total national spending than consumption, swings in investment tend to coincide with the business cycle and hence have important implications for short-run employment and unemployment levels. Indeed, most economists would agree that investment is the major propelling force in the macroeconomy and that fluctuations in private investment in particular are the main cause of upturns and downturns in the business cycle. When investment falls sharply the economy experiences serious recession. On the other hand, when investment is buoyant, the economy enjoys high rates of GDP growth.

4. The marginal productivity and cost of capital

On the supply side of the economy, firms combine capital and labour to produce goods and services for sale. But why would firms ever want to increase investment and hence the amount of capital used to produce their output? The simple answer, according to traditional neoclassical economics, is that firms aim to maximise profits in accordance with a desired level of capital. In judging how much extra capital is needed for this purpose, each period firms have to weigh up the marginal benefits and costs of acquiring extra capital.

The increase in output from employing an extra unit of capital in production is called the *marginal product of capital* (MP_K). Under competitive conditions, the *value of the marginal product of capital* (VMP_K), is the price of the firm's output times its MP_K.

The cost of acquiring additional capital is sometimes called the *rental cost* (rc). The prevailing interest rate is often used to approximate the rental cost of capital on the grounds that interest is what firms must pay when they borrow to finance the purchase of new capital equipment. If the firm has its own saving in the form of retained earnings from past profits, the interest rate is still a relevant cost measure because it reflects the opportunity cost of any retained funds. In other words, instead of acquiring plant and equipment, firms could earn interest on retained earnings at the going market interest rate.

Strictly speaking, the rental cost of capital should also include the rate of capital consumption or capital depreciation (d). Wear and tear on new capital is also part of the cost of employing capital because firms have to spend funds to maintain capital equipment in prime working condition. Therefore, the total rental cost can be expressed as $rc = r + d$.

It benefits a firm to continue investing as long as the marginal product of capital exceeds the rental cost of capital. This is because further profits can be made if the value of output from employing an additional unit of capital exceeds its rental cost. Equilibrium prevails when:

$$MP_K = r + d$$

This point of equilibrium is shown in Figure 5.3. As more capital is acquired for production, the MP_K declines. Hence the I_0I_0 schedule is downward sloping. For a given rental cost, the firm's equilibrium stock is determined.

If the rental cost of capital falls because the interest rate drops, then firms' investment should increase, as shown by the rise from OK_0 to OK_1. Alternatively, business managers might expect a higher level of output in the near future. Then the I_0I_0 schedule would shift outward and increase investment at any given rental cost because the desired capital stock would have to increase to produce the higher expected volume of production.

5. The stockmarket and investment

Fluctuations in the share market or the price of equities can also affect the volume of investment spending. Equities represent legal claims to ownership

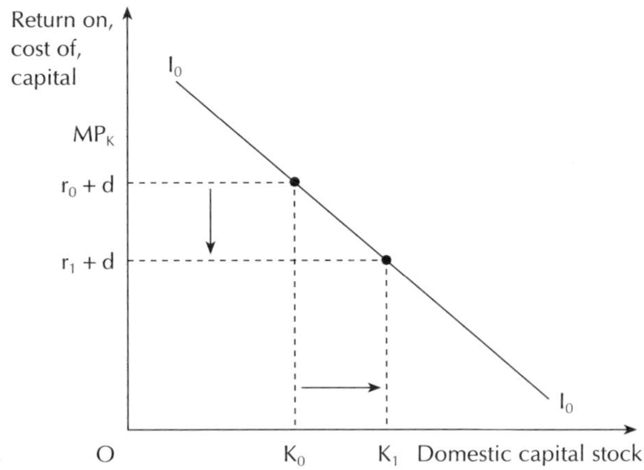

Figure 5.3 Return on capital and the cost of capital.

of firms' capital and when the price of equities is high, firms can raise substantial funds by issuing relatively few shares. However, if equity prices are low, more shares must be sold to raise a certain amount of funds. When investment is financed through equities rather than borrowing funds through financial intermediaries, the rental cost of capital is estimated as the ratio of dividends paid to shareholders to the price of the firm's equities. When equity prices rise, the rental cost falls, thus lowering the cost of capital. In this way rising share prices boost business investment spending.

Stock prices can affect firms' investment spending in another way according to the so-called *q* theory of investment proposed by Nobel laureate James Tobin. The *q* theory of investment is based on changes in the relative valuation of capital and how this influences the supply of investment. It argues that firms' investment behaviour mainly depends on a specific ratio, called Tobin's *q*. This ratio is simply,

$$q = \frac{\text{Market value of firms' capital}}{\text{Replacement value of firms' capital}}$$

The market value of firms' capital in the numerator of the expression is the value established by the stock market. This value reflects investors' assessment of the current and future profitability of the capital in use by firms. The replacement value of firms' capital in the denominator measures how much it would actually cost firms to replace their existing capital stock, as measured at today's prices.

Figure 5.4 illustrates how a change in Tobin's *q* can induce an increased flow of business investment. It shows that an increase in the demand for equities raises their market value, which increases *q* values and hence investment.

The demand for capital is shown by the downward sloping demand curve. The lower the relative price of capital as represented by the *q* ratio,

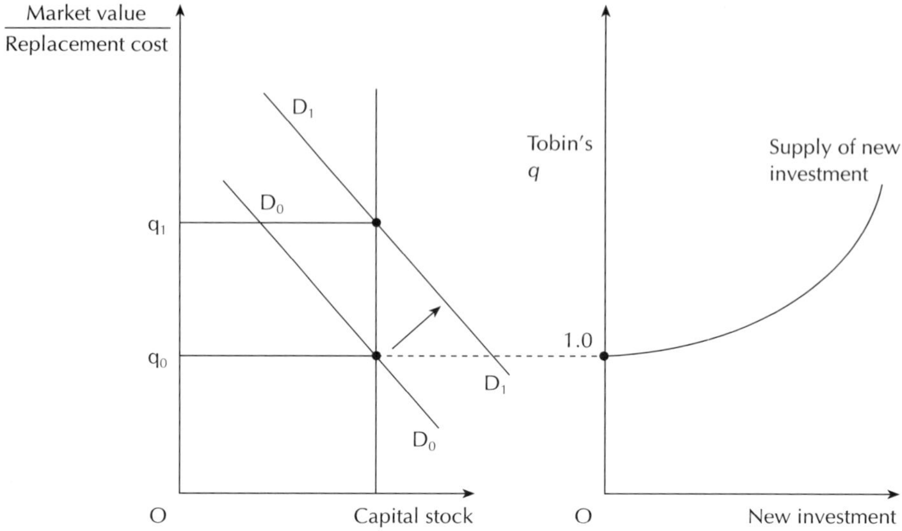

Figure 5.4 The stock market and investment.

the greater is the demand for claims to capital. Several factors determine the position of the demand curve itself. The higher is the level of wealth, the more equities economic agents would wish to own as part of their total portfolio of wealth. Second, the real return on other assets, such as government bonds or real estate, affects the demand for claims to capital. For instance, a fall in the real interest rate on government bonds would instantly make shares a more attractive part of wealthholding relative to other forms of wealth. This would shift the demand curve for capital rightward, as depicted in the left panel of Figure 5.4.

At any point in time, the relative valuation of capital is determined by the interaction of the stock demand for capital and the available stock supply, which is fixed in the short run. In Figure 5.4, the initial equilibrium relative price of q is unity since the market value and replacement cost of capital are assumed equal. An increase in the demand for claims to capital immediately raises the market price of capital above its replacement cost. This then means that the value of Tobin's q would rise above unity. As shown in the right-hand side panel of Figure 5.4, this would induce an increase in new investment after some lag. The long-run equilibrium would be reached when the replacement cost rises to meet the market value of capital. However, long-run equilibrium may never be reached in reality because there are always unexpected internal and external shocks to the economy, such as sudden changes in the terms of trade which can push the investment process off any particular adjustment path.

Keynes argued that business investment was a volatile component of aggregate expenditure because the future was inherently uncertain and that expected future demand for firms' output levels was therefore very difficult to judge. Consequently, according to the Keynesian view, business investment decisions were heavily influenced by the optimistic or pessimistic sentiments of businesspeople.

6. Dwellings and inventories

Apart from expenditure on plant and equipment, private investment in housing (usually referred to as dwellings in official statistics) is a significant part of total investment. As dwellings are also assets which form part of households' wealthholdings, they are subject to much the same influences as modelled above for equities. An increase in the demand for houses, for instance, would raise their value and subsequently induce an increased supply of houses.

Inventories are stocks of unsold goods accumulated by firms to meet future demand for goods. Inventory investment fluctuates relatively more than any other part of investment though it is only a relatively small part of total investment. Changes in stock of unsold goods are either planned or unplanned. If planned, inventory fluctuations often reflect what is called *production smoothing*, whereby firms build stocks up when seasonal demand is low and run them down when demand is seasonally high. During recessions, firms often experience unplanned inventory investment with stocks rising to uncomfortable levels. Output is then usually cut back and sales made out of existing stocks until inventories are restored to desired levels.

SAVING, INVESTMENT AND THE CAPITAL ACCOUNT

The interest rate now warrants further consideration, because it is the macroeconomic variable which plays the key role in balancing the economy-wide supply of funds arising from saving behaviour with the economy-wide demand for funds used to finance firms' investment spending.

When domestic firms invest by purchasing capital equipment, there is an increased demand for *loanable funds* in the economy. The cost of borrowing these funds is measured by the real interest rate, r. As r rises, the profitability of private investment spending falls, which is consistent with the investment demand schedule of Figure 5.3. Aggregate private investment and the associated demand for loanable funds are therefore negatively related to the interest rate.

Graphically, the demand for loanable funds, which is a derived demand, can be depicted as a downward sloping curve in real interest rate–loanable funds space, as shown in Figure 5.5.

The domestic supply of loanable funds on the other hand, depends on the rate of saving in the economy. Domestic private saving is simply

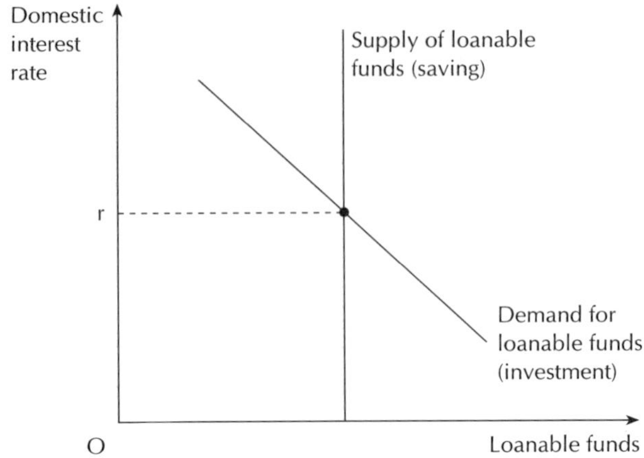

Figure 5.5 Investment, saving and the interest rate.

the pool of funds remaining out of national income after households' consumption preferences have been satisfied. For given levels of output, saving is fixed and not strongly related to the interest rate. This is consistent with the basic theories of consumption and saving, covered earlier in this chapter, none of which afforded the interest rate any significant role. Domestic saving can therefore be drawn as a vertical schedule in Figure 5.5. Together, the schedules show that the domestic interest rate is the macroeconomic variable which must adjust to balance the aggregate supply and aggregate demand for loanable funds.

If domestic saving and investment behaviour determines the interest rate in this way, it follows that the world interest rate is determined by world saving and world investment. Figure 5.5 can therefore also illustrate how the world interest rate may be determined if the domestic supply and demand schedules for loanable funds are relabelled as world supply and world demand schedules.

But what happens in a small open economy which individually has a negligible influence on world saving and investment and whose firms face a given world interest rate just as they face world prices for tradables? To adapt the loanable funds approach to the small open economy, it is necessary to recall that the capital account surplus in the external accounts is the difference between domestic investment and domestic saving. This means that for a small open economy, investment may exceed saving at the world interest rate to the extent of net borrowing from abroad by domestic firms. This is shown in Figure 5.6.

What also follows from this framework is that countries will experience a capital account deficit at the given world interest rate if their domestic saving rate exceeds the domestic demand for investment funds. This would happen, for instance, if the economy consumed much less out of given national income and saving was S_1 instead of S_0.

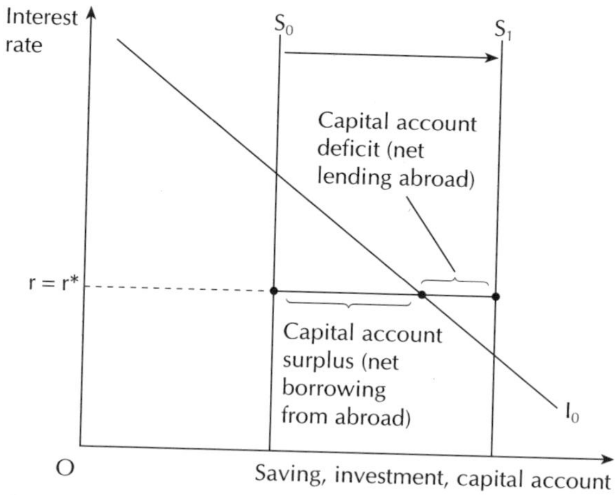

Figure 5.6 Saving, investment and the capital account balance.

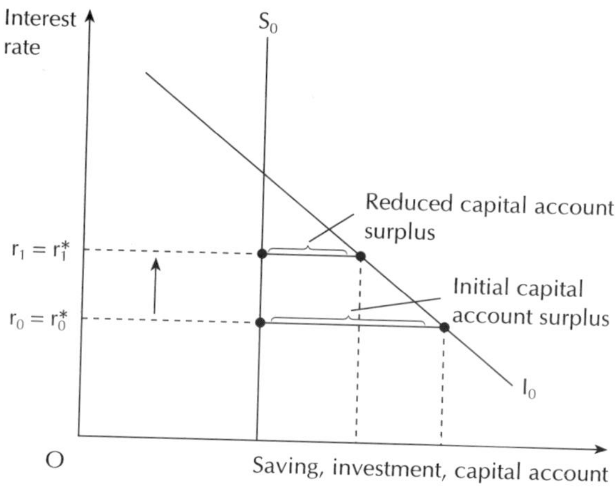

Figure 5.7 Rise in world interest rates.

If there was an outward shift of the small economy's investment schedule because domestic firms expected higher output in the future, there would also be a further widening of the economy's capital account surplus given its saving level. This is an example of a domestically sourced or endogenous shock to the economy which affects the size of its capital account balance and hence net international borrowing. Finally, consider the effect of a rise in world interest rates as shown in Figure 5.7. In this case, there would be a narrowing of the capital account surplus as there would be reduced demand for foreign funds. This is an example of a foreign-sourced or exogenous shock to the economy and to the external accounts.

Note that from a macroeconomic policy perspective there is nothing in this analysis to suggest that a capital account surplus or deficit is either good or bad. The simple flow of funds approach merely highlights the role that relative domestic saving and investment behaviour play in determining the actual size of international capital flows. Chapter 12 returns to the issue of how external account imbalances should be interpreted by policymakers. Using further theory which is fully compatible with the loanable funds approach outlined here, it actually demonstrates that an open economy's macroeconomic welfare can be improved through external account imbalances.

INTEREST RISK PREMIUM

The above analysis has presumed that foreign lenders are not averse to lending to an economy with a rising level of external debt and that consumption and saving are not responsive to changes in interest rates. These assumptions can now be relaxed to model the notion of a *risk premium* on interest rates that external borrower economies may attract which makes the domestic interest rates higher than the foreign interest rate.

As shown already, total investment spending in a closed economy must ultimately be financed out of available domestic saving with the interest rate performing the balancing role. In a financially liberalised open economy, however, domestic investment can exceed domestic saving to the extent of foreign borrowing. Borrowing countries experience international capital account surpluses which are matched by current account deficits and rising levels of foreign debt.

The left panel of Figure 5.8 shows interest responsive saving, investment and the international borrowing requirements of a small open economy. Domestic saving is the quantum of funds left out of national income after private and public consumption spending and is drawn as the upward sloping schedule. Again, the demand for funds is primarily related to investment opportunities and is shown as the downward sloping schedule. The net international borrowing requirement, and hence current account balance, is shown as the horizontal distance between the total demand for funds and the supply of domestic saving at a given world interest rate. In effect, this diagram presumes perfect international capital mobility and hence conveys only part of the story.

The framework can now be further extended to model imperfect capital mobility, involving risk aversion on the part of foreign lenders. First, however, it is necessary to highlight the small open economy's international borrowing requirement for a range of world interest rates. With reference to the right panel of Figure 5.8, if the world interest rate was at i* then, for given saving and investment behaviour, the international borrowing requirement would be equivalent to distance OP. The downward sloping excess demand for funds schedule therefore indicates the size of the international borrowing requirement at various world interest rate levels, and for a given pattern of domestic saving and investment.

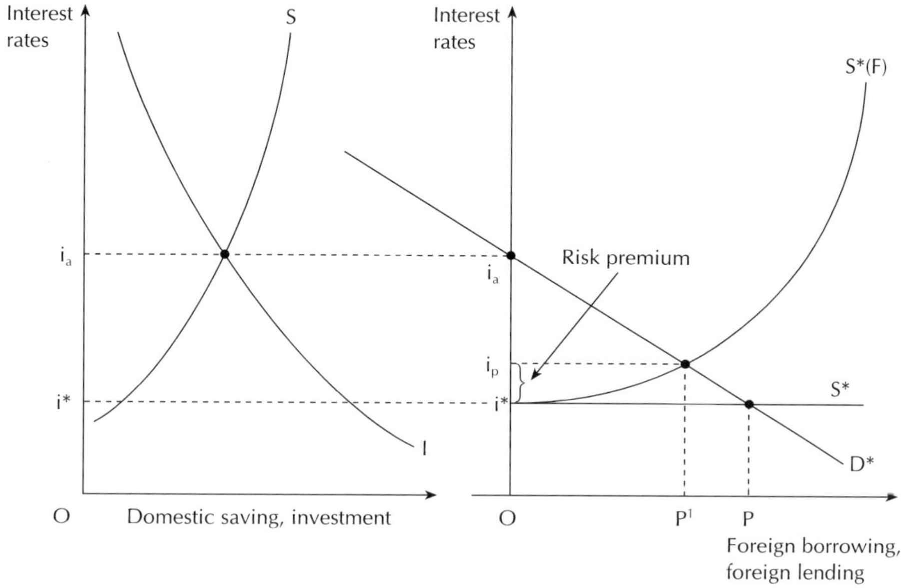

Figure 5.8 Domestic saving, investment and external borrowing.

If international capital is presumed to be perfectly mobile, as is usual in textbooks, then domestic borrowers of foreign funds effectively face an infinitely elastic supply of foreign funds. Firms can borrow as much as they want at the going world interest rate and the domestic interest rate equals the foreign interest rate. This is shown by the horizontal foreign lending schedule at i*.

But what happens if foreign lenders view rising foreign debt levels with concern? In other words, as current account deficit and foreign debt levels rise, foreigners' perceptions of default risk may become more widespread and feed back to influence their lending decisions. This phenomenon is shown by the curved foreign lending schedule rising from i*. The higher is the borrowing country's current account deficit and associated foreign debt level, the higher is the perceived default risk, and the less willing foreign lenders may be to lend to domestic borrowers. At some point, the level of default risk may be considered prohibitive, such that the foreign lending schedule becomes vertical.

The curved foreign lending schedule is drawn on the assumption that perceived risks only relate to the possibility of resident firms defaulting on their foreign loans. However, it could also encompass political or country risk, which relates to the possibility of higher withholding-type taxes being levied on foreign lenders, or exchange controls being imposed without warning by the monetary authorities of the debtor nation.

The right side of Figure 5.8 thereby shows different degrees of international capital mobility with implications for interest differentials. If capital mobility is perfect (S*), domestic and foreign interest rates remain the same,

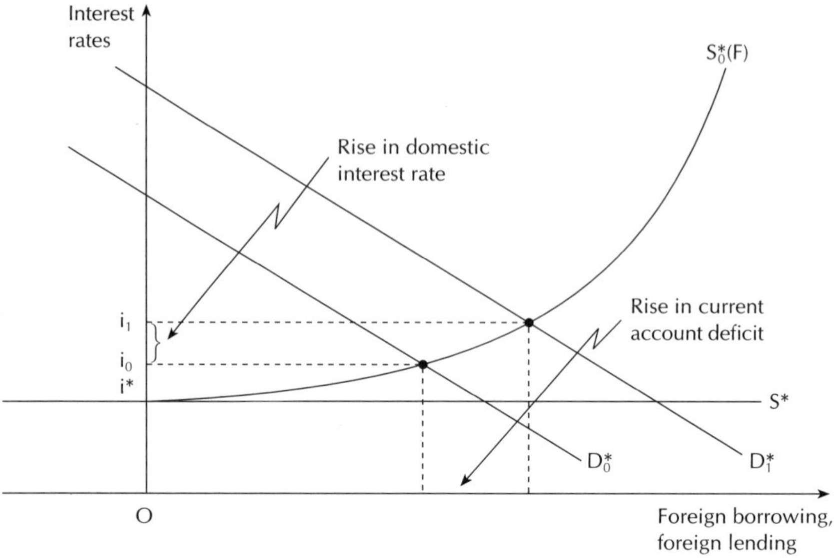

Figure 5.9 Rise in domestic investment.

if all loans are denominated in foreign currency, or, in the domestic currency denomination case, if exchange rate expectations are static. However, the greater the debt-related risk from foreigners' perspective, the wider the interest differential becomes. Nonetheless, the domestic interest rate can never be higher with foreign debt than with no external borrowing. In other words, it is possible that higher foreign debts levels could push domestic interest rates above prevailing world rates, but it is not possible for foreign debt to push domestic rates above the autarky level (i_a).

This international borrowing and lending framework can also be used to examine a number of internal and external shocks. For instance, if there is an increase in domestic investment spending, other things the same, the demand for foreign funds schedule would shift outward, as shown in Figure 5.9. This would increase the foreign borrowing requirement and push up domestic interest rates (from i_0 to i_i) if foreigners were reacting to rising external debt levels.

Of course, in the perfect capital mobility case, the domestic interest rate would not rise at all, though the increase in the external account imbalance would be larger. The rightward shift of the external borrowing schedule due to higher investment would also in that case be precisely matched by an increase in external debt.

This extended framework shows that in a financially open economy, additional domestic investment occurs if the cost of foreign funds is less than the cost of domestic funds. In addition, this approach implies that domestic firms which borrow through international capital markets may face a rising cost of foreign funds due to the international borrowing activity of other domestic firms and the government sector.

In theory, if foreigners became more reluctant to finance extra domestic economic activity as external debt rose, then the effective interest rate paid to foreign lenders would also rise, but this would also mean that foreign debt would not then increase as quickly. Such a process would eventually become self-limiting, suggesting that debt pessimists should welcome any sizeable risk premium. It also follows that if a borrower country was forced to rely on its domestic saving to finance its total domestic investment needs, then domestic interest rates would be higher than any debt-related risk premium could generate.

In economic policy discussion about the significance of external account imbalances, it has been suggested that current account deficits imply that domestic saving is 'too low' and that these deficits could be eliminated if domestic saving rose relative to domestic investment. In terms of the earlier loanable funds analysis, this simply means the domestic saving schedule should be far enough to the right to fully fund domestic investment demand.

SAVING AND INVESTMENT BEHAVIOUR

Domestic saving, defined broadly as the difference between national income and consumption, provides an economy with funds to finance its investment requirements. In turn, this additional investment augments the domestic capital stock, which allows for greater production of output, economy-wide. Consequently, the national saving rate is a key contributing factor, along with technological advance, human capital accumulation and population increase, to an economy's economic growth performance and its long-run living standards. Hence, it is important to understand what specific factors influence domestic saving behaviour.

7. Measurement issues and trends

The national accounting relationships between the private and public components of domestic saving, foreign saving, the external account imbalance and gross national investment are depicted schematically in Figure 5.10.

Saving can in principle be defined narrowly as the flow residual between income and consumption, or alternatively and more broadly as the change in the nation's stock of wealth, the market value of accumulated assets, over a given time interval. Between any two points in time, national wealth increases due to additional accumulation over the period, as well as changes in the value of the economy's pre-existing capital stock. At present, according to normal national accounting practice, saving is routinely measured as the former.

However, the standard measures of saving abstract from periodic revaluations of the capital stock. So, it is possible to devise a new broader measure of domestic saving which allows for these valuation effects and hence reflects capital gains and losses on the asset holdings of residents

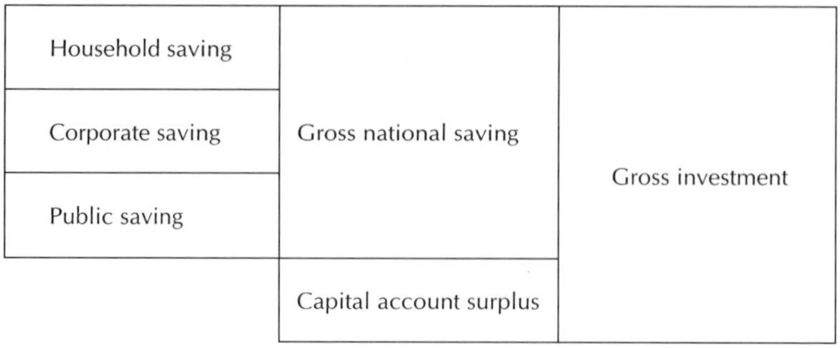

Figure 5.10 Components of saving.

(see Box 5.1). This alternative measure of saving is normally higher than the conventional measure, except during major recessions.

Of course, only saving measured in the conventional way as the residual of income and consumption measures the present flow of domestic funds available for present investment. On the other hand, the broader measure reflects total consumption possibilities available to the economy.

A second measurement problem arises because conventional saving measures are understated when national accounting convention treats public expenditure on education and health as consumption. Yet such spending may alternatively be perceived as investment in human capital and, if accordingly reclassified as such in the national accounts, would yield higher estimated values of national saving. The current practice of treating government expenditure on human capital as public consumption causes problems when making international comparisons of conventional saving measures. In particular, because governments in advanced economies spend heavily on education and health, the measured saving of these economies therefore tends to appear lower than for other economies which spend relatively less in these areas.

A third measurement problem arises when international comparisons are made on the basis of net saving data and is due to the internationally inconsistent treatment of depreciation, or consumption of fixed capital. Depreciation is difficult to define and measure, giving rise to a range of different practices being adopted worldwide. Consequently, international comparisons of saving rates should be made using gross saving data.

Numerous advanced economies have experienced declines in overall national saving over recent decades, as conventionally measured, in part because of declines in public saving, particularly during recessions. During recessions, private saving also falls dramatically as consumption is maintained in the face of lower income levels, consistent with the permanent income theory of consumption of Friedman (1957).

Within private saving there are two sub-components – household saving and corporate or business saving. The household saving component of total

Box 5.1 An alternative measure of saving.

The value of national wealth at the end of any period (W_1) exceeds the value of wealth at the beginning of that period (W_0), to the extent of domestic investment over the period (I), less net foreign liabilities incurred to fund that capital accumulation, through net foreign investment (NFI), plus any valuation effect (k) over the period. Algebraically:

$$W_1 = W_0 + I - NFI + k$$

$$= W_0 + I - (I - S) + k$$

(since NFI is just the difference between domestic investment and saving, S)

$$= W_0 + S + k$$

Hence:

$$dW = W_1 - W_0 = S + k$$

where dW is the stock change in national wealth over the period.

The main sources of growth in national wealth are therefore national saving, as conventionally measured, plus any revaluation of the total net assets of residents.

The decomposition of national wealth changes into saving and asset valuation changes allows a distinction to be made between the addition to wealth arising from forgone consumption out of present income and the addition to wealth arising from changed expectations about the stream of benefits likely to accrue from the existing capital stock. National wealth changes attributable to capital gains or losses can be unexpected, for instance as a result of stock-market collapses. On the other hand, accumulation, or saving, changes as a consequence of planned decisions to raise the level of wealth.

If national saving was actually defined differently as the full net increment to the market value of wealth, then on this definition, national saving would usually be greater than the conventional saving measures indicate.

saving has declined over recent decades in many advanced economies that have experienced substantial financial liberalisation. Interestingly, however, falls in household saving have often been offset by rises in business saving, leaving gross private saving largely unchanged.

One reason for this is that corporate saving reflects the retained earnings of incorporated enterprises. So, when the profit share rises, corporate saving rises, but this also implies a relative fall in the wage share that may reduce household saving. Moreover, the amount of corporate saving reflects companies' dividend policy, which affects the degree of offset. It should also be noted that not too much emphasis should be placed on individual components of saving. This is because significant measurement errors arise from the derivation of saving in the national accounts as a residual of other aggregates.

Demographic factors can be an important medium-term influence on domestic household saving patterns. For instance, if the age composition of the population changes, so too will saving, in so far as consumption behaviour differs between different age groups. For instance, if an economy experiences an increase in the proportion of retirees, giving rise to an increase in the so-called dependency ratio, then private saving is likely to fall. This is because retirees run down saving accumulated during their working lives consistent with the life cycle hypothesis discussed earlier in this chapter. Accordingly, significant differences in age profiles, combined with the nature of the social security system and the way it provides for retirement, can further explain differences in saving rates across countries. For instance, the more generous is the publicly funded pension scheme, the lower household saving is likely to be.

In theory, the exact response of domestic saving to interest rate movements is ambiguous. A fall in interest rates makes household consumption less expensive relative to future consumption, thus discouraging saving – the so-called substitution effect. Yet, the reduced income from interest receipts may also encourage households to save more – the income effect. Empirically, international studies have shown that on balance domestic saving only tends to be weakly responsive to interest rate changes, whereby a 1 per cent rise in interest rates affects the saving ratio by only 1 per cent.

Private saving behaviour in advanced economies tends to be relatively more stable than private investment expenditure as a proportion of GDP. In advanced economies, domestic investment, which tends to average between 20 and 25 per cent of total national expenditure, is mainly undertaken by the private sector, although public sector investment is also significant. Public sector spending on infrastructure allows for the provision of electric power, telecommunications, water supply, roads, railways, ports and airports.

A fundamental determinant of business investment is the rate of return on capital, a macroeconomic indicator of which is the ratio of gross operating surplus to the total capital stock of firms. The size of the economy's gross operating surplus is also indicative of overall corporate profitability. Sustained increases in corporate profitability also improve the ratio of the market valuation of companies to the replacement cost of capital. According to the *q* theory of investment outlined above, a rise in *q* should of itself stimulate additional real investment.

THE CURRENT ACCOUNT, CAPITAL ACCOUNT AND EXCHANGE RATE

So far in this chapter, the main focus has been the behaviour of private saving and investment and their implications for international borrowing and lending. However, where does the exchange rate, which received so much emphasis in earlier chapters, fit into this picture? To answer that, this section reintroduces the nominal exchange rate to show that its role is to

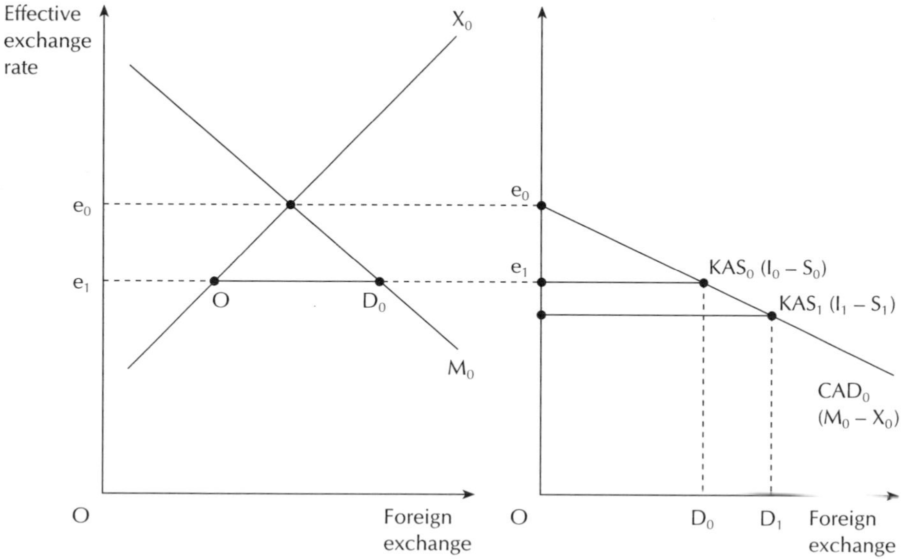

Figure 5.11 The current account, the capital account and the exchange rate.

balance the flows on both the trade and net international borrowing sides of the external accounts.

According to the simple short-run model of the exchange rate in Chapter 3, a floating exchange rate is determined by the flows of currencies in the foreign exchange market. These currency flows arise because of international goods and services transactions recorded on the current account or because of international borrowing and lending transactions recorded on the capital account of the balance of payments.

To gain a better understanding of how both sides of the external accounts simultaneously move the nominal exchange rate, another simple framework is proposed which brings together some of the basic principles outlined earlier. This framework allows us to treat international capital flows as the gap between domestic saving and investment, and to explicitly take this gap into account when thinking about the nominal exchange rate.

As a net deficit on current account transactions is financed by a net surplus on international capital transactions under a floating exchange rate, the current account deficit can be perceived in foreign exchange terms as the net demand for foreign currency, and the capital account surplus as the net supply of foreign exchange. Figure 5.11 depicts two schedules – one for each side of the external accounts.

The left panel of Figure 5.11 reproduces the flow supply and demand schedules for foreign currencies which arise from exports and imports of goods and services in the current account. The net demand for foreign currency associated with current account deficits can be derived from the left panel diagram and is shown as the downward sloping CAD schedule in the right panel of Figure 5.11. The net capital inflow schedule, the KAS schedule, is horizontal. The actual position of the KAS schedule depends most importantly on the quantity of foreign exchange supplied as a result of the difference between domestic saving and investment behaviour. A rise in domestic investment relative to domestic saving lengthens the KAS schedule, whereas a fall in domestic investment relative to domestic saving shortens it.

When the current account is balanced there is no net demand for foreign exchange. The KAS is zero and the value of the exchange rate is e_0. At e_1, however, there is a net demand for foreign currency of OD. Similarly, other points on the net demand schedule can be derived. Lower values of e (a stronger exchange rate) give rise to a larger demand for foreign currency for current account reasons, other things equal.

Domestic saving and investment behaviour determines the size of the capital account surplus and hence the exact position of the horizontal KAS schedule. Therefore, according to this framework, the nominal exchange rate is determined in the short-run by shifts in either the net demand for foreign currency (the CAD schedule), or the net supply of foreign currency (the KAS schedule), or indeed, by simultaneous shifts of both.

This framework confirms why, *ex post*, net foreign exchange flows on the current account must be equal to net borrowing flows recorded on the capital account over a given period. It also shows in a different way how nominal exchange rate movements over any period enable the balance to be struck simultaneously between exports, imports, saving, investment and international capital flows. It also implies that *ex ante* either current account or capital account transactions can drive the exchange rate over any given period.

For example, a sharp drop in the world prices of an economy's exports would cause an upward shift in the net demand for foreign currency and hence depreciate the nominal exchange rate, other things remaining the same. Alternatively, a sudden rise in domestic investment relative to domestic saving would lengthen the KAS schedule and shift it downward, thereby appreciating the nominal exchange rate and simultaneously widening the external account imbalance.

Summary

1. This chapter examined the theory of consumption, saving and investment. For a small open economy domestic saving and investment can diverge to the extent of its net foreign borrowing or lending abroad.

2. The Keynesian consumption function proposes that household consumption behaviour, and therefore total private saving, is basically related to national disposable income in the current period.

3. Alternatively, the life cycle hypothesis suggests that consumption decisions are made with lifetime considerations in mind. Saving during periods of high income

and dissaving during periods of low income, such as in retirement, allow consumption to be smoothed over longer periods.

4. Similarly, the permanent income hypothesis relates consumption spending to expected future income. It proposes that households mainly base their consumption decisions on permanent income, rather than transitory income.

5. Aggregate investment spending is more variable than consumption spending and is a major cause of the business cycle.

6. According to traditional investment theory, domestic firms will invest up to the point where the marginal return on capital equals its rental cost (the sum of the real interest rate and capital consumption). The lower are real interest rates, the higher investment will be.

7. A buoyant stock market also induces more investment. The q theory of investment suggests that investment will rise whenever the market value of firms' capital (as reflected in equity values) exceeds the replacement value of firms' existing capital.

8. The interest rate balances the demand and supply of domestic and international loanable funds. In a small open economy, the domestic interest rate is the same as the world interest rate. If the domestic demand for loanable funds exceeds the domestic supply, the economy runs a capital account surplus.

9. The exchange rate again comes into play as the variable which balances the net demand for foreign exchange arising from current account deficits and the net supply of foreign exchange arising from the capital account surplus.

Further reading

Ando, A. and Modigliani, F. (1970) 'The life cycle hypothesis of saving: aggregate implications and tests', *American Economic Review*, **53**(1), 55–84.

Friedman, M. (1957) *A Theory of the Consumption Function*, Princeton, NJ: Princeton University Press.

Keynes, J.M. (1936) *The General Theory of Employment, Interest and Money*, London: Macmillan.

Tobin, J. (1969) 'A general equilibrium approach to monetary theory', *Journal of Money, Credit and Banking*, **1** (1), 15–29.

Tsiang, S. (1989) 'Loanable funds' in Eatwell, J., Milgate, M. and P. Newman (eds) *The New Palgrave Dictionary of Economics*, London: Macmillan.

6

Fiscal policy and monetary policy

FISCAL POLICY

In advanced economies today, total government spending accounts for a third or more of total national spending. The total amount of tax revenue raised by the government sector is also roughly of the same magnitude. The public sector therefore plays a major role in advanced economies and in this chapter is brought to the forefront. Since the 1950s, the relative size of the government sector in many economies has grown markedly, although cross-country comparisons of public sector involvement in developed economies should be treated with some caution, as interpretations and measurement of public sector activity can differ.

A major reason for the rise in the size of government has been more widespread public provision of social welfare and the fact that over the course of numerous business cycles, fiscal policy has not been applied symmetrically. Governments have usually increased public spending during economic downswings, but have not fully scaled it back during upswings.

Fiscal policy is that instrument of macroeconomic policy which concerns public sector spending and taxing, and may in theory be used by the central government to influence national output, employment, the exchange rate, the external accounts and the price level in the short run. This chapter introduces the key concepts necessary for understanding the operation of fiscal and monetary policy in the open economy.

1. The budget and the fiscal stance

A central government's annual budget contains details of all expenditure and revenue-raising plans for the forthcoming fiscal year. Budgets also usually include official forecasts of the important macroeconomic variables such as GDP growth, unemployment rate, wages growth and the current account balance. They are keenly anticipated by economists and media commentators every year, because the budget documents are the medium through which the central government's fiscal intentions are revealed and through which fiscal policy is actually conducted.

Of the mass of fiscal data compiled in official budget documents, the arithmetic figure that attracts most attention is the overall budget balance. The *budget balance* (BB) is simply defined as the difference between total revenue and outlays, and is either in *deficit* or *surplus*. Total revenue earned by governments is mainly through taxation, but also includes other government receipts, such as returns on government assets (for example, rent earned on government buildings). Outlays are comprised of transfer payments, such as pensions and social welfare benefits (which are effectively negative taxes) and government expenditure on consumption and investment.

In symbols, the basic budget relationship can be stated as

$$BB = T_R - (T_r + G)$$

where BB is the budget balance, T_R is total revenue, T_r is transfers and G is government spending. BB is in deficit when outlays exceed revenue and in surplus when revenue exceeds outlays.

Budgets in advanced economies have most often been in deficit over past decades. Economic commentators use the absolute size of the budget deficit measured in absolute terms, or as expressed as a proportion of GDP, as summary indicators of the *fiscal stance*. If, for instance, the budget deficit of the UK rises from £10 billion to £15 billion from one year to the next, such a change is interpreted as a measure of the extent to which the UK government is using expansionary fiscal policy to influence macroeconomic activity.

However, some adjustments should be made to the officially published BB figure to obtain a better measure of the fiscal stance. As discussed in the Appendix to this chapter, nominal BB measures should first be adjusted for the distortionary effect of domestic inflation. This is necessary because under inflationary conditions according to the Fisher effect interest payments on the public debt should be included as part of total outlays.

Inflation-adjusted measures of budget deficits may still be misleading, however, to the extent that the state of the economy itself may affect budget outcomes. This is mainly because government revenue, especially income taxes, and to some extent indirect taxes on goods and services sold, naturally increase in line with the level of domestic economic activity and the business cycle. This suggests that budget balances may usefully be adjusted when the economy is at less than full employment to allow for cyclical influences. The cyclical effect on the budget balance is depicted in Figure 6.1. Other things equal, the higher is the level of economic activity, the higher is government revenue. The BB schedule is positively related to national income, as shown by the upward slope.

If the economy was at less than full employment at Y_E then there would naturally be a budget deficit. As the economy moves from the trough to the peak of a business cycle, there is an upswing in economic activity and the

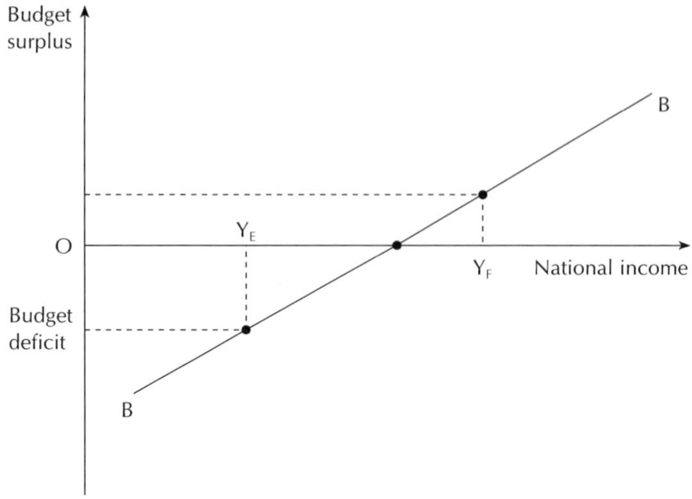

Figure 6.1 Economic activity and the budget balance.

restoration of full employment. This would automatically yield a budget surplus at Y_F.

The main message here is that the actual budget deficit should not necessarily be a focus of policy concern, in and of itself. Some economists, for example, go so far as to argue that the actual BB measure should always be adjusted to yield the cyclically adjusted BB. Such a measure would then indicate what the fiscal deficit would actually be if the economy was operating at full employment levels of national income.

Fiscal policy has been actively used as a macroeconomic instrument by governments in the post-war years to stabilise business cycles. For instance, fiscal policy has been expansionary to counter recessions and has been tightened during economic booms. Open economy factors have often motivated fiscal policy. For instance, the so-called 'twin deficits' hypothesis, relating the public accounts and the external accounts (to be outlined later in this chapter), has provided a theoretical rationale for fiscal contraction as a means of reducing trade deficits.

Nearly all of the day-to-day decisions of governments, whether they relate to issues as diverse as defence policy or policy on the environment, have some funding implications which ultimately show up as a change in some item recorded in the budget or public accounts. Revenue is mainly raised through the direct tax base (income tax and company tax) and via assorted indirect taxes (mainly excise duties, VAT, and goods and services taxes).

On the other side of budgets, the most notable feature is that government outlays in the form of defence, health, education, social security and other welfare payments comprise the major component of outlays in most advanced economies.

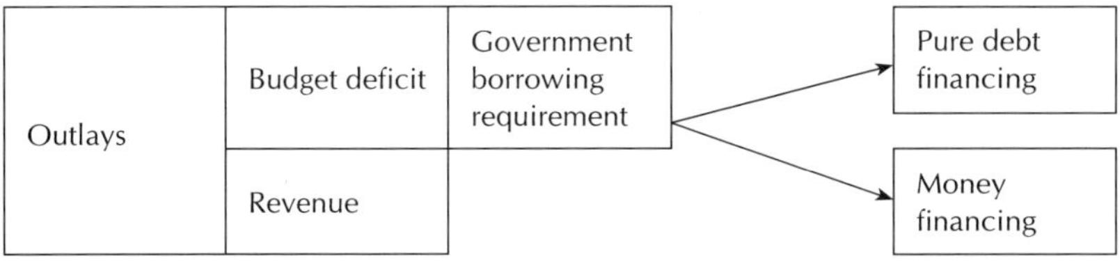

Figure 6.2 Financing budget deficits.

2. Financing budget deficits

When outlays exceed receipts, governments must borrow to fund the difference. Funds can be raised to finance budget deficits through the issue of government bonds to domestic households, firms, financial intermediaries, the rest of the world, and to the central bank. The government borrowing made necessary by budget deficits therefore increases the stock of public debt. If bonds are issued to residents or non-residents, this is termed *pure debt financing*. However, if the bonds are issued to the central bank, this is termed *money financing*. The financing options available to governments are illustrated in Figure 6.2, which is consistent with the earlier matrix showing sectoral financial positions (refer back to Chapter 2).

Yet another financing option available to government is *privatisation* of public assets, which involves the sale of real public sector assets to the private sector of the economy. Asset sales have been a frequent feature of budgets in many economies over recent decades, and funds raised by the government in this manner are akin to extra taxation revenue. Such receipts can be used to bridge the gap between outlays and traditional revenue sources without further raising the stock of public debt.

What is often forgotten in discussion of the public debt is that the government sector also has real assets which, from a balance sheet perspective, offset the government's financial liabilities in the form of public debt. Public sector balance sheets are not yet part of the budget documents of most economies. However, if they were, real assets such as buildings and roads would have to be included opposite the public debt which has at some stage financed their acquisition.

Constructing a public sector balance sheet raises a host of measurement problems. For instance, how should public assets (such as roads, national parks and national monuments) be valued when they are never actually traded in private markets? Such measurement problems partly explain why public sector balance sheets are not actually prepared. Nonetheless, we should be aware that the one-sided focus on the government's liabilities, which is often a feature of public debate on fiscal matters, may be quite misleading.

Public debt interest (PDI) is the annual cost of servicing the outstanding stock of public debt which has accumulated as a consequence of all previous budget deficits, less surpluses. As a share of total outlays, PDI rises

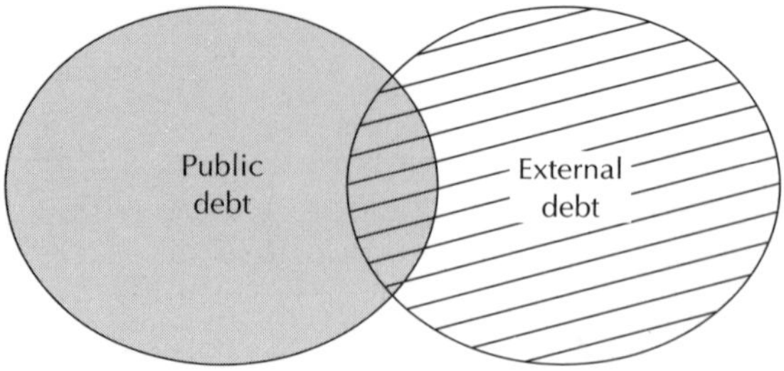

Figure 6.3 Public versus external debt.

when there are budget deficits and falls when there are budget surpluses. When there are budget surpluses, the extra revenue taken in by the Treasury is used to repay earlier borrowings. This means buying back previously issued bonds, which reduces the outstanding stock of public debt and accordingly lowers the budgetary cost of servicing it.

3. Public debt versus external debt

The public debt is a stock measure which represents the accumulation of all past budget deficits less budget surpluses. The bonds which make up the stock of public debt are the liabilities of the government acting on behalf of the nation's citizens. To the extent that domestic residents hold the bonds in their portfolio as assets, the public debt is 'owed to ourselves'.

Yet, of course not all of the public debt is owed to domestic residents in an open economy. Some bonds have been purchased by foreigners either at the time they were first issued by the nation's Treasury or Finance Ministry or through secondary trade in financial markets. This means part of public debt is also external debt and vice versa, as illustrated in Figure 6.3. To the extent that public indebtedness to foreigners must be serviced out of revenue raised domestically, the foreign part of public debt may represent a net drain on the economy, particularly if it has been used to finance public consumption expenditure. Public debt is also called *national debt*, although sometimes the term national debt is often mistakenly used to describe *external debt*.

4. The 'twin deficits' hypothesis

Many economists argue that growing budget deficits cause wider current account deficits. This proposed relationship between the fiscal and external deficits is often referred to as the *twin deficits hypothesis*. The possible causal links between the budget deficit and the current account deficit can be analysed using the saving and investment framework of the previous chapter.

First recall the definitions of private and public sector saving and investment. Private sector saving is equal to national disposable income less

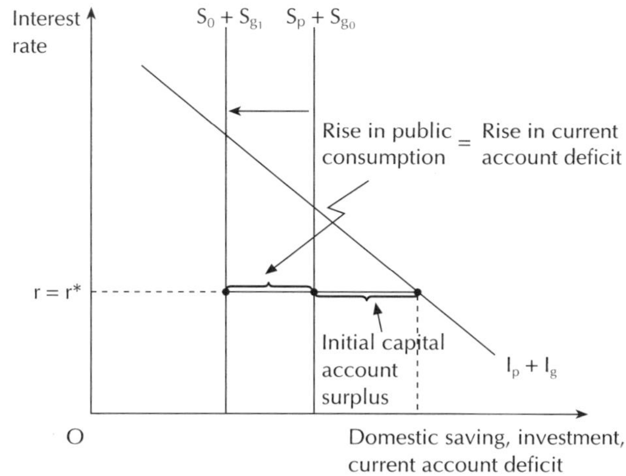

Figure 6.4 Fiscal activity and the external accounts.

private consumption. That is, $S_p = (Y_d - T_y - C_p)$ where Y_d is national disposable income, T_y is income taxes, net of transfer (including welfare) payments and C_p is private sector consumption. Public sector saving is the difference between taxes raised from the private sector less public consumption. That is, $S_g = (T_y - C_g)$ where C_g is public consumption. Total domestic saving is the sum of private saving and public saving:

$$S = S_p + S_g = (Y_d - T_y - C_p) + (T_y - C_g)$$

Consistent with the modern theories of consumption and saving behaviour outlined in the previous chapter, the supply of national saving is again assumed to be invariant to the domestic interest rate, r. Hence saving is shown by the vertical saving schedule in Figure 6.4. For a given level of national income, and total consumption, total saving is fixed.

On the investment side of the economy, there is an increased demand for available funds whenever firms invest by purchasing capital equipment, the cost of which is measured by the real interest rate (r). For a small open economy with unlimited access to world capital markets, this interest rate is the same as the world interest rate (r*). Total domestic investment is just the sum of private investment (I_p) plus public investment (I_g).

Now consider the effects of fiscal expansion on the external accounts, first by means of higher public spending. A rise in C_g implies a leftward shift of the total saving schedule. With unchanged total investment, this implies a rise in the current account deficit. Similarly, a rise in I_g would shift investment demand rightward and widen the difference between total domestic saving and investment, as reflected in a larger current account deficit.

The impact of higher income taxes on the external imbalance is much more ambiguous, however. For instance, a cut in taxes will only affect

Table 6.1 The effects of alternative fiscal measures.

	Effects on:					Budget deficit	Current account deficit
	S_p	S_g	S	I_p	I_g		
Rises in:							
Public consumption	0	↓	↓	0	0	↑	↑
Public investment	0	0	0	0	↑	↑	↑
Cuts in:							
Income taxes	↑	↓	?	0	0	↑	?

private consumption if such cuts are widely perceived as having a permanent effect on disposable income. Given the frequent and unpredictable manipulation of income tax rates, this seems most unlikely.

In other words, although a temporary cut in taxes definitely lowers public saving, if the rise in disposable income is perceived as only temporary, then any fall in public saving may be completely offset by a corresponding rise in private saving as households try to maintain living standards. Accordingly, the effect of short-run changes in taxes on domestic saving and hence on the current account deficit is uncertain.

The same sort of argument may in part apply to changing social welfare entitlements, which are here treated as negative taxes. Nonetheless, some changes to social welfare entitlements, such as raising the pensionable age for women, are more likely to be perceived as immutable and hence permanently affect private consumption behaviour.

The effects of alternative fiscal measures on saving, investment, the budget imbalance and the external account imbalance are summarised in Table 6.1. In short, although the earlier loanable funds approach suggests that the fiscal stance can influence the current account deficit, the linkages are likely to be much stronger through discretionary public spending, rather than tax changes.

Empirical studies of the 'twin deficits' hypothesis are not strongly supportive of the proposal that the two deficits are actually identical twins but perhaps more like siblings. One reason for this is that the business cycle may cause measured public and current account imbalances to move in opposite directions. For instance, during recessions, a slump in private investment may lower the current account deficit but raise the budget deficit as tax revenue falls and unemployment benefits increase government outlays.

5. Ricardian equivalence

Some economists argue that there are other reasons, apart from the nature of the exchange rate regime, that limit the effect of fiscal policy on national income. These arguments are not new. For instance, whether budget deficits and higher levels of public debt stimulate overall domestic spending behaviour was a question first raised by the classical economist David Ricardo and more recently revived by American economist Robert Barro.

In its modern form, so-called *Ricardian equivalence* proposes that households are forward looking and expect that a rise in public debt will, at some point in the future, have to be repaid. This means taxes will eventually have to rise. If so, private saving rates would tend to rise and present consumption fall in anticipation of the future tax obligations. In its strict form, Ricardian equivalence asserts that private saving will increase to the same extent as the increase in government spending that causes the budget deficit and stock of public debt to rise. In terms of the above loanable funds analysis, total saving would not actually change after fiscal expansion. This is because increased government spending (a fall in S_g) would be fully offset by a fall in private consumption (a rise in S_p).

Empirical studies have generally rejected the Ricardian equivalence proposition, however, especially in its strict form, which argues that a dollar increase in public-debt-financed government spending leads to a dollar increase in private saving. Hence, the above loanable funds analysis remains intact, although it should be borne in mind that even partial Ricardian effects would further weaken the linkage between the budget and trade deficits.

MONETARY POLICY

The importance of money as an influence on the macroeconomy has been a major issue of economic debate since the discipline of economics emerged centuries ago. In the past, these differences centred on questions such as whether the quantity of money in circulation altered the aggregate price level and output in the short run or in the long run. Most economists now agree that monetary policy can influence real economic activity over the short term although over the long-run it only affects nominal variables such as the price level and the nominal exchange rate.

Monetary policy is at least as important an instrument of macroeconomic policy as fiscal policy, and the main aim of the remainder of this chapter is to outline the mechanics of monetary policy in the open economy context. An economy's central bank issues the currency which residents use to settle all domestic transactions. Central banks conduct monetary policy by changing the amount of domestic currency in circulation for the purpose of influencing domestic liquidity conditions, interest rates and nominal exchange rates. Movements in domestic interest rates and exchange rates subsequently affect the short-run behaviour of all macroeconomic variables.

Disagreements about the way monetary policy should be conducted have, in the past, centred on the relative importance of the end goals of monetary policy, as well as on the best means of achieving those goals. At present, central bankers worldwide see inflation control as the foremost objective of monetary policy but retain considerable discretionary powers while operating with varying degrees of independence from governments.

The Monetarist school of economists led by Nobel laureate Milton Friedman proposed that a sole intermediate target, the money supply, be linked to a single end goal, low domestic inflation, on the grounds that money supply growth was the key determinant of inflation. At the same time, this proposal effectively curtailed the central bank's capacity to 'manage' overall economic activity for the purpose of pursuing other objectives, such as employment levels or the balance of payments.

Having successfully reduced inflation, central bankers are apparently all Monetarists now, at least in so far as inflation targeting has become the main objective of monetary policy. The best way to practise monetary policy has, however, been the subject of considerable ongoing debate. The *modus operandi* of monetary policy, differs somewhat across countries, both in terms of the intermediate variables actually targeted and with respect to the frequency and magnitude of central bank interventions to influence monetary conditions.

Contrary to the original policy prescription of Monetarism, central bankers in general no longer attempt to control money supplies directly as the means to limiting inflation. Instead, most central banks use short-term interest rates as their intermediate target.

6. The role of central banks

Figure 6.5 depicts the typical structure of an economy's financial and monetary system. This system is essentially a network of financial institutions which by and large act as intermediaries, or go-betweens, for savers and investors in the economy. Although they are included as one of the institutional sectors of the flow of funds accounts, financial institutions as intermediaries do not themselves ultimately contribute to the demand or supply of saving.

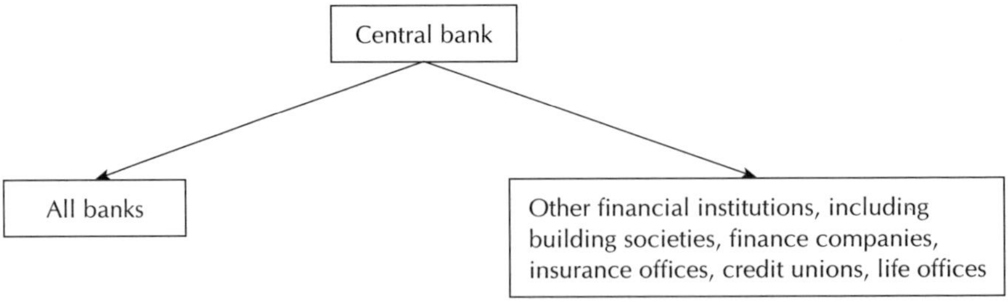

Figure 6.5 The financial and monetary system.

The main functions of a central bank include acting as major banker to the government and public authorities, acting as banker to the banks themselves and some other financial institutions, and printing the notes which circulate as money. At the international level, the central banks retain the nation's official reserves of gold and foreign exchange as well as intervening from time to time in the foreign exchange market to dampen excessive exchange rate volatility.

The central bank supplies currency and its balance sheet is:

Central bank

Assets	*Liabilities*
Government bonds	Currency
Foreign exchange reserves	Cash reserves of commercial banks

Meanwhile, the balance sheet of the commercial banks is:

Commercial banks

Assets	*Liabilities*
Cash reserves at central bank	Deposits
Government bonds	
Commercial loans	

Therefore, the balance sheet of the banking system as a whole, that is comprising the central bank and commercial banks is:

Banking system

Assets	*Liabilities*
Government bonds	Money supply:
Commercial loans	Currency
Foreign exchange reserves	Deposits

In this way, the money supply reconciles with the definition provided earlier in Chapter 2.

Central banks can also perform important supervisory and regulatory functions, although in many economies prudential supervision of the financial system to ensure it operates efficiently and effectively is undertaken by separate official bodies that are independent of the central bank.

7. Techniques of monetary policy

With deregulated financial markets, central banks can alter the stance of monetary policy through a number of channels. The most common method is for central banks to enter the domestic money market to either buy or sell government securities. This is called *open-market operations* and can be used to influence interest rates by changing the money supply. For instance, if the central bank buys domestic bonds, residents selling those bonds receive new money from the central bank in return. This increases the amount of domestic currency in circulation and so expands the domestic money supply. On the contrary, the money supply eventually contracts if the central bank sells Treasury bonds in the bond market from its own portfolio. Under such circumstances, the residents purchasing the bonds in effect reduce liquidity in the financial system.

The other major method through which the central bank can alter the money supply and hence interest rates is through *foreign exchange market intervention*. Instead of intervening in the domestic bond market, as with open-market operations, it can enter the foreign exchange market to change the money supply by either buying or selling foreign currencies from its stock of official reserves in exchange for domestic currency.

For instance, if the central bank purchases foreign exchange, this means it swaps local currency (which was previously not part of the domestic money supply) for foreign currencies held on residents' behalf by the major banks operating domestically. Therefore, foreign exchange purchases increase the domestic money supply, whereas foreign exchange sales by the central bank reduce the domestic money supply.

Any foreign exchange market intervention that involves a change in the domestic money base is called *non-sterilised intervention*. Such intervention is analogous to domestic open-market operations, except that foreign currency, rather than domestic bonds, is bought or sold by the central bank.

Sterilised intervention occurs when the central bank operates in the domestic bond market to offset the domestic money supply effects of its foreign exchange market intervention. An official purchase of foreign assets in the foreign exchange market, for instance, would lead to a rise in the central bank's holdings of foreign currency, and a simultaneous rise in the money supply. If such an operation were sterilised, then the central bank would sell domestic bonds (to the equivalent domestic currency value of its foreign exchange market intervention) to residents through the domestic bond market. Such action would restore the domestic money supply to its original level. Thus, sterilised foreign exchange market intervention does not change residents' domestic money holdings, whereas non-sterilised intervention does.

The mechanics of sterilised intervention are summarised in Table 6.2, which shows that sterilised intervention actually involves a three-stage process. Consider the case of official intervention which is designed to depreciate the nominal exchange rate. The first stage is the purchase by the central

Table 6.2 The stages of sterilised foreign exchange market intervention.

	Domestic money supply	*Foreign money supply*	*Bank of England's foreign reserves*	*Bank of England's domestic bonds*
Stage 1: Foreign exchange market intervention (Bank of England sells £ to buy forex)	+5	−5		
Stage 2: Bank of England buys foreign bonds		+5	+5	
Stage 3: Open market operations (Bank of England sells £ bonds)	−5			−5
	0	0	+5	−5

bank of foreign currency. As an example, presume the Bank of England purchases foreign currency to the value of £5 m in domestic currency terms. Through the matching sale of local currency in the foreign exchange market, this transaction increases the outstanding domestic money supply by £5 m. Next, the foreign currency acquired by the central bank through its official intervention is used to purchase foreign currency bonds on which it earns interest. These two stages are as far as unsterilised intervention goes, the net effect being a rise in the domestic money supply.

The third stage involves ordinary open-market operations by the Bank of England in the domestic bond market to offset the unintended money supply effects of the initial foreign exchange market intervention. In this final stage, the central bank would exchange £5 m worth of Treasury bonds for domestic money in the domestic bond market. Residents would acquire domestic bonds worth £5 m in place of domestic money, and the domestic money supply would be restored to its former level. In practice, what has changed is the composition of the balance sheet of the central bank. In the example, the Bank of England has gained £5 m worth of foreign reserves, but lost an equivalent value of £5 m in UK Treasury bonds.

Under the Bretton Woods exchange rate system, characterised as it was by strict controls over capital flows, current account deficits could give rise to genuine balance of payments problems. This was because the central bank's foreign reserves in effect had to be run down to meet the shortfall in foreign exchange which arose because there was an excess of imports over exports. A current account deficit therefore became unsustainable at a fixed exchange rate. Accordingly, it became necessary under such conditions to check aggregate expenditure through tight fiscal and monetary policy and at the same time devalue the currency. Currency devaluations improved the trade balance because, as shown in Chapter 4, they raised the prices of tradables, stimulating production of more tradables while simultaneously discouraging aggregate expenditure on tradables.

With floating exchange rates and greater international capital market integration, the international macroeconomic environment has changed dramatically. As explained earlier, current account deficits and international capital movements should match *ex post* over any given period, in principle. The exchange rate itself plays the major role in ensuring equality between the flows on both sides of the external accounts. If, over any period, the net demand for foreign currency arising from current account transactions does not match the net supply from capital account transactions the exchange rate either depreciates or appreciates.

In effect, the decision by governments to float exchange rates means that floating exchange rates bear the pressure of external adjustment. Despite the adoption of an independently floating exchange rate, most central banks retain powers to intervene in foreign exchange markets for the purposes of smoothing short-run exchange rate fluctuations. Although it should not strictly be necessary for central banks to maintain large holdings of official reserve assets with which to influence exchange rates under a floating rate system, they have nonetheless maintained sizeable foreign currency reserves.

8. The yield curve

The discussion of the flow of funds in the previous chapter referred to the interest rate prevailing in the economy. In reality, however, there is always a spectrum of interest rates on offer at any particular time. For instance, different interest rates are paid on 90-day bank bills, 5-year Treasury bonds and personal loans. The *yield curve* describes the various interest rates payable on financial assets that are the same in all respects except the time period over which borrowings must be repaid. This time period is called the *term of maturity*.

The yield curve is simply a graph in interest rate–term to maturity space. It typically depicts the interest rates paid on short- versus long-term government bonds. An *ascending* yield curve shows that at any given time, short-term rates are lower than long-term rates, whereas a *descending* yield curve shows that interest rates on short-term securities are higher than rates on longer-term securities. These types of yield curves are depicted in Figure 6.6. They can also be flat or hump-backed, and the slope and position of the yield curve can vary from day to day.

Various theories have been expounded over the years to explain why it is that short- and long-term market interest rates differ. The three main theories of the term structure of interest rates which have been advanced are the *expectations theory*, the risk or *liquidity preference approach* and the *segmented markets theory*. Of these, the expectations theory and the closely related liquidity preference approach are widely accepted explanations of the term structure.

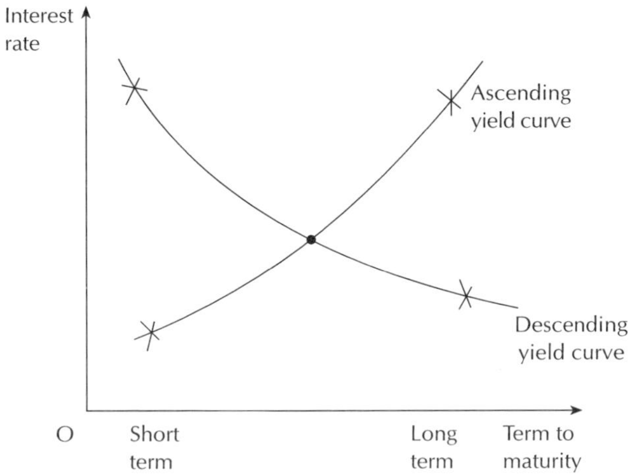

Figure 6.6 Ascending and descending yield curves.

The expectations theory presumes that default-free securities, like Treasury Notes, which are issued by the same entity but which differ with respect to their terms to maturity, are perceived as perfect substitutes by investors. Accordingly, the interest rate paid on the longer term security, say a hypothetical 60-day Treasury Note, equals the average of the current rate on a hypothetical 30-day Treasury Note, and the markets' expectations of the rate to be paid on 30-day Treasury Notes in a month's time. In formula terms, the expectations hypothesis suggests that:

$$\text{60-day rate} = \frac{\text{30-day rate + next month's expected 30-day rate}}{2}$$

Or, more generally:

$$i_{2t} = \frac{i_t^s + i_t^e}{2}$$

where i_{2t} is the longer term rate, i_t^s is the current, or spot, short-term rate and i_t^e is the short-term rate expected in the next period.

As an example, if the spot interest rate on a 30-day Treasury Note is 5 per cent and the market expects that the interest rate on a 30-day Treasury Note next month will be 7 per cent, then according to this theory, the spot interest rate on a 60-day Note would be 6 per cent. It follows that an ascending yield curve depicting the short rate at 5 per cent and the long rate at 6 per cent contains information about the money market's expectation of the future short-term rate.

In other words, this approach suggests that it is market opinion about what future short-term rates will be which essentially drives longer-term rates. The accepted corollary for monetary policy is that long-term interest rates can therefore be changed by fixing the official short-term rate for sustained periods because money and bond markets will base their expectations of future short-term rates on the current official rate.

The risk, or liquidity preference, theory of the term structure is effectively an augmented version of the expectations hypothesis. It suggests that investors consider short-term securities to be more attractive than longer-term bonds due to uncertainty about future short-term rates and that, accordingly, a premium is required on longer-term securities to make them as appealing to investors as short-term securities. The longer the maturity, it is argued, the higher this premium will be.

The segmented markets theory of the term structure is diametrically opposed to the expectations theory because it presumes that securities of different maturities, issued by the same entity, are completely non-substitutable. Accordingly, the slope of the yield curve results from the interaction of the demand and supply of bonds in distinct, or segmented, markets. In other words, no linkage exists between officially controlled short-term interest rates and longer-term rates.

The corollary for monetary policy here is that targeting short-term rates is largely pointless as a means of influencing long-rate-sensitive investment spending and macroeconomic activity. Instead, it implies that central banks should be intervening in longer-term securities markets in order to directly influence long-term interest rates. However, this approach has few advocates and little empirical support.

The earlier discussion of the role interest rates play in balancing domestic and foreign saving and investment flows essentially related to the long-term interest rate. A small open economy's (long-term) interest rate was earlier assumed to be equivalent to the world interest rate, and the external capital account balance and net foreign borrowing were measures of the difference between domestic saving and investment at that (long-term) interest rate. In subsequent discussion of the short-term effects of monetary policy on the open economy, the focus will shift more to short-term interest rate behaviour, for it is at the short end of the interest rate spectrum that monetary policy has its major impact.

The yield curve itself can be used as an indicator of the stance of monetary policy. If the yield curve is ascending, this may suggest that the *monetary stance* is relaxed or expansionary. This simply means that short-term interest rates are lower than long-term rates, which are tied to international rates. On the contrary, a descending yield curve may indicate a tighter or contractionary monetary policy. As we will see, international investment funds very quickly flow in and out of the open economy as short-term rates are manipulated by the monetary authorities.

9. The impact of monetary policy

Higher or lower interest rates are thought to have an impact on the spending patterns of households and firms through liquidity, wealth, exchange rate and expectations channels. For instance, higher interest rates can curb

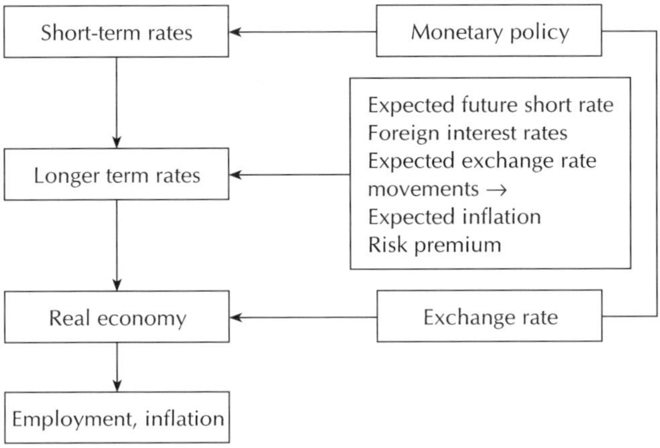

Figure 6.7 Monetary policy, interest rates and the economy.

firms' investment expenditure because the cost of capital rises relative to its productivity. Higher interest rates are also likely to reduce equity values, as investors switch from shares to bonds, thus lowering the market value of firms' capital relative to its replacement cost. According to standard theory, this further weakens the incentive for firms to invest. Moreover, to the extent that lower equity values depress aggregate household wealth, consumption spending may also be reduced.

For monetary policy to operate effectively along these lines, it is important that interest rates at the short end of the spectrum influence rates at the long end, since investment spending in particular is likely to be more sensitive to longer-term interest rate movements, given business planning horizons. The interrelationship between monetary policy, interest rates and the economy is shown schematically in Figure 6.7.

In many economies with floating exchange rates, central banks alter the stance of monetary policy by focusing on short-term interest rates for the purpose of influencing longer-term rates. Thus, the linkage between short- and longer-term interest rates plays a major role in the transmission of changes in the stance of monetary policy to the real economy. International arbitrage ties long-term rates to foreign long-term rates, with any difference between domestic and foreign interest rates likely to arise from the market's expectation of future exchange rate changes according to the standard uncovered interest parity (explained in Chapter 8). Gaps between similar long-term rates domestically and abroad will also reflect market expectations of domestic inflation and liquidity and risk premia which vary over time.

10. Central bank independence

Monetary policy can be manipulated far more readily by the authorities than fiscal policy and in general is subject to less public scrutiny and accountability. It has been argued that making central banks more independent of governments would be a means of avoiding undue political influence over the conduct of monetary policy. Such influence may be exercised by governments seeking to improve their chances of re-election. Those countries noted for the stability of their monetary policies, such as New Zealand, Switzerland and Germany, have central banks which are very independent of government control. At the other end of the scale, developing countries with relatively unstable monetary policies have central banks which come directly under the influence of governments. Some economists argue that, according to past experience, the more independent of government a central bank tends to be, the lower that country's inflation rate. At the same time, however, the more independent a central bank is from government, the less accountable it is to the government and the electorate for any major mistakes it makes, such as raising interest rates too high and inducing recession and unemployment.

An important reason for maintaining low inflation is that a reversion to higher and more variable inflation causes arbitrary income redistribution. There are several well-known channels through which even moderate inflation may affect income distribution and worsen inequality. For instance, inflation will have an adverse direct impact on household disposable income when nominal wages are less than fully indexed, or even if wages are fully indexed, when marginal income tax rates are not. Indirectly, inflation can also increase inequality by slowing output growth and hence employment through channels which distort relative prices and worsen allocative efficiency.

Changes in inflation arbitrarily redistribute income and wealth between savers and borrowers when it is unanticipated. Such unintended redistributions are far reaching in any economy since every household unit must be either a saver household or a borrower household, except for that proportion whose expenditure always coincides exactly with their income.

After several prior decades of relative price stability in advanced economies, the high-inflation regime that emerged in the early 1970s surprised domestic borrowers and savers (lenders) and enabled a transfer of income to occur from savers to borrowers, which sector included governments running sizeable fiscal deficits. Hence, the notion that unanticipated inflation was a form of theft because it effectively eroded the real value of savers' wealth. In practice, this erosion occurred because the Fisher effect took time to assert itself and savers were not compensated for the loss in purchasing power of their accumulated funds through higher nominal interest rates.

Summary

1. This chapter explained key aspects of fiscal and monetary policy.
2. Fiscal policy involves the manipulation of government spending and taxing as recorded in the budget to influence aggregate expenditure and saving in the economy.

3. To ascertain the fiscal stance, it is necessary to go beyond the official measures of the overall budget deficit or surplus to account for the effects of economic activity and inflation.
4. Pure debt financing of budget deficits entails borrowing from residents and foreigners. A budget deficit funded through borrowings from the central bank is money financing, which increases the money base.
5. The 'twin deficits' hypothesis causally links budget and current account deficits by suggesting that higher budget deficits affect domestic saving and investment behaviour and hence the economy's international borrowing requirement.
6. Ricardian equivalence proposes that households will reduce consumption spending to offset any extra government spending.
7. The main function of a central bank is to conduct monetary policy to ensure low inflation and full employment. Central banks or other independent public authorities are also often responsible for prudential supervision of an economy's financial system.
8. Monetary policy can be implemented through open-market operations or foreign exchange market intervention. Sterilised foreign exchange market intervention involves offsetting domestic bond market transactions which leave the domestic money supply unchanged.
9. The yield curve relates short-term and long-term interest rates. The central bank mainly exercises control over short-term rates, and changes in the yield curve are indicative of the stance of monetary policy.
10. Advocates of central bank independence argue that an economy's inflation performance improves when monetary policy is not subject to political interference.

Further reading

Seater, J. (1993) 'Ricardian equivalence', *Journal of Economic Literature*, **31** (1), 142–90.

Appendix

Inflation-adjusted budget and current account imbalances

Unlike most of the other macroeconomic data published by national statistics agencies, the sectoral accounts making up the flow of funds accounts are not officially adjusted for the distortionary effects of domestic inflation. One reason for this is that inflation adjustment of sectoral balances raises some tricky measurement issues which do not arise for other components of the national accounts.

First consider the budget or public account imbalance. In the absence of inflation, nominal and real budget outcomes for a closed economy have the same numerical value and are the accounting equivalents of changes in the nominal and real stocks of public debt over time. In an inflationary environment, however, the real purchasing power embodied in public debt held as an asset by bond holders and as a liability of the government falls. Any net decrease (increase) in the inflation-adjusted stock of public debt can be thought of as a measure of the 'real' budget surplus (deficit) over that time.

An unchanged stock of real public debt means a balanced real budget, as a simple numerical example should make clear. If, for instance, the stock of public debt was \$100 m, inflation was 10 per cent and the budget deficit was \$10 m, the level of real public debt would remain the same since inflation has reduced the purchasing power value of the debt to the same extent as the nominal budget deficit has increased it.

Taxpayers effectively pay off the public debt through the inflation premium included in the nominal interest rate due to the Fisher effect. From a portfolio perspective, such income transfers are compensation for inflation and represent principal repayments to preserve the capital value of bonds to asset holders. In effect, rising public debt interest payments caused by inflation are no less inflation-adjusted transfer payments than, say, indexed old age pensions. In both cases, recipients are insulated from any erosion of the purchasing power of their taxpayer-sourced income.

To actually measure the real public account imbalance for a financially open economy, it is important to note that, *ex post*, any change in the nominal domestic currency value of public debt must equal the primary public account imbalance (defined as non-interest outlays less revenue), plus public debt interest. Putting this more formally:

$$\frac{d}{dt}(H_g + eF_g) = B + i_g H_g + r_g eF_g + seF_g$$

where H_g is nominal home currency denominated public debt, F_g is nominal foreign currency denominated public debt, B is the primary public account imbalance, i_g is the average interest rate paid on H, r_g is the average interest rate paid on F and s is the rate of currency depreciation.

Deflating by the price level (P), the change in real public debt:

$$\frac{d}{dt}\frac{(H_g + eF_g)}{P} = \frac{\left(\frac{dH_g}{dt} + seF_g + \frac{edF_g}{dt}\right)P - (H_g + eF_g)\frac{dP}{dt}}{P^2}$$

$$= \frac{\left(\frac{dH_g}{dt} + seF_g + \frac{edF_g}{dt}\right) - (H_g + eF_g)\pi}{P}$$

where π is inflation, $\frac{dP}{dt}/P$.

Substituting:

$$\frac{d}{dt}\frac{(H_g + eF_g)}{P} = \frac{(B + i_g H_g + r_g eF + seF_g) - (H_g + eF_g)\pi}{P}$$

$$= \frac{B}{P} + (i_g - \pi)\frac{H_g}{P} + (r_g - \pi + s)\frac{eF_g}{P}$$

The real budget imbalance is therefore the sum of the primary part of the public account imbalance, deflated by the price level, as well as the real costs of servicing total public debt outstanding. The servicing cost on public debt previously issued in domestic currency can be measured by simply applying the real interest rate to public debt, whereas the servicing cost on foreign currency denominated debt is additionally influenced by exchange rate movements.

Similarly, inflation distorts the other sectoral balances. For instance, a lower inflation rate automatically means a lower adjusted current account deficit since, in an inflationary environment, part of the nominal income payments made to foreigners in the form of profit remittances, interest and dividends and shown as income paid abroad in the current account, effectively represents repayment of capital and should be offset against recorded foreign investment in the capital account.

Inflation-adjusted measures of external imbalance could therefore indicate the extent of the real transfer of capital which takes place between current account surplus and current account deficit nations. Essentially, the transfer process itself involves foreign borrowing recorded, of course, in the capital account of the debtor country, being reflected in an overall deficit on the current account due to higher imports of investment goods or higher imports of consumption goods which allow the release of real resources for domestic capital production.

Inflation adjustment of the external and public account balances has direct implications for private sector saving. The inflation-adjusted external imbalance as a proportion of GDP should be less than the actual measure, because net capital inflow is effectively over-recorded. Therefore, measured domestic saving, comprising both private and public saving, must be similarly understated for given gross investment.

7

Macroeconomic policy in the short run

National governments are always changing the stance of their fiscal and monetary policies to try to influence domestic financial and expenditure conditions. Such macroeconomic policy activism is due to the influence of Keynesian thinking, which generally presumes that fiscal and monetary policy can satisfactorily stabilise the business cycle and achieve the objectives of full employment and low inflation. In circumstances where international markets have become more integrated, it is necessary to understand how international capital mobility affects the overall behaviour of open economics and the potency of macroeconomic policies. Macroeconomic policy prescriptions based on closed-economy assumptions very seldom transfer without modification to the open economy.

This chapter covers standard theoretical approaches to modelling the impact of fiscal and monetary policies on the open economy in the short run. First, it outlines what is known as the *Mundell–Fleming* model of national income determination, which remains the 'workhorse' of international macroeconomic analysis. The model is presented in its conventional format, but also in an alternative way which allows us to explicitly trace the balance of payments and exchange rate effects of fiscal and monetary policy. The chapter later narrows the focus somewhat to concentrate on how the different techniques of monetary policy, as explained in the previous chapter, influence the domestic interest rate and exchange rate under conditions where international capital mobility is less than perfect. The theoretical vehicle used for this purpose is known as the *portfolio balance* approach to the exchange rate.

THE MUNDELL–FLEMING MODEL

The macroeconomic model most often used to analyse how fiscal and monetary policies may work in the open economy is the Mundell–Fleming model. Named after its authors, Robert Mundell (1963) and John Fleming (1962), this model explains short-run fluctuations in national income, taking exchange rates, consumption, investment, government spending, international trade and international capital flows into account. Also known as the IS-LM-BP model, it is popular because it predicts how effective fiscal and monetary policies are as macroeconomic policy instruments, under either fixed or floating exchange rate regimes.

There are several building blocks to this model. These foundations will be outlined first before showing how the model may be used to assess the effectiveness of fiscal policy and monetary policy.

1. Deriving the IS curve

To develop the Mundell–Fleming model, it is first necessary to construct the IS curve. This curve is a locus which shows a relationship between the domestic interest rate and the associated level of equilibrium national income.

The fundamental condition for equilibrium in the market for goods and services in the economy is that total expenditure (C + I + G + NX) equals total national income, Y. That is, C + I + G + NX = Y.

The behaviour of the consumption (C) and investment (I) aggregates was covered earlier in Chapter 6. The simple Keynesian consumption function and the investment function capture the spending behaviour of households and firms. The behaviour of private consumption and investment can now be summarised as:

$C = C(Y)$

$I = I(r)$

Therefore, total private spending by residents in the economy (A) can be shown as:

$A = C(Y) + I(r)$

The derivation of the IS curve is shown graphically in Figure 7.1. Notice first that the horizontal axes in the figure are the same. In the top panel, the total expenditure function is drawn for a particular interest rate. If the interest rate (i) is 10 per cent, then the total spending at that interest rate determines a particular equilibrium level of income and output, Y_0. This allows us to associate the interest rate of 10 per cent with the equilibrium income level of Y_0 as shown in the bottom panel.

Now, if the interest rate is lower, at say 8 per cent, then investment would be higher and the total expenditure function would be higher, as shown by A_1 in the top panel. Equilibrium income would also be higher at Y_1. So a lower interest rate is associated with a higher level of national income, as shown in the bottom panel.

The IS curve connects all points which associate interest rates and corresponding equilibrium income levels. If there is any rise in autonomous spending in the economy (that is, spending unconnected to the interest rate) the IS curve will shift rightward.

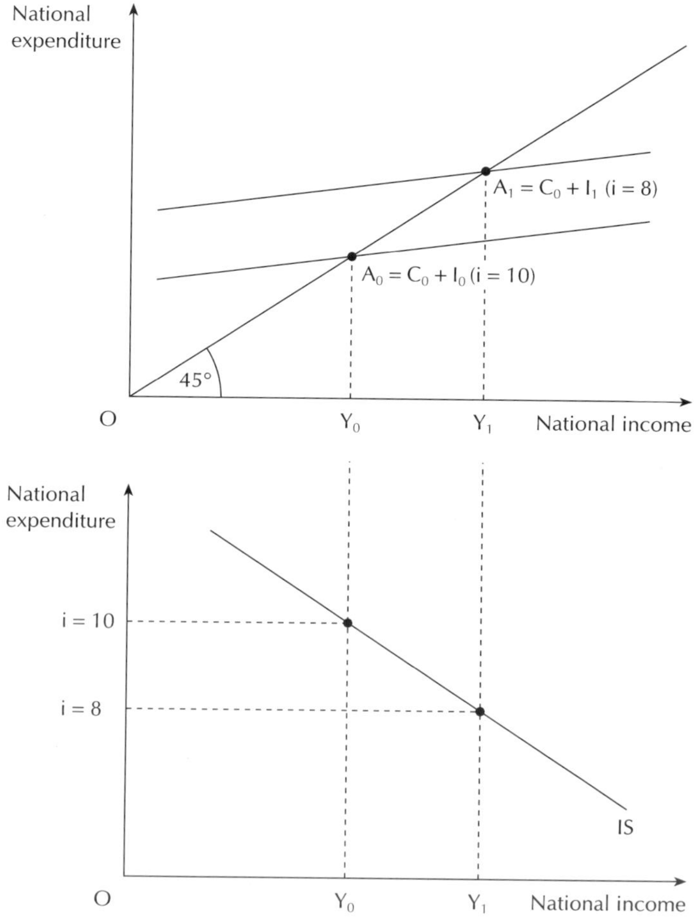

Figure 7.1 Deriving the IS curve.

2. Net exports, competitiveness and the IS curve

In the basic Mundell–Fleming model, changes in the nominal exchange rate cause equivalent changes in the conventionally defined real exchange rate, R, since the foreign and domestic price levels are fixed in the short-run by assumption (that is, R↓ as *e*↓). These changes in competitiveness in turn influence export and import flows. In particular, improved competitiveness raises exports and lowers imports, thereby increasing net exports, NX. Higher national spending and income (Y) also means more spending by residents on imported goods and services. Hence, in summary we can write:

$$NX = NX(R, Y)$$

With reference to Figure 7.1, net exports are added to C + I so that the total expenditure schedule now represents C + I + NX. If net exports rise, following an improvement in competitiveness, total spending on nationally

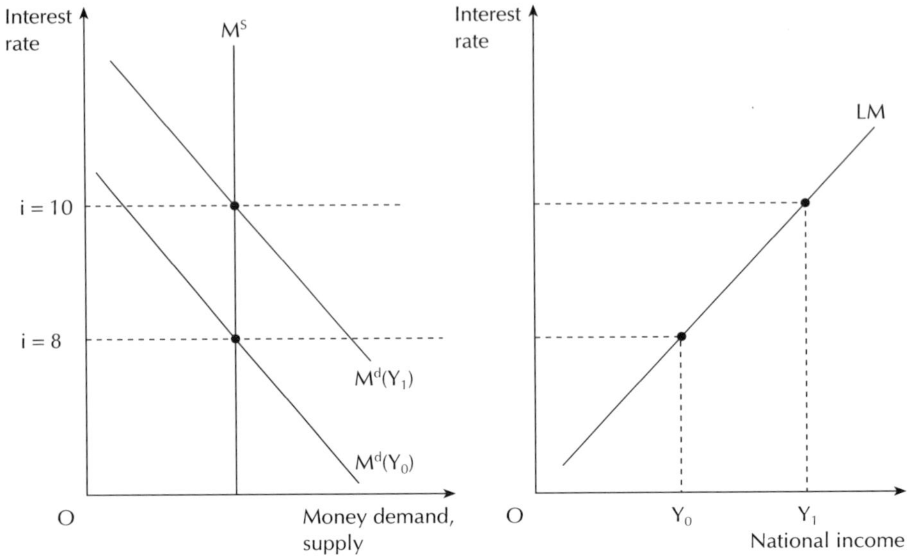

Figure 7.2 Deriving the LM curve.

produced goods and services also rises. This means the IS curve shifts to the right. If competitiveness worsens net exports fall, and the IS curve shifts leftward.

3. Deriving the LM curve

So far, the analysis has been about equilibrium in the goods and services market. In this section, attention turns to the money market. Equilibrium in this market is represented by the LM curve. The derivation of the LM curve is shown in Figure 7.2. Note here that the vertical axes are the same.

The left panel of the figure depicts the money market. Residents' demand for money, or liquidity preference, can be represented in functional form as:

$$M^d = M^d(i, Y)$$

That is, the amount of money demanded in the economy depends on both the interest rate and the level of income. It depends negatively on the interest rate because the higher the interest rate, the greater is the opportunity cost of holding non-interest-earning cash balances. Therefore, the demand for money schedule in interest–money space is downward sloping. It depends positively on the level of income because the higher the level of income, the more spending there is in the economy and the greater the need for money to conduct daily transactions. The supply of money is fixed by the central bank and is shown as a vertical schedule.

The equilibrium interest rate is determined at the intersection of the money demand and supply schedules. Hence money demand associated with national income at Y_0 implies on interest rate of, say, 8 per cent. A higher level of income at Y_1 suggests a stronger demand for money and is paired with a higher interest rate of, say, 10 per cent. The LM curve in the right panel connects all points showing equilibrium in the money market and is drawn for a given money supply. The LM curve shifts to the right if the money supply increases as a result of the actions of the central bank (expansionary monetary policy). It shifts to the left if the central bank contracts the money supply (contractionary monetary policy).

4. Capital mobility and the BP curve

Over recent decades, international financial markets have become highly integrated. This now means that if domestic interest rates tend to rise above foreign rates, then international capital will immediately flow into the country as foreigners purchase higher yielding debt instruments denominated in the domestic currency. Other things being equal, this increases the supply of foreign exchange relative to the demand for foreign exchange. This tends to appreciate the external value of the currency. On the contrary, if domestic interest rates tend to fall relative to foreign rates, there would be capital outflow in search of higher interest returns abroad and a tendency for the exchange rate to depreciate.

If financial capital movements are infinitely responsive to interest differentials, capital mobility is said to be *perfect* and the domestic and foreign interest rates must be equal in equilibrium. This is another way of stating the small-country assumption of Chapter 5, where the domestic interest rate was equal to the world interest rate. It also implies that domestic and foreign bonds are perfect substitutes in the eyes of investors. In the opposite case, where exchange controls and risk premia prohibit international capital movements, domestic and foreign interest rates can be quite independent of each other. International capital is then said to be *immobile*.

If capital is perfectly mobile and the economy is small, the balance of payments (BP) schedule is horizontal at the world interest rate, r^*. If the exchange rate floats, all points above the BP line in Figure 7.1 imply that the exchange rate is appreciating. This is because international capital will continue to flow into the country, creating an excess supply of foreign currency, as long as domestic interest rates are above the world rate. All points below the BP line imply a depreciating exchange rate because international capital will flow out of the economy, if the domestic interest rate falls below the world rate.

On the other hand, if the exchange rate is fixed or centrally managed, points above the BP line suggest an overall balance of payments surplus. This surplus reflects the build-up of official reserve assets resulting from the central bank's intervention in the foreign exchange market to purchase an excess supply of foreign currency. Likewise, points below the line suggest a balance of payments deficit, or a run-down of official reserve assets as the central bank intervenes, selling its foreign currency reserves in exchange for domestic currency.

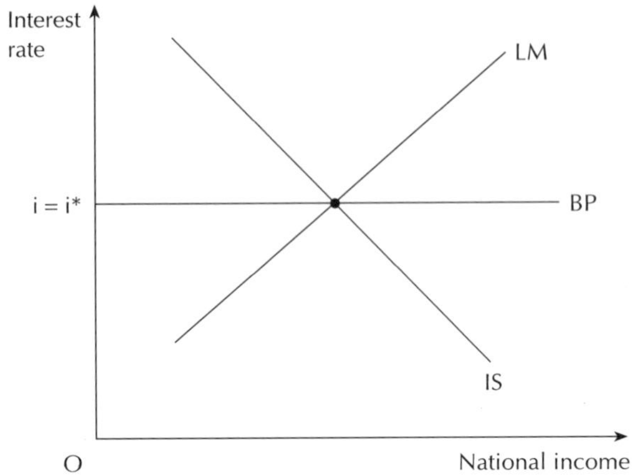

Figure 7.3 IS-LM-BP framework.

The Mundell–Fleming model is also known as the IS-LM-BP model as it is based on the three loci which have just been derived. In summary, the IS curve shows the pairings of interest rates and national income levels consistent with equilibrium in the goods and services sector of the economy, whereby planned expenditure equals planned output. The LM curve shows the combinations of interest rates and income, consistent with equilibrium in the monetary sector, whereby the domestic demand for money equals the domestic supply of money. The BP curve shows equilibrium in the foreign exchange market.

The point of intersection of all three schedules shows where goods, services, and domestic and foreign exchange money markets are all simultaneously in equilibrium. This is depicted in Figure 7.3.

FISCAL AND MONETARY POLICIES IN AN OPEN ECONOMY

This standard version of the IS-LM-BP model can now be used to analyse the effects of internal and external disturbances on the open economy. For instance, such disturbances may be generated on the goods and services side of the economy, such as when there are autonomous changes in consumption, investment, government spending or foreign trade, or on the monetary side, such as when there are autonomous changes in the domestic money supply or demand.

Most often, the model is used to examine the impact of fiscal and monetary policy on national income and hence employment levels under either floating or fixed exchange rates. As discussed in the previous chapter, fiscal policy involves a change in government spending and taxing, whereas monetary policy involves a change in the domestic money supply.

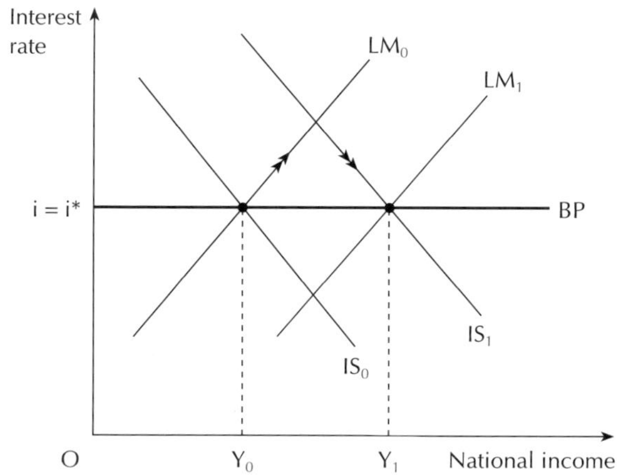

Figure 7.4 Fiscal expansion under fixed exchange rates.

Throughout the following exposition, it is assumed that the economy is small and that international capital mobility is perfect. Hence, the domestic interest rate must be equal to the world interest rate in equilibrium. Under the perfect capital mobility assumption, if there is any tendency for domestic and foreign interest rates to diverge, international financial capital movements would be so large as to immediately restore interest rate equality.

5. Fixed exchange rates

It is now possible to examine the comparative static effects of fiscal and monetary policy under alternative exchange rate systems.

Consider first the case of fiscal expansion under fixed rates with perfect capital mobility. Fiscal expansion may come about because government spending increases or because tax cuts boost households' disposable income, enabling consumption to be higher. Either way, with an easing of the fiscal stance the government budget tends to greater deficit and national spending increases.

In terms of the IS-LM-BP framework, the following stages of adjustment occur, as shown in Figure 7.4:

1. As government spending rises (G↑) or taxes fall (T↓), the IS schedule shifts rightward.
2. Domestic interest rates initially rise above foreign rates.
3. Capital inflow tends to strengthen the exchange rate.
4. To prevent an appreciation, the central bank must intervene in the foreign exchange market, buying foreign currency. This raises official reserve assets.
5. The domestic money supply thereby increases (M^s↑), shifting LM rightward until the domestic interest rate again equals the foreign interest rate.

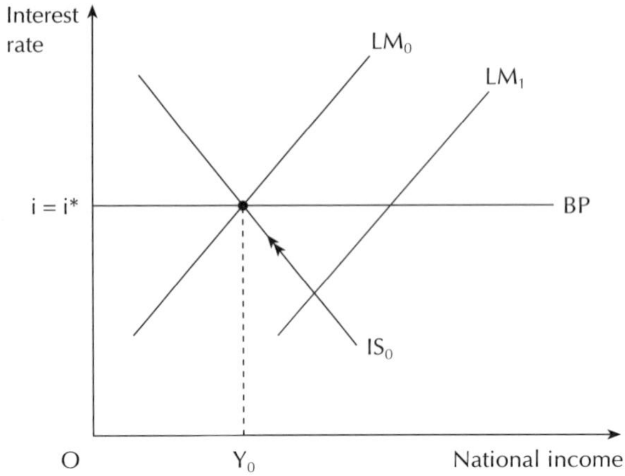

Figure 7.5 Monetary expansion under fixed exchange rates.

As a result, fiscal expansion under fixed exchange rates has been very effective in the sense that it has raised domestic income (from Y_0 to Y_1) and hence employment in the short run.

Next consider what happens with an easing of the monetary stance under fixed exchange rates.

Figure 7.5 demonstrates the following causal sequence of economic events:

1. As the domestic money supply expands ($M^s\uparrow$), the LM curve initially shifts rightward.
2. Domestic interest rates initially fall below world rates, inducing capital outflow.
3. Capital outflow tends to weaken the exchange rate.
4. To prevent depreciation, the central bank must intervene in the foreign exchange market, selling foreign currency. This lowers official reserve assets.
5. The domestic money supply thereby decreases ($M^s\downarrow$), shifting LM leftward until the domestic interest rate again equals the foreign rate.

It is important to note that the end result of this process is that nothing has really changed. In particular, the level of equilibrium income is the same as before the monetary expansion. Hence, we have shown that monetary policy under fixed exchange rates is ineffective.

6. Floating exchange rates

Interestingly, very different results about the effectiveness of fiscal and monetary policy arise under a floating exchange rate system.

If the central bank is not committed to any particular exchange rate, fiscal expansion works in the following way, as depicted in Figure 7.6:

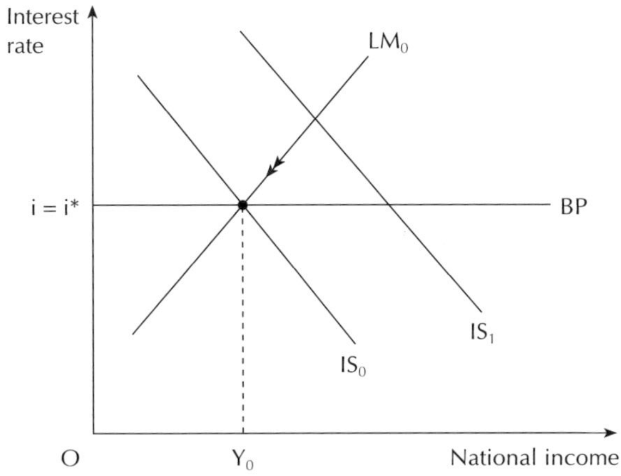

Figure 7.6 Fiscal expansion under floating exchange rates.

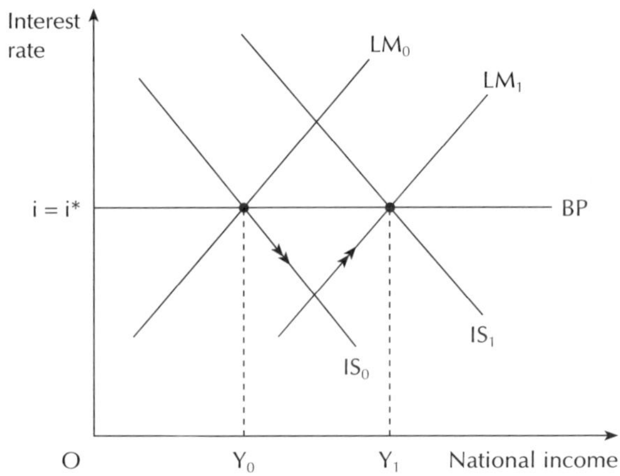

Figure 7.7 Monetary expansion under floating exchange rates.

1. As government spending rises (G↑) or taxes fall (T↓), IS again shifts to the right.
2. Domestic interest rates initially rise above foreign rates.
3. This time, however, international capital inflow is allowed to appreciate the exchange rate.
4. The attendant worsening of competitiveness then reduces net exports.
5. Falling net exports shift the IS curve back, leaving the level of income unaffected.

Consequently, fiscal policy under floating exchange rates is ineffective because national income has not increased from its initial value of Y_0.

Finally, consider monetary policy under floating exchange rates. Here the stages are as mapped in Figure 7.7:

1. As the domestic money supply expands ($M^s\uparrow$), the LM curve shifts rightward.
2. Domestic interest rates initially fall below world rates.
3. Capital outflow depreciates the exchange rate.
4. Improved competitiveness boosts net exports.
5. Rising net exports shift the IS curve rightward.

Monetary policy under floating exchange rates is therefore very effective because national income rises from Y_0 to Y_1.

The key effectiveness results of the basic Mundell–Fleming analysis are summarised in Table 7.1.

Table 7.1 Basic Mundell–Fleming results.

Policy instrument	*Exchange rate regime*	
	Fixed	*Floating*
Fiscal policy	Effective	Ineffective
Monetary policy	Ineffective	Effective

FISCAL AND MONETARY POLICIES IN EXCHANGE RATE–INCOME SPACE

It is also possible to examine the effectiveness of fiscal and monetary policy on an exchange rate–national income graph. This way of presenting the Mundell–Fleming approach is somewhat simpler than the standard IS-LM-BP version in that it reduces the analytical framework to only two loci. It is also useful for re-examining the issue of exchange rate management in the face of internal and external shocks to the open economy. In this alternative version, the market definition of the exchange rate (E) is used. Recall that a rise in E is an appreciation, whereas a fall is a depreciation.

To derive the goods market schedule in this framework, recall that as the exchange rate depreciates, improving competitiveness, net exports rise and this contributes to higher national income. Therefore, the better competitiveness is (the lower is E), the higher equilibrium national income should be. This means that the IS schedule in this variation of the model slopes downward.

On the monetary side of the economy, a rise in output, other things the same, causes a rise in relative demand for domestic currency and a rise in the domestic interest rate. With high (though not necessarily perfect) capital mobility, this strengthens the currency. Therefore higher levels of output are associated with an appreciating currency. Hence, the LM curve in this framework slopes upward. These alternative IS and LM curves, denoted IS* and LM*, are shown in Figure 7.8.

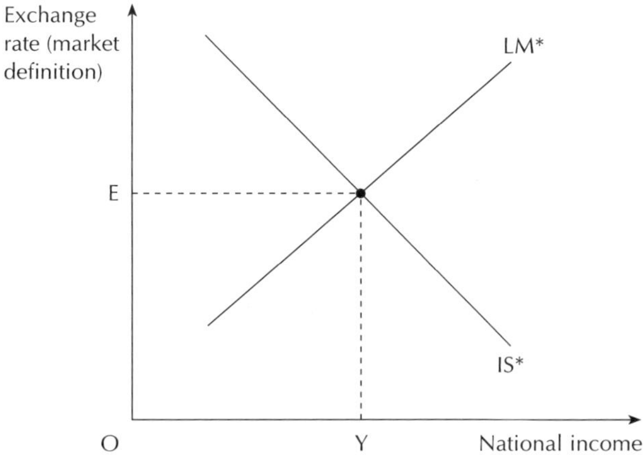

Figure 7.8 IS-LM in exchange rate–income space.

7. Fixed exchange rates

In this framework, if the exchange rate is fixed at a level such as Ē, then any tendency for it to appreciate would result in a rise in official reserves assets as the central bank purchases foreign exchange with local currency. In contrast, if there is a tendency for the exchange rate to depreciate, central bank reserves would run down as it sold foreign exchange for local currency.

The comparative static effects of fiscal expansion in the IS*-LM* framework under fixed exchange rates are shown in Figure 7.9. Here, the sequence of events following fiscal expansion are as follows:

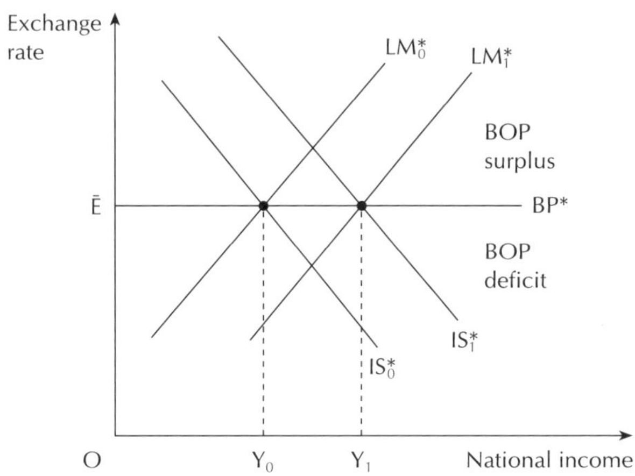

Figure 7.9 Fiscal expansion under fixed exchange rates.

1. IS* shifts rightward.
2. The exchange rate tends to appreciate.
3. Foreign reserves accumulate as the central bank buys foreign currency in the foreign exchange market.
4. The domestic money supply increases.
5. The LM* curve also shifts rightward.

Therefore, fiscal policy is again very effective under fixed exchange rates. National income rises from Y_0 to Y_1.

In the case of monetary expansion under fixed exchange rates (see Figure 7.10):

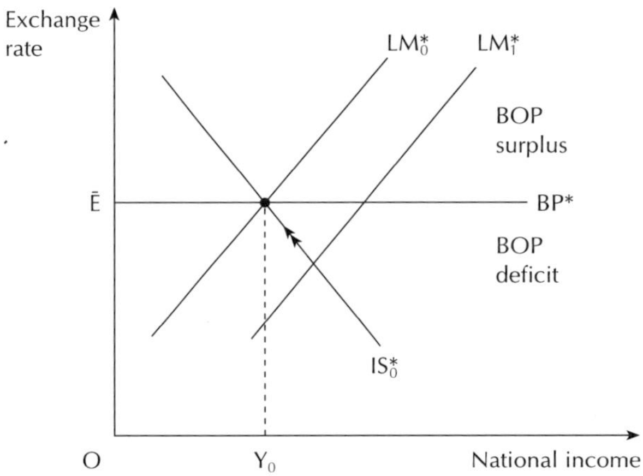

Figure 7.10 Monetary expansion under fixed exchange rates.

1. The domestic money supply increase shifts LM* rightward.
2. The exchange rate tends to depreciate.
3. Foreign reserves run down as the central bank buys domestic currency in the foreign exchange market.
4. The money supply decreases.
5. The LM* curve shifts back.

Monetary policy is therefore ineffective under fixed exchange rates. National income remains at Y_0.

8. Floating exchange rates

Under floating exchange rates in this framework, fiscal expansion is as shown in Figure 7.11:

1. IS* shifts rightward.
2. The exchange rate appreciates and worsens competitiveness.
3. National income rises, though there would be some crowding out of net exports.

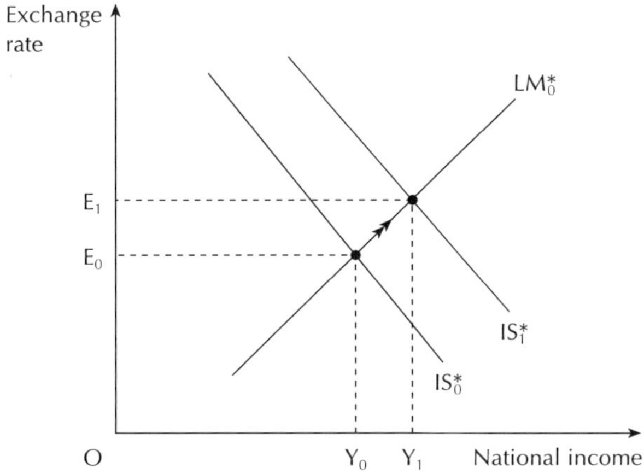

Figure 7.11 Fiscal expansion under floating exchange rates.

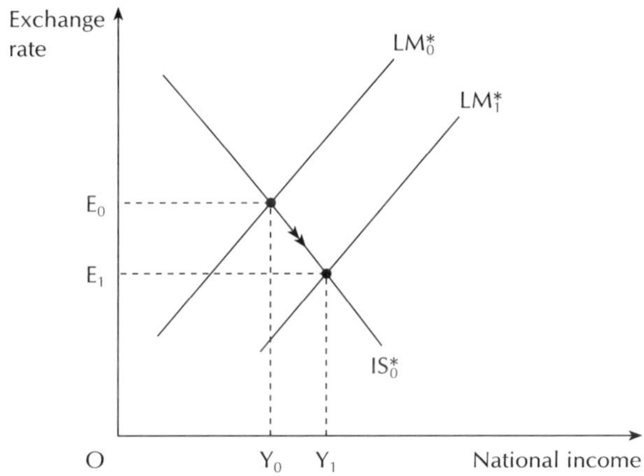

Figure 7.12 Monetary expansion under floating exchange rates.

Fiscal policy retains some effectiveness, in contrast to the special case of the IS-LM-BP approach considered earlier. However, the steeper the LM* schedule, the less effective fiscal policy would be and the greater the crowding out of net exports. In the limiting case of a vertical LM* schedule, the results of the IS-LM-BP and IS*-LM* framework are identical. Hence, a vertical LM* curve corresponds exactly with the perfect capital mobility assumption of the earlier IS-LM apparatus.

Finally, under floating exchange rates in this version of the model, monetary expansion operates as shown in Figure 7.12:

1. LM* shifts rightward.
2. The exchange rate depreciates and competitiveness improves.
3. National income rises.

FIXED VERSUS FLOATING EXCHANGE RATES AGAIN

The IS*-LM* model can be used to re-examine the issue of fixed versus floating exchange rates, first introduced in Chapter 3. The questions for resolution in this context are the following. Which exchange rate regime (fixed or floating) is preferable in the face of frequent money market disturbances? Is the same system still preferable if persistent goods market disturbances are a greater concern for the economy?

A major difficulty which macroeconomic policymakers face everywhere is that in reality the IS* and LM* schedules move about unpredictably. When this happens, national output fluctuates and hence so do employment levels. The objective of policymakers should therefore be to minimise the extent of these fluctuations. In what follows, it becomes apparent that the choice of exchange rate regime can influence just how large the fluctuations in income and employment will be over short periods.

If, for instance, the economy is more prone to monetary disturbances in the form of shifts in domestic money demand, the LM* curve would move about, as shown in Figure 7.13. With a floating exchange rate, the level of output would vary between Y_0 and Y_1. With a fixed exchange rate, however, the output level would remain fixed at Y_2. This is because the central bank would be intervening in the foreign exchange market to accommodate any shock on the monetary side and maintain the exchange rate at $\bar{E}$. Therefore, under circumstances where there are frequent shifts in the domestic demand for money, the optimal exchange rate policy is to hold the exchange rate fixed.

Now consider a different set of circumstances, such that the disturbances or shocks emanate mainly from the goods market side of the economy.

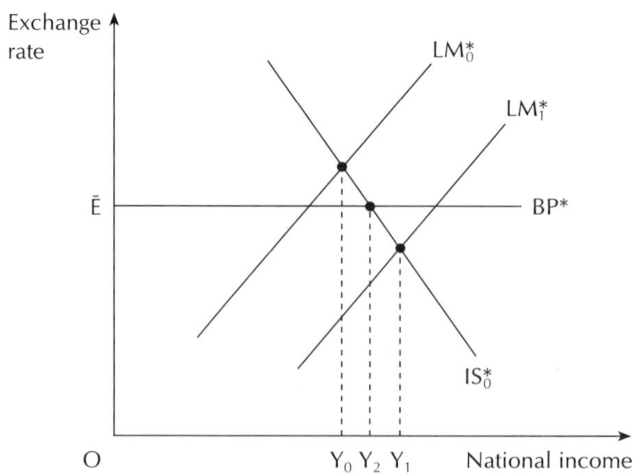

Figure 7.13 Monetary shocks and the exchange rate.

This would imply that the IS* curve is relatively unstable and would shift about between IS_0^* and IS_1^*. As discussed earlier in Chapter 4, a major source of shocks to the goods side of many economies is the terms of trade (TOT). In that chapter, we saw that rises in the TOT appreciated the exchange rate, whereas falls in the TOT depreciated the exchange rate. Improvements in the TOT also have the same effect on national income as a rise in total expenditure. Under a floating exchange rate system, the exchange rate would appreciate and national income would increase in response to a TOT improvement, as shown in Figure 7.14. The IS* schedule shifts right from IS_0^* to IS_1^*, with an improvement in the TOT. A worsening TOT would imply a leftward shift. This is an example of an *external shock* shifting the IS* curve.

Frequent fluctuations in private investment expenditure exemplify a source of *internal shock* for an open economy. Higher investment would shift IS* rightward and lower investment would shift IS* leftward. If the nominal exchange rate is held fixed in the face of such shocks, however, there will be accommodating changes in the domestic money supply. Following a move in the IS* curve from IS_0^* to IS_1^*, the domestic money supply would also rise with a fixed exchange rate as the central bank intervened to prevent the exchange rate appreciating. This would shift the LM* curve from LM_0^* to LM_1^*, which causes an even greater fluctuation in output to level Y_2.

What general conclusion follows from this analysis? It is best to allow the exchange rate to float if the disturbances in the economy are primarily occurring on the goods side. Under these conditions, fluctuations in national income and hence employment levels are minimised. What the IS*-LM* model also shows is that a floating exchange rate *insulates* the economy from TOT shocks in the sense that variations in national income are much less than would be the case under a fixed exchange rate.

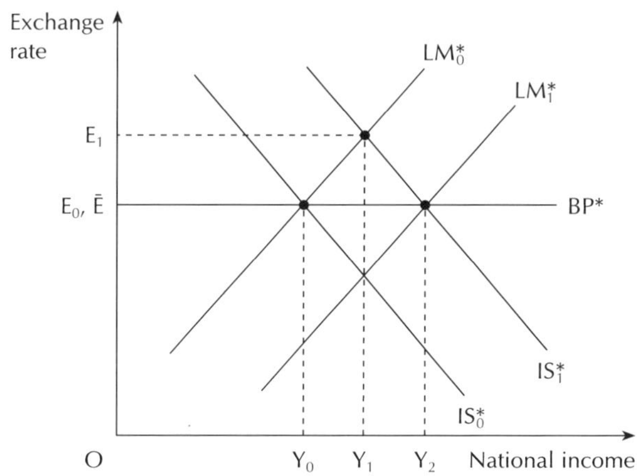

Figure 7.14 Output shocks and the exchange rate.

The models of this chapter can also be adapted to show that budget deficits may influence trade deficits through the competitiveness channel, in the absence of other shocks such as private investment booms. For instance, recall that under floating exchange rates with perfect capital mobility, a rise in government spending shifts the IS curve rightward. This puts upward pressure on interest rates, the exchange rate appreciates and the net exports are reduced. Therein lies another theoretical rationale for some linkage between government budget deficits and trade deficits. Note, however, that the analysis does not suggest any one-for-one relationship between the two deficits.

Also note that if Ricardian equivalence happened to hold, then any relationship between the budget and trade deficits would be broken as private saving would rise to offset the increase in government spending. In the above models with Ricardian equivalence, the IS curves would not shift in the first instance.

Summary

1. This chapter introduced the Mundell–Fleming model, which predicts how fiscal and monetary policy may work to minimise short-run fluctuations in national income.
2. The IS curve of the IS-LM-BP version of the model shows combinations of the interest rate and national income consistent with equilibrium on the goods and services side of the economy.
3. The LM curve shows combinations of the interest rate and national income consistent with equilibrium on the monetary side of the economy.
4. The BP curve depicts balance of payments equilibrium. Under the small country and perfect capital mobility assumptions, the domestic interest rate equals the world interest rate and the BP curve is horizontal at that interest rate.
5. Fiscal policy is effective under fixed exchange rates and ineffective under floating rates, whereas monetary policy is ineffective under fixed rates and effective under floating rates.
6. The IS*-LM* version of the Mundell–Fleming model relaxes the perfect capital mobility assumption and more explicitly highlights the exchange rate and balance of payments effects of fiscal and monetary policy.
7. Under conditions where the monetary sector of the economy is relatively unstable, the IS*-LM* model suggests that a fixed exchange rate will minimise national income and employment fluctuations.
8. On the contrary, if the goods and services sector of the economy is relatively more unstable because of its exposure to external and internal shocks then a floating exchange rate will best minimise national income and employment fluctuations.

Further reading

Dornbusch, R. (1980) *Open Economy Macroeconomics*, New York: Basic Books, chapters 10 and 11.

Gartner, M. (1993) *Macroeconomics under Flexible Exchange Rates*, London: Harvester Wheatsheaf, chapter 1.

Makin, A. (2000) *Global Finance and the Macroeconomy*, London: Palgrave, chapters 6 and 7.

8

Asset markets, exchange rates and interest rates

There are many theories of exchange rate behaviour, although there is not complete agreement among academics and practitioners about what factors primarily drive floating exchange rates. Key differences centre on the validity of purchasing power parity and the importance of real and monetary fundamentals, such as current account imbalances, relative money supply growth and interest rate differentials.

At one end of the spectrum, there is the view that macroeconomic fundamentals and inflation differentials between economies are influential, whereas at the other, economy-wide explanations are thought irrelevant because foreign exchange markets are inherently unstable and prone to speculative bubbles and herd behaviour. Explaining exchange rate movements is therefore not unlike explaining stockmarket fluctuations. Theories of stockmarket behaviour also range from those based on the premise that stockmarkets are at times less than fully rational to those stressing economic fundamentals. This chapter further considers exchange rate behaviour with reference to perspectives that stress the role of asset markets.

UNCOVERED INTEREST PARITY

Capital flows are also especially sensitive to changes in investors' expectations, including expected exchange rate changes. If, for instance, investors expect a future currency collapse, they will rush to sell financial instruments denominated in that currency to avoid capital losses. An important equilibrium that incorporates exchange rate expectations and the relationship between short-term interest rates at home and abroad is known as either *uncovered interest parity* or *open interest parity*. As uncovered interest parity (UIP) has important implications for international investment decisions and also for the conduct of monetary policy, it is useful to know how the relationship is actually derived.

To derive UIP, imagine there are only two financial instruments – a domestic bond paying nominal interest at the rate i each year and denominated in the domestic currency, assumed here to be pounds sterling, and a foreign bond paying nominal interest at the rate i* and denominated in a foreign currency. The nominal exchange rate, e, is the quantity of domestic units of currency required to buy a unit of foreign currency (the academic definition).

If the two bonds have the same term to maturity and are both risk free, then one pound used to purchase the domestic bond would generate (1 + i) after a year. Alternatively, a pound used to purchase a foreign bond would yield

$$\frac{1}{e}(1 + i^*)$$

units of foreign exchange over the same period.

To be able to judge whether purchasing foreign bonds would provide a greater return than buying domestic bonds, resident investors have to predict the nominal exchange rate likely to prevail in a year's time. This is because the foreign currency earnings must be converted back to domestic currency to compare alternative investment strategies. Foreign exchange earnings eventually have to be converted into local currency values in any case if they are to be spent at home by resident investors.

What characterises equilibrium in the UIP relationship is the cessation of cross-border movements of funds. This happens when the expected return on the domestic bond equals the expected return on the foreign bond, after allowing for the anticipated change in the nominal exchange rate. Equilibrium prevails when investors in the bond markets are satisfied that:

$$\begin{array}{ccc} \text{The yield on the local bond} & = & \text{The yield on the foreign bond} \\ (1 + i) & = & \frac{1}{e}(1 + i^*)e^f \end{array} \qquad (8.1)$$

where e^f is the nominal exchange rate predicted a year ahead.

Note also that

$$\hat{e} = \frac{(e^f - e)}{e}$$

where $\hat{e}$ is the expected rate of depreciation of the currency. It follows that, solving for e^f:

$$e^f = (1 + \hat{e})e \qquad (8.2)$$

Substituting Equation (8.2) into Equation (8.1):

$$(1 + i) = \frac{1}{e}(1 + i^*)(1 + \hat{e})e$$

$$= 1 + \hat{e} + i^* + i^*\hat{e}$$

Rearranging:

$$i \approx i^* + \hat{e}$$

The two sides of this relationship are only approximately equal because we ignore the term $i^* \hat{e}$ which would not usually be significant. (For instance, if $i^* = 10$ per cent and $\hat{e} = 5$ per cent, their product is only 0.5 per cent.) Accordingly, the uncovered interest parity (UIP) relationship is usually expressed as:

$$i - i^* = \hat{e} \qquad (8.3)$$

Equation (8.3) suggests that, as an equilibrium condition, any domestic–foreign interest differential is exactly equal to the change in the nominal exchange rate expected by investors in financial markets. When UIP prevails resident investors are completely indifferent between holding a domestic or foreign bond even though observed interest rates abroad may be higher than those at home.

Another important implication of UIP is that any observed interest differential actually provides a measure of the expected appreciation, or depreciation, of the nominal exchange rate. Consequently, if domestic interest rates happen to be higher than foreign interest rates, this does not suggest it would necessarily be advantageous, in terms of lower interest servicing costs, to take out foreign currency denominated loans. As many domestic borrowers of foreign funds have discovered, sharp currency depreciations which occur after the borrowing has been undertaken quickly eliminate the benefits of lower interest rates quoted on foreign currency denominated loans.

The UIP relationship suggests a wedge may develop between domestic and foreign interest rates attributable to the financial markets' expectations about the likely path of the nominal exchange rate. In this sense, UIP is an indicator of possible future exchange rate movements. If the observed foreign interest rate happens to be lower than the domestic interest rate, then a depreciation of the local currency may well follow.

Note, however, that this assumes financial markets are in equilibrium at any given time and that all bond market participants have similar expectations about likely exchange rate movements. These expectations may be formed on the basis of what financial markets believe are the central bank's exchange rate intentions.

Importantly, not only may UIP offer a guide to future exchange rate movements, it also implies that the central bank can widen cross-border interest rate differentials if it alters the financial markets' exchange rate expectations.

If financial markets expect that the future exchange rate will be the same as the present exchange rate, they possess what are called *static exchange rate expectations*. Static exchange rate expectations suggest that in equilibrium and in the absence of a risk premium the domestic and foreign interest rates will be equal, as assumed in the treatment of international investment in the loanable funds framework of earlier chapters. This is because expected currency depreciations will be zero if markets believe the exchange rate will be the same in the future as it is in the present.

REAL INTEREST PARITY

UIP can also be reconciled with two other fundamental financial relationships introduced in preceding chapters. The first is the Fisher interest rate relation (the 'Fisher effect'), first introduced in Chapter 2, which proposes that the nominal interest rate reflects a real interest rate component, plus a premium for expected domestic inflation (π^f). At home and abroad the Fisher effect can be specified as:

$$i = r + \pi^f \text{ and } i^* = r^* + \pi^{*f}$$

Hence, the nominal interest differential is:

$$i - i^* = (r - r^*) + (\pi^f - \pi^{*f})$$

The real interest differential must therefore be

$$r - r^* = (i - i^*) - (\pi^f - \pi^{*f}) \quad (8.4)$$

Recall also that purchasing power parity (PPP) in relative form as outlined in Chapter 4, provided a relation between the exchange rate and inflation at home and abroad. That is, $\hat{e} = \pi - \pi^*$. If relative PPP is restated in terms of the expected future values of domestic and foreign inflation, then relative PPP may be rewritten as:

$$\hat{e} = \pi^f - \pi^{*f} \quad (8.5)$$

That is, expected currency depreciation is equivalent to the difference between expected domestic inflation and expected foreign inflation. Substituting Equation (8.5) into Equation (8.4):

$$r - r^* = (i - i^*) - \hat{e} \quad (8.6)$$

Recall that UIP is

$$i - i^* = \hat{e} \quad (8.7)$$

If UIP applies as well as expected relative PPP, then by substitution of Equation (8.7) into Equation (8.6),

$$r - r^* = \hat{e} - \hat{e} = 0 \quad (8.8)$$

That is, real interest rates at home and abroad will only be equal if both PPP and UIP hold in a strict sense. If this is true, then the real interest differential between two countries is zero and *real interest parity* prevails. In practice, however, real interest parity is unlikely to hold in a strict sense. This is because of the many qualifications to PPP and UIP, as well as the presumption that there is no risk premium.

OUTPUT, EXPENDITURE AND THE EXCHANGE RATE

The balance of payments accounts record the international factors that affect the demand and supply of the economy's currency in flow terms, and as current account transactions make up one complete side of the balance of payments, they continue to have major implications for exchange rate behaviour. The exchange rate must either depreciate or appreciate over any given period if the net demand for foreign currency arising from current account transactions does not match the net supply from capital account transactions. This principle forms the basis of the analytical framework to be outlined shortly.

To assist understanding of the many factors that can determine exchange rates, the following outlines a basic framework relating macroeconomic fundamentals, the current account, expectations and capital flows. In this framework, exchange rate variation simply reflects the external price adjustment necessary for equalising foreign exchange flows arising from current and capital account transactions. It implies that the capital account, exchange rate expectations and the current account are central to exchange rate determination.

The following is based on the distinction between production and spending in an open economy, as captured in the equation:

$$A - Y = CAD \tag{8.9}$$

where A is national expenditure (equal to C + I + G), Y is national output or income and CAD is the current account deficit. The real exchange rate, R, influences aggregate output and expenditure, and hence the current account balance, and is defined as:

$$R = \frac{eP^*}{P} \tag{8.10}$$

where e is the nominal effective exchange rate, P^* is the foreign price level and P is the domestic price level. The foreign and domestic price levels are assumed to be invariant, so that nominal exchange rate movements alone affect the real exchange rate over shorter periods.

The national expenditure function can then be written as:

$$A = f(R;\ C,I,G) \tag{8.11}$$

The stronger is the exchange rate, the higher is total spending including imports, enabling us to draw a downward-sloping absorption schedule in expenditure–real exchange rate space as depicted in Figure 8.1.

The aggregate output function is specified as:

$$Y = f(R;\ L(w),K,\tau) \tag{8.12}$$

where L and K are the factor inputs, labour and the capital stock, and T is technology or overall productivity (to be discussed further in Chapter 11).

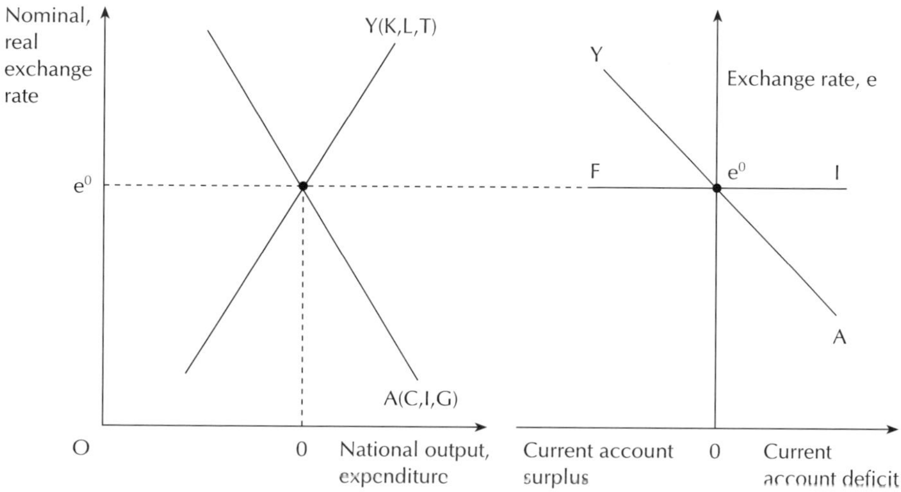

Figure 8.1 Output, expenditure, the current account and exchange rate.

Hours worked, L, depend on the prevailing wage, w, presumed sticky over the period of analysis. Real exchange rate depreciations improve competitiveness and hence increase exports of goods and services.

Since national product includes that part of output sold abroad as exports, total output is positively related to the exchange rate and is represented by the upward-sloping schedule in exchange rate–output space shown in Figure 8.1. In the absence of capital flows, the trade (current) account is balanced and the nominal exchange rate settles at the point where national spending equals national product.

EXPECTATIONS AND THE EXCHANGE RATE

The negatively sloped YA schedule in the right panel of Figure 8.1 shows the excess demand for foreign currency arising from divergences between domestic expenditure and output, whereas the FI schedule depicts the inflow of foreign exchange to finance the economy's output–expenditure gap. In general, if foreign investors expect additional domestic expenditure in one period to generate the minimum necessary extra production to enable repayment in the next, then in this framework they expect the YA schedule to return to its initial position and the exchange rate neither appreciates or depreciates.

If international capital mobility is perfect, foreign exchange will flow into the small economy whenever foreign investors expect the total return from holding newly issued domestic bonds to exceed the world interest rate. The time horizon is limited to two periods only, the present (period 1) and the future (period 2). The key point is that the exchange rate itself becomes pivotal to the external adjustment process.

If in initial equilibrium, the domestic interest rate, i, equals the world interest rate, i*, any differential between effective returns on domestic versus foreign bonds in period 1 is then only attributable to expected exchange rate movements, consistent with the open interest parity relationship derived above:

$$i^1 + \hat{a} = i^{*1}$$

where â is the exchange rate appreciation expected between the beginning of period 1 and the end of period 2. Capital inflow depends on the take-up by foreigners of domestic debt instruments issued in the local currency to fund *ex ante* increases in domestic expenditure over output. This provides a supply of foreign exchange and increases the stock of foreign debt that must be repaid in the second period, with interest, to satisfy the intertemporal budget constraint. With these foundations, it is possible to show how macroeconomic factors can jointly determine the current account deficit, capital inflow and the exchange rate.

1. Productive versus unproductive spending

First, imagine there is extra domestic investment spending by resident firms because the real prospective return on new capital equipment is expected to exceed the world interest rate, other things being equal. This shifts the left panel expenditure schedule in Figure 8.2 rightwards in period 1 from A to A′ and creates a CAD and foreign financing requirement equivalent to distance e^0f in the right panel.

If the capital inflow in the first period equals the CAD, the economy's capital stock will rise and produce more output in the second period. Hence, the YA schedule is eventually expected to shift back in the future, implying

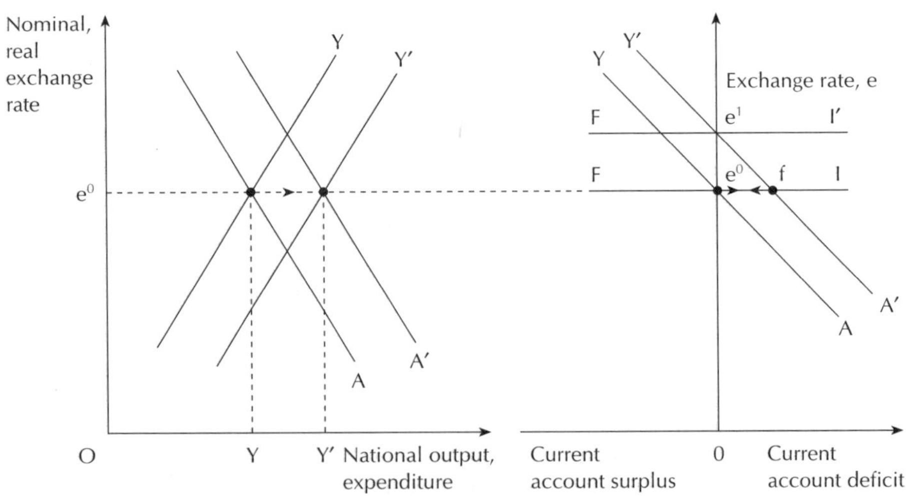

Figure 8.2 Investment, the external accounts and exchange rate.

that the future exchange rate will not depreciate. This is because the additional output attributable to the initial CAD should at least cover capital and interest repayments and even any additional consumption arising from the higher income.

If foreigners expected the future exchange rate to be e^0, yet the nominal exchange rate actually tended to rise above e^0 as domestic investment expenditure increased, an international interest differential would open up to the extent that an exchange rate appreciation was expected in the second period, in line with the predicted expansion of output and rewind of the initial CAD. This momentary differential would remain open until all the foreign currency required to fund the output–expenditure imbalance was forthcoming and the equilibrium exchange rate of e^0 was restored in the first period.

This follows because the segment of the Y′A′ schedule labelled fe^1 is actually the supply of foreign currency curve read from right to left, provided the exchange rate at the end of period 2 is expected to be the same as at the beginning of period 1.

Now consider what happens when there is a rise in domestic consumption, stemming, for instance, from higher public spending or monetary expansion. This would also shift the *ex ante* YE schedule rightward, although in this case the additional spending would not enhance the economy's future potential output. Accordingly, foreign investors anticipating a future depreciation would not finance any *ex ante* CAD, causing an upward shift in the FI schedule.

The exchange rate immediately depreciates, with adverse longer-term implications for the domestic price level and aggregate output as wages rise. The above model therefore suggests that exchange rate movements may be related to changes in domestic saving behaviour, other things being equal. Decreased thrift, for instance, could depreciate the nominal, and hence real, exchange rate over the medium term, to the extent that foreigners are unlikely to underwrite consumption expenditure outpacing output growth. On the other hand, improved productivity that enables output to outpace expenditure, other things being equal, would appreciate the currency.

It is also possible to consider the link between excessive monetary expansion, the exchange rate and domestic inflation over the longer term. Money supply growth is generally considered an important influence on long-term inflation. In this framework, a monetary expansion that lowers domestic interest rates below the world rate in the first instance would generate unsustainable spending relative to output that would not be externally funded. Therefore, the exchange rate must depreciate over time, as reflected in an upward-shifting YA schedule. However, as foreigners would not fund extra money-induced spending, it would not manifest in a larger measured CAD.

In turn, higher domestic inflation stemming from the weaker currency would feed into firms' costs through wage increases, reducing aggregate output. This would cause a further upward shift in the YA schedule and further currency depreciation. Note, however, that this suggests that depreciations precede inflation, not the other way around. Such a sequence could describe an apparent longer-term relationship between economies' relatively poor inflation performance and their exchange rates.

2. Current account sustainability

In the above framework, capital inflow forthcoming to fund additional domestic spending over production depends on foreigners' expectations about the future exchange rate. It assumes foreign investors continually assess whether the CADs they fund through the purchase of debt instruments are likely to generate sufficient extra output in the future to enable servicing and eventual repayment of their loans at an exchange rate at least no weaker than the current rate.

In this way, the framework provides another dimension to the notion of current account sustainability. *Ex ante* CADs are sustainable in the sense that foreigners fully finance them and the exchange rate does not immediately depreciate to narrow them, whereas *ex post* CADs reveal how much additional domestic spending foreign investors actually funded on the grounds it was deemed sufficiently productive.

By focusing on exchange rate expectations, the above analysis shows that the sustainability of exchange rates and external account imbalances should ultimately depend on macroeconomic fundamentals such as whether increased domestic expenditure is on consumption or investment and how well informed foreign investors are. In short, CADs only persist on the understanding that such deficits will eventually be self-financing. The corollary is that nominal exchange rate movements quickly check unsustainable deficits.

Economies like Australia, Canada, the United States and New Zealand may continually experience CADs over some time provided international investors continue to underwrite additional real capital accumulation period by period on the understanding that it will be sufficiently productive into the future. If a large part of the foreign debt is denominated in domestic currency and CADs do prove unsustainable and the exchange rate depreciates, then foreign investors bear much of the exchange rate risk.

EXPLAINING MISALIGNMENTS

So far, it has been implicitly assumed that the foreign exchange market is efficient and bases exchange rate expectations on the correct macroeconomic fundamentals. However, there is considerable evidence to suggest that exchange rates can become seriously misaligned at times, seemingly detached from fundamentals. There have been notable episodes of such misalignments, especially between the US dollar and the yen, since the early 1990s.

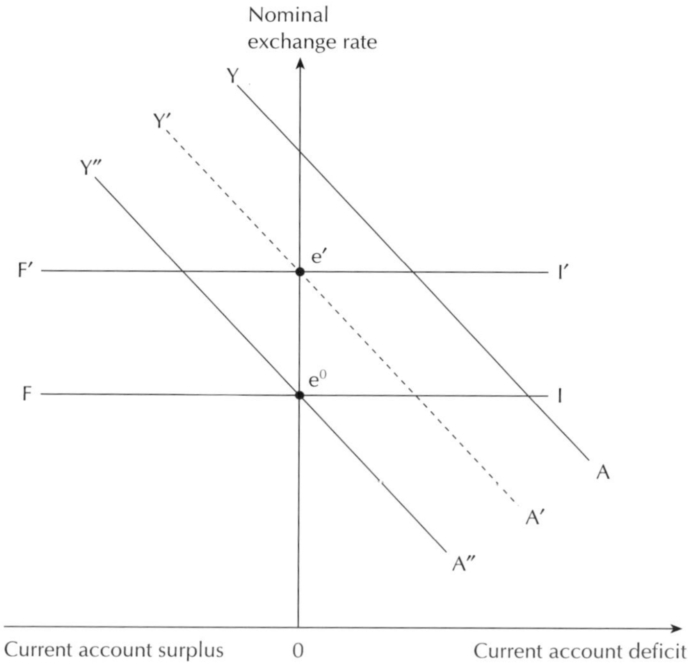

Figure 8.3 Exchange rate misalignment.

Nonetheless, there is also evidence that fundamentals, especially those related to inflation differentials, do eventually reassert themselves over time and rewind the exchange rate misalignments that have occurred.

The most likely reason exchange rates could depart from fundamentals is that there may be serious information problems, including asymmetries that distort exchange rate expectations and persist for extended periods. For example, if international investors become more pessimistic about the sustainability of a given CAD than underlying fundamentals actually warrant, they would then expect the exchange rate to depreciate in the future. Consequently, there would be insufficient foreign exchange available to finance the existing CAD and the exchange rate must depreciate immediately.

With reference to Figure 8.3, the FI schedule shifts up on the basis of an expected return of the YA schedule to Y′A′ only (the broken line) rather than to Y″A″. This would imply an expected depreciation to e′ that reduces the actual CAD as measured in foreign exchange.

Importantly, however, if investors' expectations turn out to be wrong and the economy performs better than was expected, with the net currency demand schedule actually returning to Y″A″, then investors have lost potential income. As investors realise their mistake, exchange rate expectations are revised and the earlier exchange rate depreciation rewinds to once again reflect fundamentals.

ECONOMIC POLICY IMPLICATIONS

The above approach to understanding exchange rate determination is based on the macroeconomic fundamentals of national spending and production, rather than on narrower monetary underpinnings that feature prominently in the next chapter. Furthermore, it has important implications for the conduct and effectiveness of fiscal and monetary policies. It suggests that under conditions where international capital is highly mobile, investors can exercise a strong external discipline over domestic policymakers by rebalancing portfolios.

For instance, on the fiscal front if there is a rise in unproductive government expenditure, international investors may quite rightly expect a future depreciation of the currency because the extra public spending may only add to the future demand for foreign currency and not to future supply via increased production in the economy. In other words, international investors may deem the fiscal expansion is unsustainable in the above sense, in which case the exchange rate will depreciate, creating inflationary pressures.

Similarly, the increased integration of domestic and international capital markets has imposed an even greater discipline over monetary policy that may help explain how inflation outcomes improved for so many economies, whether advanced, emerging or less developed, throughout the 1990s.

In this model, expansionary monetary policy characterised by official interest rates being set too low will only spark excess spending in the economy relative to production. In an increasingly globalised economy, such spending will mainly be curbed through currency depreciation, which forces up the prices of tradables. The higher is the share of tradable output in the economy, the harder it is for the central bank to ignore depreciation-induced inflation. For many economies, the tradable share of output has risen relative to the nontradable share and continue to rise as internationalisation of economies proceeds, suggesting that the exchange rate has become an important variable to watch for inflation-control purposes.

In general, supply-side factors that promote greater productivity relative to unproductive spending should strengthen the currency, whereas factors encouraging unproductive spending relative to output depreciate it. This suggests that the exchange rate provides a useful signal to policymakers that further productivity-enhancing reform may be necessary to prevent the now stronger inflationary pressures that build in the wake of significant depreciations.

MONETARY POLICY, INTEREST RATES AND THE EXCHANGE RATE

The loanable-funds approach to the open economy of Chapter 5, the UIP condition and the standard IS-LM-BP version of the Mundell–Fleming model outlined earlier all assumed that domestic and foreign bonds were perfect substitutes in the portfolios of domestic and foreign investors. This assumption rules out the possibility that foreign bonds may be perceived as riskier than domestic bonds and hence require some additional premium to induce investors to hold them.

Under circumstances where foreign bonds are deemed riskier, then cross-border interest differentials can be explained by both expected exchange rate movements, and a risk premium. That is, in the presence of risk, the earlier UIP condition can be written as $i - i^* = \hat{e} + r\rho$ where $r\rho$ is the risk premium.

There are many factors which influence the size of the risk premium. For instance, as mentioned earlier in Chapter 5, there are risks called *country risks* which arise because of uncertainties about the possibility of governments defaulting on loans, reimposing exchange controls or levying new taxes on foreign investors. There are also so-called *currency risks* due to uncertainty about the expected foreign inflation rate. This leads us to consider another approach to short-run exchange rate and interest rate determination which allows for different perceptions of risk. This approach is called the asset market or *portfolio balance approach* to exchange rate determination.

The portfolio balance model is largely in the spirit of the work of Nobel prize-winner James Tobin and the Yale school of monetary economics. It was developed by a number of academic economists, most notably William Branson. The portfolio approach to the exchange rate is based on the recognition that domestic money is just one form of financial asset in a world of many alternative financial assets exhibiting a variety of yields. The approach extends the precepts of the portfolio theory of financial behaviour to the open economy with the focus on the linkages between domestic and foreign interest rates and the nominal exchange rate.

The general theory of portfolio behaviour explains how financial asset prices and yields adjust to equate overall asset demands and the available supply (which is a measure of overall financial wealth). The degree of substitutability between financial assets depends on subjective risk assessments, which are influenced by uncertainty about the future. Hence, the demand for alternative financial assets depends on both their riskiness and their yields. A key assumption of portfolio theory is that the demand for any particular financial asset responds positively to increases in its own rate of return and negatively to increases in the yields on alternative assets. This is called the *gross substitutability*[1] assumption.

The portfolio balance approach to the exchange rate assumes that domestic residents satisfy their demands for financial assets by choosing between national money, domestic bonds and foreign bonds. Domestic bonds represent the class of all interest-earning financial assets denominated in domestic currency, whereas foreign bonds include all interest-earning assets denominated in foreign currency. It is further assumed that domestic residents have no demand for foreign money.

The basic equations of the model are:

$$M^s = \alpha(i, i^*) \cdot Q$$

$$B = \beta(i, i^*) \cdot Q$$

$$eF = \gamma(i, i^*) \cdot Q$$

$$Q = M^s + B + eF$$

$$\alpha + \beta + \gamma = 1$$

where M^s is domestic money, B is the stock of domestic bonds, F is the stock of residents' foreign bond holdings, and Q is the level of total financial wealth held by domestic residents. The variables α, β and γ must sum to unity, because they represent the proportions of total wealth held in the three alternative assets. F can be positive or negative according to whether the particular country is a net creditor or debtor.

In what follows, for expositional purposes it is assumed that the small open economy is a net creditor, such that its residents are net holders of foreign assets in the form of foreign currency denominated bonds. The nominal exchange rate (academic definition e) converts foreign currency bond holdings into domestic currency values.

The proportion of wealth held in the form of domestic money (α) depends on both domestic and foreign interest rates. As either domestic or foreign interest rates rise, the demand for money will fall. However, the share of domestic bonds in the portfolio (β) rises with an increase in the domestic interest rate because this makes domestic bonds a more attractive asset. The value of β falls with an increase in the foreign bond interest rate, though, because foreign interest rate rises would make foreign bonds relatively more attractive to investors than domestic bonds.

Hence, the gross substitutability assumption guarantees that the share of foreign bonds in the portfolio (γ) increases as the foreign interest rate rises but decreases as the domestic interest rate falls. Higher overall levels of financial wealth raise the demand for all assets. From the above equations, it follows that the nominal exchange rate must be determined in the short run through the role it plays in balancing asset demands with any given supply of financial assets on issue.

Diagrammatically, the portfolio balance model is shown in Figure 8.4. The figure is drawn in domestic interest rate–nominal exchange rate space and includes three schedules, each of which depicts equilibrium in a particular asset market. Note that the nominal exchange rate is again defined as e.

Why are the MM, BB and FF loci sloped as drawn in the diagram? Starting with the MM schedule, this reflects various combinations of the domestic interest rate and exchange rate which ensure the demand for money is satisfied by the available money supply. To understand the slope of the MM schedule, imagine that the exchange rate increases. An exchange rate depreciation raises the domestic currency value of foreign asset holdings

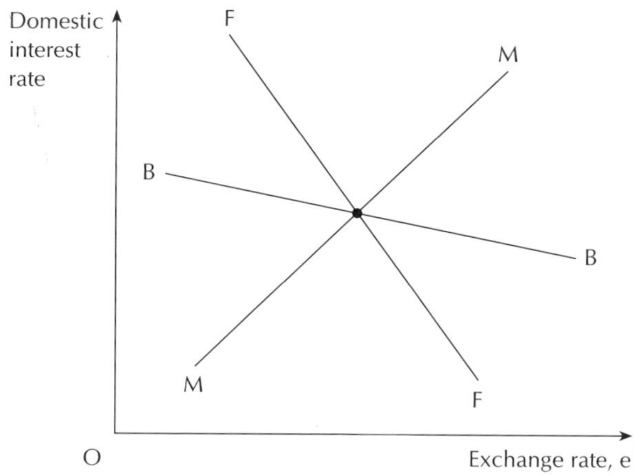

Figure 8.4 Portfolio balance model of exchange rate.

(as eF↑). This raises the value of total wealth holdings, which increases demand for all financial assets, including money. Equilibrium therefore requires a rise in the domestic interest rate to reduce the excess demand for money. This means that a weaker exchange rate (as e↑) is associated with a higher domestic interest rate, thus explaining the upward-sloping MM schedule.

Consider next the BB schedule. A depreciation of the nominal exchange rate also raises the demand for domestic bonds because of the wealth effect on the demand for all three assets. In this case, asset market equilibrium requires that the domestic interest rate falls to eliminate the excess demand for domestic bonds. Hence, a weaker exchange rate is associated with a lower domestic interest rate, thus explaining the downward-sloping BB schedule.

Lastly, consider the FF schedule. If the exchange rate rises, wealth again increases through the higher value of residents' foreign bond holdings. The increase in wealth would also raise demand for foreign assets, as for the other assets. In this case, things are slightly different because the wealth-induced increase in demand for foreign bonds would be more than offset by the higher domestic currency value of the supply arising from the rise in e. This results in a tendency for an excess supply of foreign bonds, relative to residents' demand for them in their portfolios.

Only if the return on the competing interest earning asset falls (that is, i paid on the domestic bond) will there be sufficient further portfolio switching to foreign bonds out of domestic bonds. If the yield on domestic bonds does fall sufficiently, this eliminates the excess supply of foreign bonds, thereby restoring balance between the demand and supply of foreign bonds. This explains why the FF schedule is also downward sloping. The FF schedule is steeper than the BB schedule because a change in the domestic interest rate impacts more on the demand for domestic bonds than on the demand for foreign bonds.

The portfolio balance framework, as just outlined, is particularly useful for examining how the central bank may use monetary policy to influence domestic interest rates and the nominal exchange rate in the short run. In what follows, we consider the comparative static effects on the domestic interest rate and the exchange rate of the several alternative methods of implementing monetary policy.

3. Open-market operations

Let us first examine the domestic interest rate and exchange rate effects of open-market operations carried out by the central bank. With expansionary open-market operations, the central bank buys domestic bonds. This reduces residents' holdings of domestic bonds, but increases their holdings of domestic money. The consequences are shown in Figure 8.5.

As residents now hold more domestic money than before, the domestic interest rate (as the opportunity cost of holding non-interest-earning money) would have to be lower at all levels of the exchange rate. This is to ensure that residents are satisfied with holding the higher level of money holdings. Accordingly, the MM schedule moves downward.

Since there are now fewer bonds for residents to hold, the excess demand for domestic bonds can only be satisfied by a fall in the domestic interest rate. Therefore, nominal exchange rate values are associated with lower domestic bond yields in the new equilibrium. This means the BB schedule moves downward also.

The FF schedule remains unaffected throughout because the central bank has done nothing to affect the outstanding supply of foreign bonds. Consequently, as shown by the intersection of the new MM and BB schedules with the FF schedule, domestic interest rates fall from i_0 to i_1 and the exchange rate depreciates from e_0 to e_1 following expansionary open-market operations.

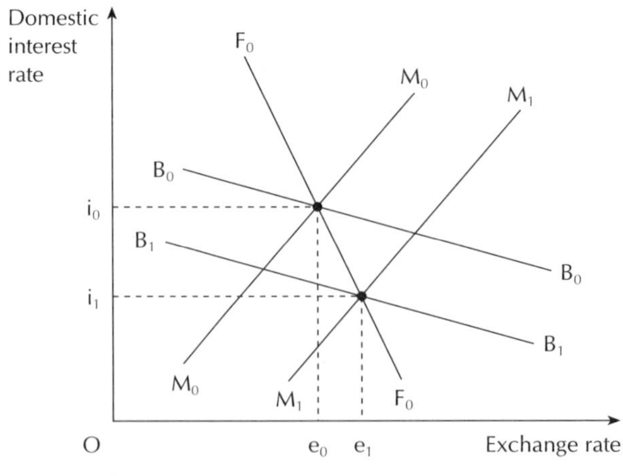

Figure 8.5 Open-market operations.

4. Non-sterilised intervention

Another technique through which the central bank may alter the domestic money supply is *foreign exchange market intervention*. In other words, instead of intervening in the domestic bond market, as with open-market operations, the central bank can enter the foreign exchange market, either buying or selling foreign currencies from its stock of official reserves in exchange for local currency.

For instance, as outlined in Chapter 6, if the central bank purchases foreign exchange, this means it swaps domestic currency which was previously not part of the domestic money supply for residents' foreign currency assets. Remember that foreign exchange purchases by the central bank increase the domestic money supply, whereas foreign exchange sales reduce the domestic money supply.

Also recall from Chapter 6 that any foreign exchange market intervention that changes the domestic money is called *non-sterilised intervention*. Such intervention is analogous to domestic open-market operations except that foreign rather than domestic bonds are bought or sold by the central bank.

In terms of the above analytical framework, if the central bank buys foreign bonds from residents in exchange for domestic money, there will be a fall in residents' holdings of foreign bonds and an offsetting rise in residents' domestic money holdings. The FF schedule shifts rightward and the MM schedule shifts downward. To induce residents to hold the increased supply of domestic money there must be some reduction in the domestic interest rate. The exchange rate must also depreciate, given the increased relative supply of domestic money on the foreign exchange market. The short-run interest and exchange rate effects of non-sterilised intervention are depicted in Figure 8.6.

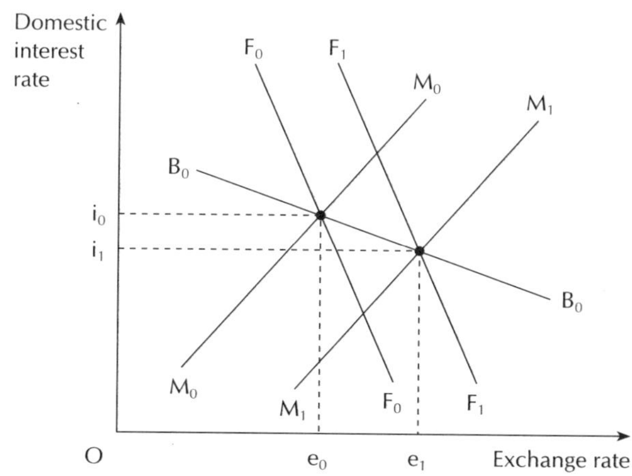

Figure 8.6 Non-sterilised foreign exchange market intervention.

5. Sterilised intervention

Sterilised intervention is the third monetary technique which the central bank can use to try to influence the exchange rate and the domestic interest rate in the very short run. The exchange rate and interest rate effects of sterilised foreign exchange market intervention are depicted in Figure 8.7. When the central bank buys foreign bonds from domestic holders of foreign bonds, the FF schedule shifts rightward. When it then sterilises the expansionary monetary consequences of such intervention by selling domestic bonds, the BB schedule also shifts rightward. As a result, the domestic interest rate rises and the nominal exchange rate depreciates. Note that the MM schedule does not shift because the domestic money supply remains unchanged.

The results of the three forms of central bank intervention outlined above – open-market operations, and unsterilised and sterilised foreign exchange market intervention – are summarised in Table 8.1.

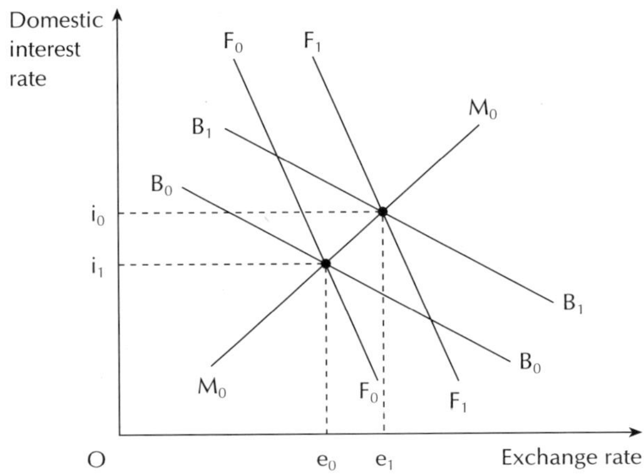

Figure 8.7 Sterilised foreign exchange market intervention.

Table 8.1 Effects of alternative techniques of monetary policy on short-term interest rates and exchange rates.

Technique of monetary policy	*Effect on:*		
	Domestic money supply	*Domestic interest rate*	*Exchange rate*
Open-market operations	Rises	Falls significantly	Depreciates
Unsterilised forex intervention	Rises	Falls	Depreciates significantly
Sterilised forex intervention	No change	Rises	Depreciates

Table 8.1 reveals that if domestic and foreign bonds are imperfect substitutes, expansionary monetary policy will always lower domestic interest rates and depreciate the exchange rate in the short run. It also reveals that expansionary monetary policy has a bigger effect on the financial variable immediately determined in the market in which the central bank directly operates. For instance, in the case of open-market operations (direct intervention in the bond market), domestic interest rates are most significantly affected. On the other hand, direct intervention in the foreign exchange market has a bigger impact on the exchange rate than any of the other techniques.

Note that it is possible for monetary policy to be implemented directly through the foreign exchange market. For instance, if the central bank does not sterilise its intervention, the domestic money supply would change just as it does with standard open-market operations. Many central banks in practice pursue a policy of sterilised intervention if their currencies are floating.

Summary

1. Uncovered interest parity suggests that if domestic and foreign bonds are perfect substitutes, then in equilibrium the domestic interest rate should equal the sum of the foreign interest rate and the expected change in the exchange rate.

2. Real interest parity implies the equality of domestic and foreign real interest rates. Real interest parity can only hold if the conditions for both purchasing power parity and uncovered interest parity are met.

3. The sustainability of exchange rates and current account imbalances ultimately depends on the expectations of foreign investors with respect to macroeconomic fundamentals of spending, productivity and output.

4. Exchange rate misalignments can occur from time to time due to short-term information problems.

5. The portfolio balance approach can be used to analyse the short-run impact of central bank intervention in the domestic bond and foreign exchange markets on the domestic interest rate and exchange rate.

6. Open-market operations which increase the domestic money supply simultaneously lower the domestic interest rate and depreciate the exchange rate.

7. Unsterilised foreign exchange market intervention, which increases the money supply, depreciates the nominal exchange rate by more in the short run than sterilised intervention, which leaves the money supply unchanged.

8. In general, monetary policy has a greater impact on the financial variable immediately determined in the market in which the central bank operates.

Note

1. More formally, it implies that the partial derivative of the demand function for any particular asset with respect to that asset's yield is positive (the own rate effect) whereas the effect on other assets is negative (the cross effect). If, for example, the demand for asset A, was A^D, and the demand for asset B was B^D then:

$$\frac{\partial A^D}{\partial r^A} > 0, \text{ and } \frac{\partial B^D}{\partial r^A} < 0$$

where r^A is the yield on asset A.

Further reading

Branson, W. and Henderson, D. (1985) 'The specification and influence of asset markets', in R. Jones and P. Kenen (eds) *Handbook of International Economics*, vol. 2 Amsterdam: North-Holland.

Frenkel, J. and Mussa, M. (1985) 'Asset markets, exchange rates and the balance of payments', in R. Jones and P. Kenen (eds) *Handbook of International Economics*, vol. 2 Amsterdam: North-Holland.

Isard, P. (1995) *Exchange Rate Economics*, New York: Cambridge University Press.

Makin, A. (2000) *Global Finance and the Macroeconomy*, London: Palgrave, chapter 5.

9

Macroeconomic policy in the longer run

The Mundell–Fleming model of the open economy outlined in Chapter 7 explained how interest rates, exchange rates, national income and hence employment may be related in the short run. However, neither the IS-LM-BP nor related IS*-LM* versions of the approach allow for the inflationary consequences of fiscal and monetary policy in the open economy. This is because the Mundell–Fleming model centres on the aggregate expenditure or demand side of the economy, without explicit mention of the aggregate output or supply side. Effectively, it assumes that aggregate output supplied by firms in the economy is automatically forthcoming in response to increased aggregate demand at the given national price level.

It is now possible to extend this short-run approach to allow for aggregate supply-side and price-level effects of fiscal and monetary policy. To do this, the chapter first develops the aggregate demand–aggregate supply (AD–AS) framework. Later in the chapter, longer-run monetary influences on the price level and the exchange rate are considered.

DERIVING THE AGGREGATE DEMAND CURVE

An *aggregate demand* curve, depicted in price level–income space for an open economy, shows the relationship between the overall price level and the economy-wide quantity of goods and services demanded. This schedule can be derived as follows using the earlier IS-LM-BP framework.

In the top panel of Figure 9.1 equilibrium national income is initially at Y_0. The domestic interest rate is the same as the world interest rate (i^*) under the simplifying assumption of perfect capital mobility.

The aggregate demand curve can be derived under assumptions of either floating or fixed exchange rates. Let us consider the fixed-rate case, which is relatively straightforward. An increase in the domestic price level from P_0 to P_1 under fixed rates appreciates the real exchange rate and worsens competitiveness, other things equal. This shifts the IS_0 curve backwards to

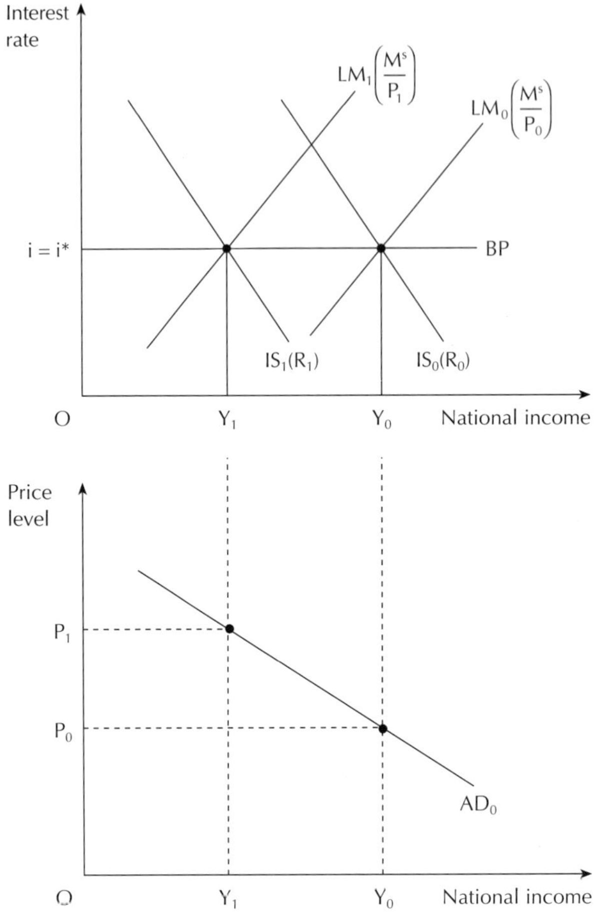

Figure 9.1 Deriving the aggregate demand curve.

IS_1 because net exports will fall. At the same time, the rise in the domestic price level from P_0 to P_1, for a given nominal money supply (M^s), reduces the real money supply

$$\text{(i.e. } \frac{M^s}{P_1} < \frac{M^s}{P_0}\text{)}$$

This shifts the LM curve back as well.

With perfect capital mobility, the new equilibrium associated with the higher price level of P_1 is Y_1. In the lower panel of Figure 9.1, the combination of the initial price level P_0 and national income Y_0 yields a point on the aggregate demand curve drawn in price level–income space. Similarly, the higher price level P_1 is associated with a lower equilibrium level of equilibrium income Y_1. Both of these points lie on the aggregate demand curve for the open economy, which is always downward sloping.

DERIVING THE AGGREGATE SUPPLY CURVE

An *aggregate supply* curve can also be depicted in price level–income space. It shows how aggregate production, the total output of all firms in the open economy, is related to the domestic price level. An important distinction in analysing the output side of the economy is the behaviour of firms' production in the short run versus firms' production in the long run. First let us consider long-run behaviour.

The *long-run aggregate supply* curve (LRAS) is actually vertical. To understand why this is so, consider a simple aggregate production function specified as Y = f(K, N) where Y is aggregate output or GDP, K is the economy's capital stock and L is the number of workers employed. This suggests that for a given capital stock, Y increases as more workers are employed, as shown in the top panel of Figure 9.2. Diminishing marginal returns explain why the slope of the production frontier is concave from below. Quite simply, as employment of workers increases, so too does aggregate output but at a declining rate.

The next question to arise is what determines the number of workers employed. To answer this question, it is necessary to consider the labour market itself. Figure 9.2 shows that as long as wages are completely flexible, the labour market will always clear, ensuring that all workers who want to work will obtain jobs. Because workers are concerned about the purchasing power of their wages, they make their decisions about how much labour to supply on the basis of real wages – the nominal wage, W, deflated by the price level, P

$$(\text{real wage} = \frac{W}{P})$$

The higher is the real wage, the greater the number of people willing to supply their labour, or participate in the total labour force. Hence, the supply of labour schedule slopes upward in real wage–labour force space, demonstrating that the participation rate is, in effect, a function of real earnings.

Firms on the demand side of the labour market essentially employ extra labour according to its marginal cost. The lower the level of real wages, the more workers are employed, whereas the higher are real wages, the fewer workers are employed. Accordingly, the demand for labour is a downward-sloping schedule in real wage–labour force space. In combination, the demand and supply schedules of labour determine both the equilibrium real wage and the number of people employed.

Now consider what happens if the domestic price level changes. Say the price level rises from P_0 to P_1, thus reducing the real wage

$$\left(\frac{W_0}{P_1} < \frac{W_0}{P_0}\right)$$

The lower real wage reduces the supply of labour at the same time as it raises firms' demand for labour. Such effects are, however, unsustainable at

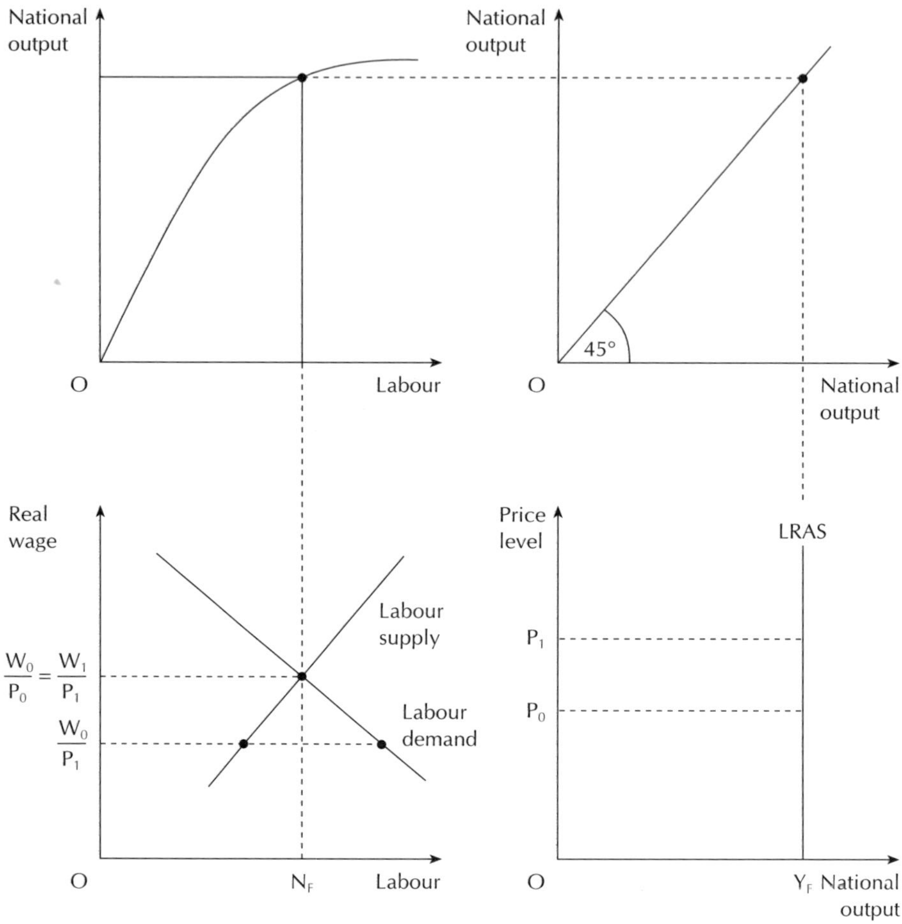

Figure 9.2 Deriving long-run aggregate supply.

prevailing nominal wages. There is an excess demand for labour at the new price level, which means that nominal wages will have to be bid up until the labour market clears. Nominal wages must therefore rise from W_0 to W_1, such that the real wage reverts to its former level

$$\left(\frac{W_1}{P_1} = \frac{W_0}{P_0}\right)$$

Consequently, following an overall price level increase, equilibrium will be restored in the labour market through a catch-up rise in nominal wages to preserve the value of real wages. Note from the diagram that at the higher nominal wage, there is still full employment, in the sense that everyone who wants to work has a job.

The long-run aggregate supply curve is always vertical because the number of employed persons, a real macroeconomic magnitude, is invariant with

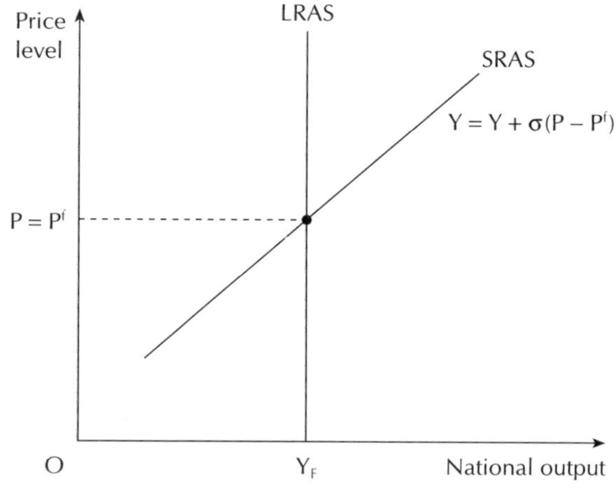

Figure 9.3 Short-run and long-run aggregate supply.

respect to a changing overall price level. Only the number of employed persons and the quantity of other factor inputs determine the volume of aggregate output. Aggregate output is therefore not fundamentally affected in the long run by the price level, which is a nominal variable.

Over shorter periods, however, aggregate output can be responsive to the aggregate price level. Accordingly, the *short-run aggregate supply* (SRAS) schedule is upward sloping in price level–output space. It reflects the behaviour of workers and firms when there are certain information problems or when wages are inflexible. These inflexibilities may arise because of negotiated labour contracts between workers and private firms which set wages over given periods, or because of other government-influenced wage fixing arrangements, as under a centralised wage system. The relationship between the SRAS and LRAS schedules is depicted in Figure 9.3.

There are several theoretical explanations of aggregate supply behaviour in the short run, each of which provides a rationale for an upward-sloping SRAS. For instance, one approach stresses the fact that many nominal wages are set under contracts lasting for a certain time. Under such circumstances any expansion of aggregate demand which puts upward pressure on the general level of prices therefore leads to a reduction in the real wage. This raises firms' demand for labour and temporarily allows more workers to be employed. Aggregate output can therefore rise above the normal level. At the expiry of the labour contracts, however, workers will renegotiate higher nominal wages in an attempt to at least restore former real wage levels.

Another theoretical explanation of SRAS emphasises information problems in production. Firms might make the mistake of confusing general price rises occurring throughout the economy with changes in the relative prices of their particular products. This would cause aggregate production to be higher than otherwise until such time as firms realise their mistakes.

Alternative explanations of SRAS behaviour therefore differ in terms of whether they highlight information problems affecting firms' pricing behaviour or highlight the presence of rigidities in the labour market. Taken as a whole, however, these various perspectives are broadly consistent and can be summarised by the following general equation:

$$Y = Y_F + \sigma(P - P^f)$$

where Y_F is full employment output, σ is some parameter which governs the rate of adjustment and P^f is the expected price level. Full employment output (Y_F) or normal output is the level of output above which the LRAS is vertically drawn. This is the real level of aggregate output, which was determined in Figure 9.2.

The above equation suggests that if the actual price level (P) is above the expected price level (P^f) associated with 'full' employment output, then output will be greater than normal. If the actual price level is less than the expected price level, then output will be less than normal and employment will be less than full employment.

For example, according to the misinformation view of SRAS, if firms misinterpret a rise in the overall price level as an increase in the relative price of their particular output, they would raise production in response. The economy would move up the SRAS schedule until firms realised their errors, at which time the economy would return to its initial point on the LRAS.

COMBINING AD, SRAS AND LRAS

To obtain full equilibrium in the economy, the aggregate demand and aggregate supply sides must be brought together as shown in Figure 9.4. This full equilibrium simultaneously determines national output and the overall price level.

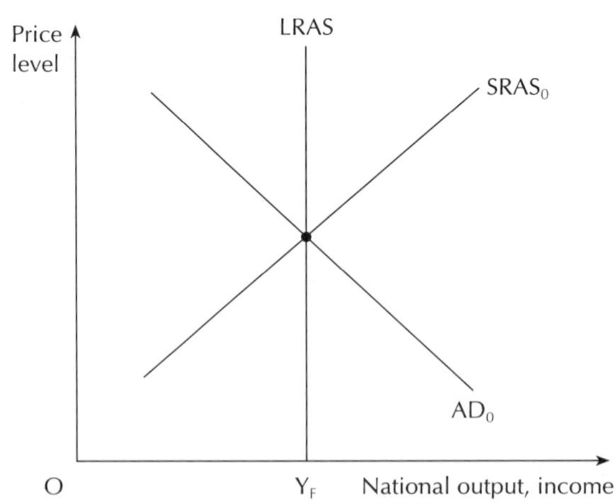

Figure 9.4 AD, SRAS and LRAS for an open economy.

In the short run, equilibrium in the economy will be at the intersection of any AD and SRAS curve, such as AD_0 and $SRAS_0$. If AD then shifts unexpectedly, for instance as a result of monetary expansion under floating exchange rates, the price level will rise above the expected price level and output will rise above the normal level. The economy will then be moving up along the SRAS, producing a higher short-run level of output. However, over time the expected price level itself rises. As workers bid up nominal wages to preserve real wages, this raises firms' costs and shifts the SRAS up.

In the long run, the price-level expectations of workers and firms must again coincide with the actual price level. The final equilibrium is therefore at a point of intersection between AD, SRAS and LRAS. The important thing to note is that, despite the transitory increase in economic activity following the short-run AD shift, the economy eventually returns to the initial normal level of output, but at a higher overall price level.

In an open economy, long-run equilibrium requires not only that:

$$AD = SRAS = LRAS \text{ and } P = P^f$$

but also that there is equilibrium in the foreign exchange market and on the external accounts.

MACROECONOMIC POLICY IN THE AD-SRAS-LRAS FRAMEWORK

It is now possible to subsume the earlier discussion of the effects of monetary and fiscal policy under alternative exchange rate regimes, as conveyed by the IS-LM-BP and IS*-LM* models, into the basic AD-AS framework. Because the earlier analysis of Chapter 7 only captured the aggregate demand side of the economy, it effectively presumed that firms' output was perfectly elastic at the given national price level. In other words, the earlier Mundell–Fleming analysis can be seen as a special case, where the SRAS curve is horizontal at any given price level. Such an SRAS curve is often referred to as a Keynesian AS curve.

The objective now is to translate the earlier Mundell–Fleming results about the effectiveness of fiscal and monetary policy to price level–output space under normal circumstances of an upward-sloping SRAS curve. To do this, first it is necessary to examine the initial effects of fiscal and monetary policy on the AD curve, according to the kind of exchange rate system the economy has.

Recall that fiscal policy was effective under fixed exchange rates, yet ineffective under floating exchange rates, whereas monetary policy was ineffective under fixed exchange rates, but effective under floating exchange rates. In thinking about what this means in the AD-SRAS-LRAS framework, the main thing to keep in mind is that any macroeconomic policy that shifts the IS or LM curves in the earlier frameworks also shifts the AD curve in the same direction.

1. Fiscal and monetary policy under fixed exchange rates

To illustrate, consider what happens when there is fiscal expansion under fixed exchange rates, as in Figure 9.5, where the economy is initially assumed to be in normal equilibrium. As the fiscal expansion shifts the IS curve rightward, the AD curve shifts from AD_0 to AD_1 up along $SRAS_0$.

Then, however, because the central bank must intervene to maintain the fixed exchange rate (by buying foreign exchange in the face of capital inflow), the domestic money supply also rises. This shifts the LM curve, which means there must also be a further shift in aggregate demand (from AD_1 to AD_2). This was the end of the story in the earlier IS-LM-BP analysis of short-run aggregate expenditure effects.

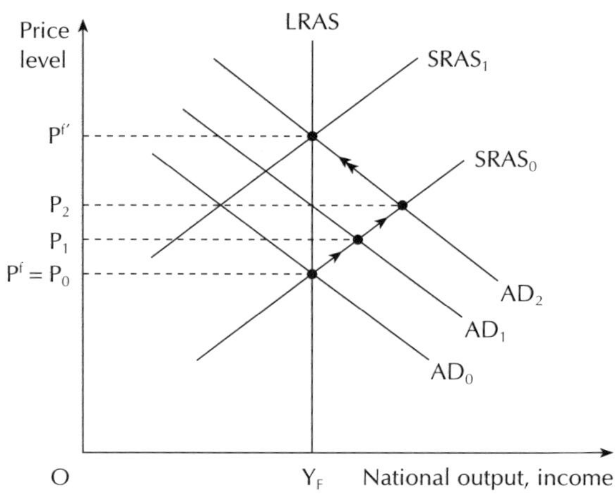

Figure 9.5 Fiscal expansion under fixed rates.

Now, however, consider the economy's aggregate supply-side behaviour. As the economy moves up its SRAS, the expected price level rises. Workers then bid up nominal wages to maintain the purchasing power of their pay packets. Consequently, the SRAS curve drifts upward (to $SRAS_1$) because higher wage costs, in the economy, mean all firms must eventually charge higher prices for their output. In the long run, the economy has therefore moved back to the LRAS and hence to the normal rate of output, Y_F.

In the case of monetary expansion under fixed rates, the LM curve shifts rightward, also moving the AD schedule from AD_0 to AD_1 as in Figure 9.6.

Yet, as discussed earlier, because international financial capital immediately flows out in response to the reduction in domestic interest rates, the exchange rate constraint makes central bank intervention in the foreign exchange market necessary. Official foreign exchange market intervention

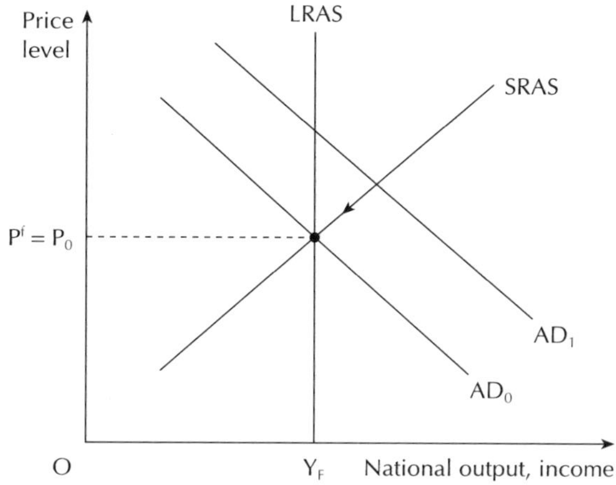

Figure 9.6 Monetary expansion under fixed rates.

means the central bank purchases domestic currency with foreign currency, and the domestic money supply therefore contracts. Hence, the LM curve shifts back, as will the AD curve. In this case, there are no lasting effects on either the price level or the level of aggregate output.

2. Fiscal and monetary policy under floating exchange rates

Fiscal expansion under floating exchange rates, as shown in Figure 9.7, yields a similar result to monetary expansion under fixed exchange rates. In the IS-LM-BP framework, the IS curve initially moves out, but because the higher domestic interest rate generates massive short-run international investment flows, the exchange rate appreciates and worsens competitiveness. This crowds out net exports and subsequently moves the IS schedule

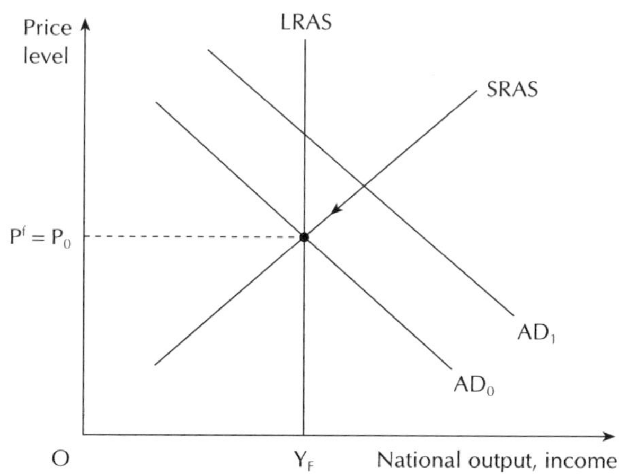

Figure 9.7 Fiscal expansion under floating rates.

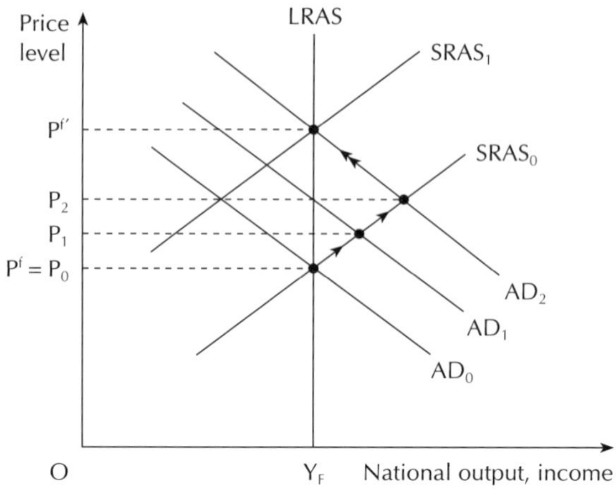

Figure 9.8 Monetary expansion under floating rates.

back. Hence in the AD-SRAS-LRAS framework, the AD curve moves only temporarily from AD_0 to AD_1 and eventually returns to its initial position, with no lasting effect on the overall price level or level of aggregate output.

Lastly, there is the case of monetary expansion under floating exchange rates, as shown in Figure 9.8. Here, the LM schedule first shifts rightward, the exchange rate depreciates and competitiveness improves. The AD curve shifts (AD_0 to AD_1). The improved competitiveness also boosts net exports so that the IS schedule also shifts. The AD curve will therefore shift again (AD_1 to AD_2). Thereafter, as nominal wages are again bid up, the SRAS curve shifts up over time. Eventually, the economy returns to the normal output level at Y_F, but with a higher price level.

The above modelled macroeconomic policy outcomes are summarised in Table 9.1, which extends the earlier Mundell–Fleming effectiveness results

Table 9.1 The effectiveness of monetary and fiscal policy in the short run and longer run.

Macroeconomic policy instrument	*Exchange rate regime*	
	Fixed	*Floating*
Fiscal policy		
Short run	Effective	Ineffective
Longer run	Ineffective	Ineffective
Monetary policy		
Short run	Ineffective	Effective
Longer run	Ineffective	Ineffective

by distinguishing between the short run and the longer run. Note again that by effectiveness, what is meant is whether macroeconomic policy has a lasting impact on equilibrium national income.

The table reveals that, in theory, neither fiscal nor monetary policy is effective in the long run, although they can raise the overall price level. This again brings us to the issue of monetary policy and inflation in the open economy.

THE MONETARY APPROACH TO THE OPEN ECONOMY

Chapter 4 developed a model of inflation in the small open economy based on the tradables/nontradables dichotomy of goods and services. This earlier approach assumed the economy's exchange rate was fixed. The purpose of this section is to present an alternative approach to thinking about inflation in the open economy which, on the contrary, assumes exchange rates are floating. Known as the monetary approach to the open economy, this model highlights the role of the domestic money supply and its long-run effects on the exchange rate and domestic inflation.

In Chapter 3, nominal exchange rate movements over longer periods were explained in terms of price and inflation differences between nations using the notion of purchasing power parity. However, the earlier exposition of PPP did not explain exactly how open economies' aggregate price levels and rates of inflation were determined in the first place.

An important building block of the monetary approach to the open economy, which is used to explain what causes domestic inflation, is known as the *Quantity Theory of Money* (QTM). The QTM is an ancient economic doctrine the antecedents of which can be traced back as far as 500 BC, when the Chinese adopted its precepts to understand how the domestic money supply and domestic price level were related.

In its modern and simplest form, the QTM asserts that monetary equilibrium – meaning the equality in the domestic money markets between the demand and the supply of money – sets the domestic price level.

In algebraic form, the QTM can be expressed as:

$$M^s \cdot V = P \cdot Y_F$$

where M^s is the nominal domestic money supply, V is the velocity of money, P is the domestic price level and Y_F is real full employment output. The variables M^s, P and Y_F should all be familiar from earlier material and have exactly the same macroeconomic meaning as before. The newly introduced variable is the velocity of money, which is the number of times the domestic money supply turns over in a given period, such as a quarter or a year.

More formally:

$$V \equiv \frac{P \cdot Y_F}{M^s}$$

which shows that V is the ratio of the amount of total nominal spending (PY_F) to domestic money in circulation. This suggests, for example, that if V had a value of 3.0, then each local currency unit on average turns over three times a year to facilitate final domestic spending on GDP. Note that if V is defined in this way, then the equation $M^sV = P \cdot Y_F$ must follow more or less as an identity.

The QTM is a theory of domestic inflation which becomes more obvious when the basic equation is rearranged as:

$$M^s = P \cdot \frac{Y_F}{V}$$

When V and Y_F are held constant over time, that is,

$$\frac{Y_F}{V} = \text{constant}$$

causality may then run from the size of the domestic money supply to the overall price level itself. Because the rate of change of a constant is zero, the original QTM equation in rate of change form therefore reduces to:

$$\hat{M}^s = \hat{P} = \pi$$

Alternatively, the QTM can be expressed as residents' demand for real cash balances, defined as L. That is, the demand for real cash balances can be shown as:

$$L = \frac{M^s}{P} = \left(\frac{1}{V}\right)Y_F$$

Accordingly, the demand for real cash balances is proportional to full employment output if velocity is invariant. This equation is known as the Cambridge cash balance version of the QTM. If the real supply of money M^s/P, is willingly held in equilibrium, it follows that:

$$P = M^s/L(Y_F)$$

The above equation also implies that, for a given demand for real cash balances, an increase in the domestic money supply will cause an equi-proportionate rise in the domestic price level. Essential to this proposition is the assumption that the real demand for money is a relatively stable function of real output over time.

Now recall from Chapter 3 the absolute PPP relationship stated in absolute form. That is:

$$P = e \cdot P^*$$

where P is the domestic price level, e is the exchange rate against the currency of a particular economy and P* is just the overall price level of that other economy. PPP is important in this context because it provides the link between the domestic and foreign price levels.

Through rearrangement and substitution of terms, a reduced form equation for the exchange rate can be derived as shown below:

$$e = \frac{M^s}{L(Y_F)} \cdot \frac{1}{P^*} \qquad (9.1)$$

In the foreign economy's market for money, it also follows that:

$$P^* = \frac{M^{s*}}{L^*(Y_F^*)}$$

where asterisks simply denote foreign variables.

By further substitution, Equation (9.1) can then be written as:

$$e = \frac{M^s}{L(Y_F)} \cdot \frac{L^*(Y_F^*)}{M^*}$$

or

$$e = \frac{M^s}{M^{s*}} \cdot \frac{L^*}{L}$$

which in rate-of-change form is:

$$\hat{e} = (\hat{M}^s - \hat{M}^{s*}) + (L^* - L) \qquad (9.2)$$

where the 'hats' again signify the percentage rate of change in the variables.

Equation (9.2) conveys the central points of the monetary approach to the exchange rate. It shows that changes in the exchange rate depend solely on relative rates of change in domestic and foreign money demands and money supplies.

For instance, an increase in the rate of domestic money supply growth relative to foreign money supply growth leads to a long-run depreciation of the nominal exchange rate for given domestic and foreign money demands. Alternatively, if there was an exogenous increase in domestic money demand, all other things constant, the nominal exchange rate would appreciate.

The monetary approach to the exchange rate can also be depicted diagrammatically as in Figure 9.9. The left-hand side panel of the figure summarises the QTM relationship between money and prices. A domestic money supply increase from M_0 to M_1 raises the domestic price level from P_0 to P_1 in order to keep real balances constant. The slope of the ray from the origin in the left panel is given by

$$\frac{1}{L}$$

The right panel of Figure 9.9 reflects the absolute PPP relationship

$$P = e \cdot P^*$$

The slope of the ray from the origin on the right side is given by the foreign price level (P^*), which is taken as given.[1] Starting at the left panel of

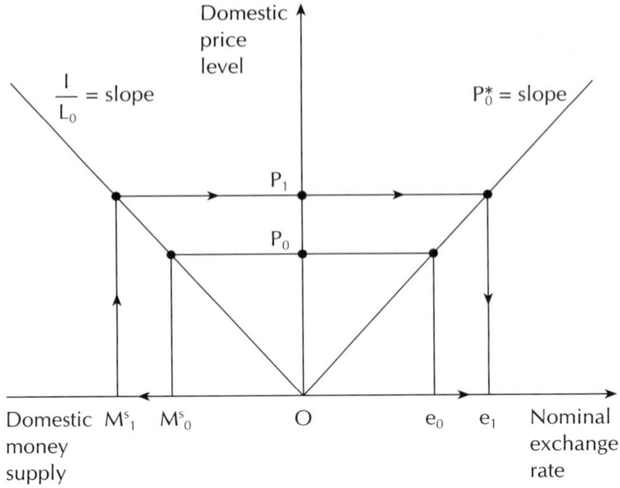

Figure 9.9 Increase in the domestic money supply.

the diagram, an increase in the domestic money supply first causes the domestic price level to rise from P_0 to P_1 through the QTM relationship. The ray reflecting the PPP relationship then shows that as the domestic price level increases, the nominal exchange rate depreciates, given the foreign price level. Therefore, a domestic money supply increase from M_0 to M_1 eventually leads to a currency depreciation from e_0 to e_1, other things remaining constant. The percentage depreciation of the exchange rate is equivalent to the percentage increase in the domestic money supply, consistent with Equation (9.2).

Now consider the case where there is an exogenous fall in the domestic demand for real cash balances with no change in the domestic money supply. Residents' demand for domestic currency may for instance fall in the wake of widespread financial deregulation or financial innovation which reduces the need to hold liquid cash balances. As illustrated in Figure 9.10, a fall in residents' demand for real cash balances would lead to a fall in the demand for money from L_0 to L_1, although the domestic money supply would remain at M_0.

With the supply of domestic money constant, the fall in money demand would, according to the QTM, raise the domestic price level in the first instance. Consequently, to maintain PPP, the higher price level would depreciate the exchange rate from e_0 to e_1 for a given foreign price level.

A number of lessons can be drawn from the monetary approach to the open economy. First, it suggests that under a floating exchange rate domestic inflation is primarily caused over longer periods by growth in the domestic money supply. Second, higher ongoing inflation at home than abroad will be reflected in a persistently depreciating nominal exchange rate. What this means for macroeconomic policy is that if the central bank, which creates the domestic money supply, exercises tight control over its

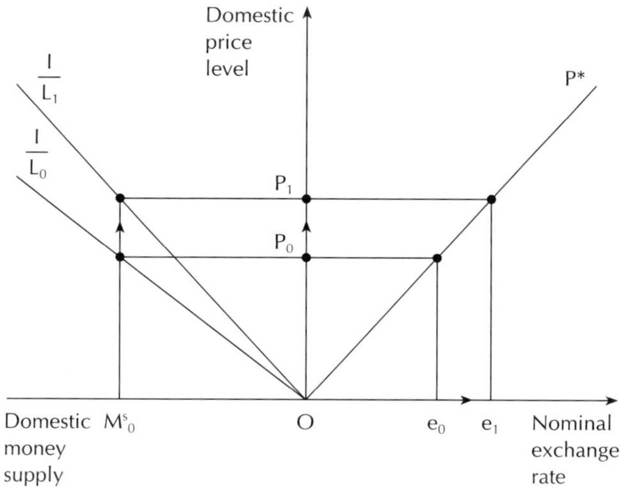

Figure 9.10 Fall in residents' demand for money.

growth, then domestic inflation also will come under control and the nominal exchange rate should stabilise. Under floating exchange rates, inflation is therefore largely a home-grown phenomenon for an open economy. This contrasts with the Scandinavian model of inflation from Chapter 4 which shows that under fixed exchange rates, domestic inflation may largely be externally determined.

THE NEUTRALITY OF MONEY

A macroeconomic notion sometimes associated with the QTM is the so-called *neutrality of money* proposition. This proposition states that if growth in the domestic money supply eventually only raises the domestic price level, then real variables like real output and employment remain unaffected. In other words, money has a nil, or neutral, effect on real macroeconomic variables. The neutrality of money proposition is illustrated in Figure 9.11.

With reference to the earlier AD-AS framework of this chapter, assume the economy is initially in long-run equilibrium at the normal full employment level (Y_F). If the domestic money supply is suddenly increased by the central bank, the AD curve would shift out. But in the long run this only raises the overall domestic price level. According to the QTM, the percentage change in the domestic money supply which caused the AD to shift ultimately generates a one-for-one rise in the domestic price level. There is no change in any real macroeconomic variable in the long run, including real output, employment or even the real exchange rate. In short, the domestic money supply eventually exerts a neutral influence over real macroeconomic variables, and only affects nominal magnitudes.

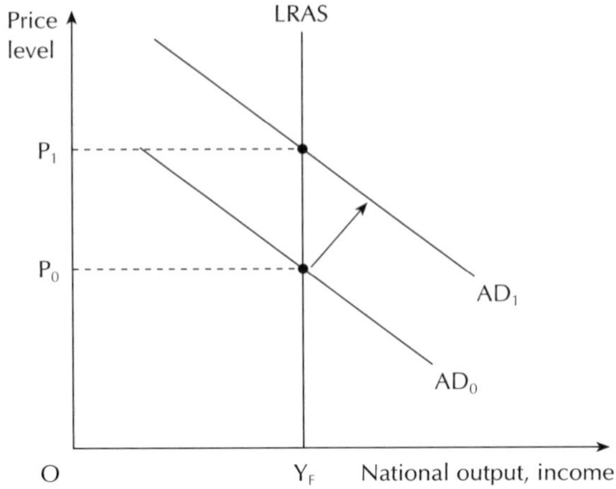

Figure 9.11 The neutrality of money.

RULES VERSUS DISCRETION

The question of how monetary policy should actually be conducted by central banks is one of those perennial issues in macroeconomics that generate strong disagreement among economists and policymakers. The Keynesian view that governments are responsible for stabilising the economy is founded on the assumption that disastrous international macroeconomic shocks like the Great Depression of the 1930s (when unemployment reached over 30 per cent of the workforce in most English-speaking countries) are likely to happen regularly. Accordingly, discretionary macroeconomic policy reactions are generally deemed both effective and timely.

Views about whether discretionary macroeconomic policy is beneficial or harmful usually depend on whether macroeconomic interventions are considered capable of stabilising or actually destabilise the normal business cycle. Because of the time lags involved between the implementation of a macroeconomic policy change and the time it takes to have an impact on the economy, policy activism may not always smooth the peaks and troughs of the business cycle.

In practice, if monetary policy is exacerbating, not smoothing, the business cycle, it follows that the conduct of monetary policy may be improved through a commitment to a fixed money growth rule. Related to this, a way of eliminating the influence of governments over the operation of discretionary monetary policy in particular is to formally establish the independence of the central bank from popularly elected politicians. This issue was raised earlier in Chapter 6.

Consistent with the neutrality proposition explained in the previous section, the so-called New Classical approach to monetary policy analysis argues that monetary expansion, of itself, has no lasting effect on the real economy because well-informed economic agents immediately seek higher compensa-

Table 9.2 Policy discretion versus policy rules.

Those favouring discretion believe:	*Those favouring rules believe:*
1. The economy is inherently unstable because of perpetually changing business expectations.	1. The economy is inherently stable, though mistakes are made by the private sector from time to time.
2. Macroeconomic policymakers are well placed to stabilise economic fluctuations because they possess superior information about the economy.	2. Macroeconomic policymakers possess less information than the sum of the knowledge of all households and firms transacting in domestic and international markets.
3. Activist fiscal and monetary policies can be well timed to stabilise the business cycle.	3. Activist fiscal and monetary policies usually exacerbate the business cycle because of time lags.
4. Inflexible prices and wages prevent adjustments that would restore full employment.	4. Over time, prices and wages would eventually adjust to correct for any external or internal shocks.

tion for the effects of rising domestic prices. Workers bid for higher nominal wages or lenders demand higher nominal interest rates, in anticipation of a rise in expected inflation. As a result, inflation increases almost instantaneously, leaving the real economy and employment levels the same.

The policy implication of the New Classical approach is that monetary policy itself is quite ineffective at any time. If this is true then it follows that money growth should be fixed to minimise uncertainty about future inflation. Note at this point that there is some similarity between the New Classical approach to monetary policy and the Ricardian equivalence proposition about the ineffectiveness of fiscal policy. Central to the New Classical and Ricardian equivalence approaches is the idea that residents are forward looking and make the most of all available information about the ultimate effects of policy changes. Such behaviour assumes residents have what are called *rational expectations* about all economic phenomena.

The debate between economists favouring policy rules and those favouring policy discretion can be summarised in the set of competing propositions shown in Table 9.2.

Another view of macroeconomic behaviour proposes that fluctuations in the business cycle are mainly caused, not by demand-side disturbances, but by occasional shocks to the supply side of the economy, such as sudden breakthroughs in technology. So-called *real business cycle* theory implies that, under such circumstances, economic fluctuations are actually optimal and that policymakers should not even try to stabilise the economy. This still controversial perspective has yet to find widespread support among economists, however.

Over longer periods, economists of all persuasions agree that expansions and contractions in the money supply mainly influence the rate of inflation in the economy. A money rule approach must choose a particular money supply measure to target. One possibility is to fix the growth rate of the money base, year in and year out. Because the money base consists of the total value of the central bank's liabilities and is the measure of money over which the central bank exercises a monopoly, it should in principle be the easiest measure to control. A rule of this kind could restrict the growth rate of the money base to, for example, between 2 and 5 per cent, in accordance with the economy's average long-term output growth. A money rule would also necessarily be accompanied by a pure floating exchange rate regime, since foreign exchange market intervention would be at odds with a transparent money-growth objective.

An alternative to a fixed money-growth rule pursued irrespective of the behaviour of the private economy is a so-called *feedback* or activist rule that in theory could specify how policy should react to evolving economic circumstances. For example, if the unemployment level starts to rise in the wake of an investment slump, the money supply could be automatically expanded and short-term interest rates lowered. The nominal exchange rate would further depreciate, thus cushioning the impact of the fall in investment on the economy. However, given the real-world complication of variable lags already discussed, such an activist money rule may be difficult to design with precision.

Another qualification to the fixed money-growth proposition is that, although the money-growth rule ensures constancy on the supply side of the money market equation, from time to time residents' demand for money may shift for other reasons, such as further financial innovation. As discussed earlier, autonomous money demand shifts may also ultimately affect the overall price level, irrespective of money supply growth.

Summary

1. This chapter introduced the AD-AS framework in price level–national income space. This framework can be used to predict the short- and longer-run effects of fiscal and monetary policy on the price level and output in the open economy.

2. The AD curve is derived from the IS-LM-BP framework and shows that a lower domestic price level is associated with a higher level of equilibrium national income.

3. The LRAS rises vertically above the full employment, or normal, aggregate output level. Because nominal wages are assumed to be completely flexible in the long run, the labour market will eventually clear to ensure that everyone who wants to work will be employed at the equilibrium real wage.

4. The SRAS is upward sloping. This can be explained by wage rigidities due to labour contracts or by firms' misunderstanding of price movements.

5. Any macroeconomic policy initiative which shifts the IS or LM curves in the Mundell–Fleming framework also shifts the AD curve in the same direction, thereby affecting the domestic price level.
6. The Quantity Theory of Money, $M^s.V = P.Y_F$, becomes a theory of domestic inflation if the velocity of money is stable and national income is at the normal level.
7. Combined with purchasing power parity, the QTM provides a monetary model of exchange-rate determination in the longer run.
8. According to the monetary approach to the exchange rate, domestic inflation generated by excessive domestic money supply growth eventually depreciates the nominal exchange rate.
9. The neutrality of money proposition asserts that in the long run, money only changes nominal variables, such as the price level and the nominal exchange rate. The money supply has no lasting effect on the values of real variables such as employment, real output and the real exchange rate.
10. Some economists favour central banks adhering to set money-growth rules instead of allowing them wide discretionary powers. Conceivably, the exercise of discretionary monetary policy could exacerbate the open economy's business cycle or generate excessive domestic inflation.

Note

1. The slopes of the rays can be derived by differentiating the two basic equations of the model

$$P = \frac{M^s}{L} \text{ and } P = e \cdot P^*$$

Hence

$$\frac{dP}{dM^s} = \frac{1}{L} \text{ and } \frac{dP}{de} = P^*$$

Further reading

Clements, K. (1981) 'The monetary approach to exchange rate determination: a geometric analysis', *Weltwertschaftliches Archiv*, **117**(1), 20–25.

Fischer, S. (1990) 'Rules versus discretion in monetary policy', in B. Friedman and F. Hahn (eds) *Handbook of Monetary Economics*, Amsterdam: North-Holland.

Scarth, W. (1988) *Macroeconomics: An Introduction to Advanced Methods*, Toronto: Harcourt Brace Jovanovich, chapter 2.

10

Wages, employment and unemployment

In the previous chapter, the behaviour of the domestic labour market was central to explaining the causes of inflation and unemployment in the open economy. In particular, the labour market and wages were pivotal in the AD-AS analysis of output, employment and price-level adjustment under alternative exchange rate regimes. Recall also that wage-setting behaviour played a crucial role in generating domestic inflation under fixed exchange rates in the tradable/nontradable framework of Chapter 4.

This chapter examines the macroeconomic implications of labour market arrangements in more depth than previously and presents some further perspectives on wage setting, employment and unemployment. Why is the achievement of low unemployment an important goal of macroeconomic policy? The costs of unemployment to individuals include loss of current income and loss of future income if skills deteriorate during unemployment. The consequent fall in standard of living, loss of self-esteem and possible deterioration in health are also costs associated with unemployed individuals.

From the perspective of the economy as a whole, unemployment represents a loss in output of goods and services, increased government expenditure on social welfare and a reduction in the nation's stock of human capital. In addition, there may be costs to the rest of society arising from the health and social problems that result from unemployment. In order to discuss the causes of and policies to reduce unemployment, it is first necessary to examine the workings of the labour market and, in particular, the crucial role of wages.

LABOUR DEMAND, LABOUR SUPPLY AND UNEMPLOYMENT

Figure 10.1 reproduces the labour market diagram used to derive the LRAS curve of the previous chapter. The demand for labour (N^D) measured in

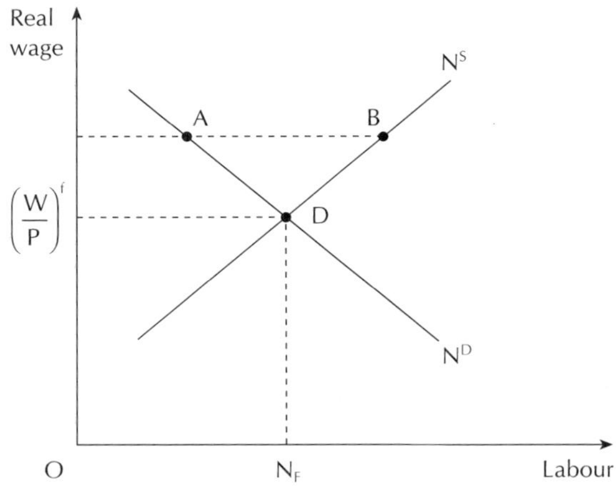

Figure 10.1 Demand and supply of labour.

terms of the number of workers is a downward-sloping function of the real wage (W/P) where W is the nominal wage rate and P is the price level. The supply of labour is an upward-sloping function of the real wage rate. Empirical studies have actually established the existence of these curves for many countries.

The question of if and how the labour market reaches equilibrium is at the heart of macroeconomic debate and will be discussed later in the chapter. However, it is convenient here to observe that, in Figure 10.1, full employment will be at the point D where demand for labour is equal to supply. It follows that if the real wage rate is above the equilibrium wage, demand for labour will be at a point such as A while supply will be greater than this at a point such as B' and there will be unemployment.

To fully understand unemployment it is necessary to expand on the basic measurement issues first introduced in Chapter 2. The labour force (LF) – that is, employed (E) plus unemployed (U) persons – is often taken to be synonymous with the labour supply. However, there are a number of people, the *hidden unemployed*, who, because they believe there is no work available, are not actively looking for work. In addition there are a number of workers who would prefer to work more hours, or, although working part time, would prefer to work full time. Such factors make it somewhat difficult to define the labour supply with precision.

Labour demand is often taken to be the number employed (E) plus the number of vacancies (V). It is difficult to estimate the number of vacancies. Estimates are usually based on surveys, notification of vacancies with employment agencies and newspaper advertisements. While the available series may be good indicators of *trends* in vacancies they are unlikely to be reliable estimates of the *level* of vacancies.

It is important to note that unemployment is a stock, the total number of unemployed at a point in time. The magnitude of this stock is determined by flows of people moving in and out of unemployment and by the average duration of unemployment. The unemployment rate is related to flows and duration by the following formula:

$$UR = \frac{F}{LF} \times ad$$

where UR is the unemployment rate, F is the number of people entering unemployment, LF is the number of people in the workforce and ad is the average duration of unemployment in years. As an example, consider an unemployment rate of 10 per cent. This is consistent with 10 per cent of the labour force being unemployed for a year or 100 per cent of the labour force being unemployed for 0.1 year (about five weeks). From a policy perspective, these two extremes may be quite different. Focusing solely on the unemployment rate may therefore be misleading if the structure and duration of unemployment are not taken into account.

TYPES OF UNEMPLOYMENT

There are several types of unemployment, and the extent to which aggregate unemployment is made up of each kind implies quite different policy responses. Indeed, some unemployment, rather than being a problem, is necessary for the efficient allocation of labour in the economy.

For instance, structural and frictional unemployment arise even when the aggregate demand for labour is equal to the aggregate supply of labour. *Structural unemployment* relates to the unemployment following structural changes in government policy, technology and shifts in demand. *Frictional unemployment* refers to unemployment due to the time it takes to leave one job and find another or to find a first job. These types of unemployment are in the sphere of microeconomic policy and will not be considered further.

Demand-deficient unemployment is a major concern of macroeconomic policy and dominates debate about which policy prescriptions are most appropriate. It is usual to contrast two types of demand-deficient unemployment. The first, 'Classical' unemployment, is caused by real wages being too high. The second, 'Keynesian' unemployment, is caused by the demand for goods and services being too low. However, as discussed below, wages still play an important role in Keynesian unemployment.

The Classical model assumes that all prices, including wages, are perfectly flexible and hence all markets, including the labour market, clear. This is illustrated in Figure 10.2.

Consider first the situation where equilibrium exists in both the goods and labour markets. In the goods market, the equilibrium price level is given by P^f and the aggregate demand for goods is equal to the aggregate supply of goods. In the labour market the equilibrium real wage is at $(W/P)^f$ where the demand for labour equals the supply of labour. Consider next a situation where, in the goods market, the actual price level, P_1, is

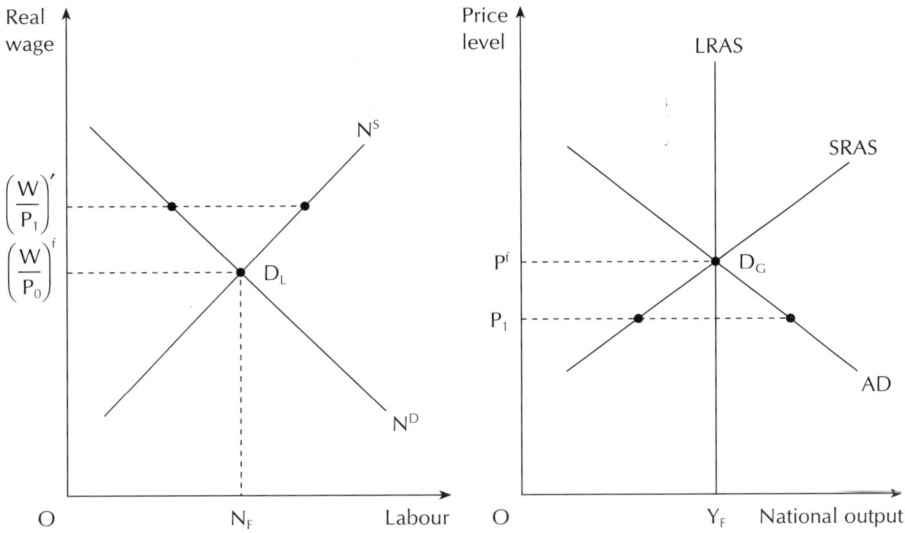

Figure 10.2 Market clearing in the Classical model.

below equilibrium and there is an excess demand for goods. The 'too low' price level corresponds to a 'too high' real wage rate $(W/P)'$ in the labour market and hence excess supply of labour – that is, unemployment. This 'rule' that excess demand for goods must imply excess supply of labour is another example of *Walras's law*.

Given the Classical assumption that nominal wages and prices are flexible, from the well-known foundations of microeconomics, prices will rise in markets with excess demand and fall in markets with excess supply. Therefore, both the goods and labour markets will move to their respective equilibrium positions D_G and D_L. It follows from the above analysis that either the economy will always move to full employment or the failure to move to full employment must be due to wages failing to adjust.

Figure 10.3 presents an explanation of the Keynesian case. Again D_G and D_L represent the equilibrium in the goods and labour markets, respectively. Consider a shock causing a fall in aggregate demand for goods from D_G to A, with a drop in the price level to P_1. In the Classical model of flexible wages and prices, the nominal wage would fall together with the price level to maintain the real wages at $(W/P)^f$ and employment would be unchanged at N_F. The aggregate supply curve for goods would shift downwards to SRAS, and the new equilibrium (B) would be at the original equilibrium output Y_F.

The Keynesian view is that firms are unlikely to expand supply in the face of excess supply and rising real wages. Rather, they will perceive that they are selling all the goods they can. Therefore, although the 'notional' demand curve is along N^D, the 'effective' demand curve is given by the vertical line CF.

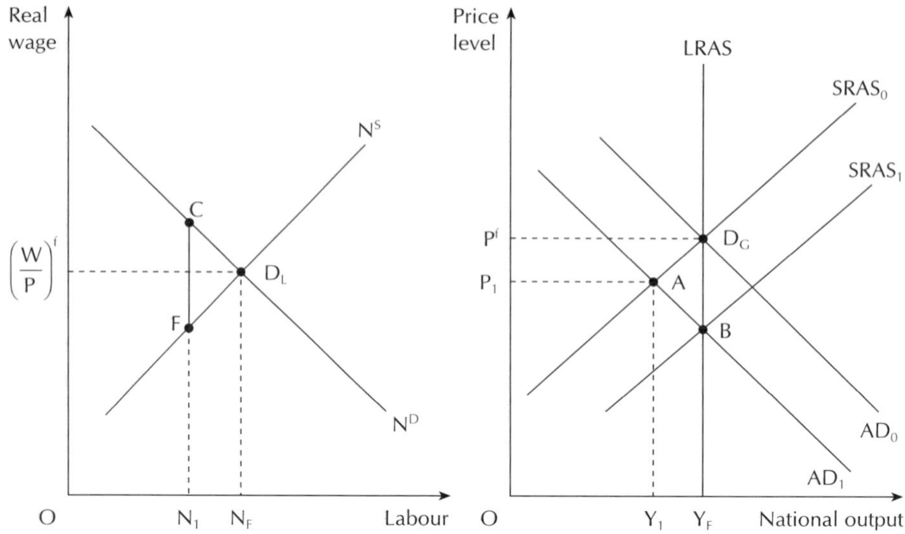

Figure 10.3 Keynesian unemployment.

FULL EMPLOYMENT AND THE 'NATURAL' RATE OF UNEMPLOYMENT

Full employment is a major goal of macroeconomic policy. The question, therefore, arises as to what is meant by *full employment*. In theory, it is simply when the demand for labour is equal to the supply of labour. However, as we saw above, involuntary frictional and structural unemployment exists, even though vacancies are available. In addition, a number of people are *voluntarily unemployed* in that they are willing to work, but a job with the desired wage or desired characteristics is not available.

The rate of voluntary unemployment will depend on the time taken for the unemployed to revise their expectations of the appropriate wage for their labour services. As the search for a job proceeds, workers should revise downwards their expectations of the appropriate wage. It should be noted here, although this issue will be discussed fully later, that the appropriate wage is itself to fall with the length of time unemployed.

Clearly, the size of the wage obtained from work relative to income from not working will influence the incentive to search for a job. The higher the *replacement ratio*, the ratio of income earned when out of work to income earned when in work, the higher the level of voluntary unemployment.

The unemployment rate when the economy is at full employment, as defined above, is called the *natural rate of unemployment*. This is a rather unfortunate name, as it implies there is something natural about unemployment which cannot be influenced by economic policy. Labour market and social security reform, the province of structural policy, can change the natural rate. In addition, recent evidence discussed later in this section

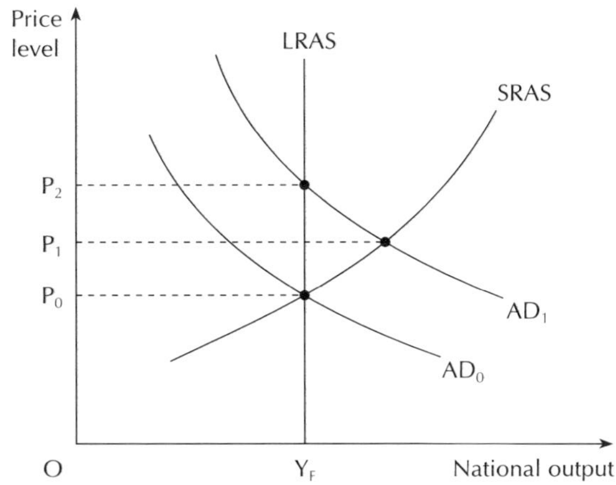

Figure 10.4 The NAIRU.

suggests that the natural rate is not a constant but depends on past macroeconomic performance, and hence can be affected by macroeconomic policy after all.

Another concept virtually identical to that of the natural rate is the non-accelerating inflation rate of unemployment (NAIRU). This concept is associated with Milton Friedman and is simply illustrated in Figure 10.4, which is similar to the analysis used in Chapter 9.

Assume the economy is at full employment output Y_F. Although there is a notional portion of the SRAS curve to the right of full employment, this can only be temporary since the economy cannot produce more output for very long when it is at full employment. Consider a shift in the AD_0 curve to AD_1 due to, say, an increase in the money supply. The price level will rise to P_1 and, as long as wages do not rise by as much as prices, then firms will increase output along SRAS. This arises because workers will be 'fooled' into thinking the rise in money wages is a real rise and will increase labour supply. However, eventually money wages will rise by the rate of inflation and real wages will remain unchanged. Firms will therefore reduce output back to Y_F and prices will eventually rise to P_2. Note that at any output less than Y_F there will be a rise in both employment and prices but at Y_F output cannot rise for very long and there is inflation – hence the reason for the name NAIRU, for it is the unemployment rate when the economy is at Y_F.

It is worth noting that the upward-sloping, as opposed to vertical, SRAS curve assumes that workers interpret the price rise as a rise in their own price rather than an increase in all prices – that is, inflation. For this reason, this model is often referred to as the 'fooling' model. The idea that individuals are 'fooled' by inflation has, generally, been rejected by economists in favour of the *rational expectations hypothesis*, to be discussed shortly.

One way of examining what has happened to the natural rate of unemployment is to examine the locus of inflation and unemployment,

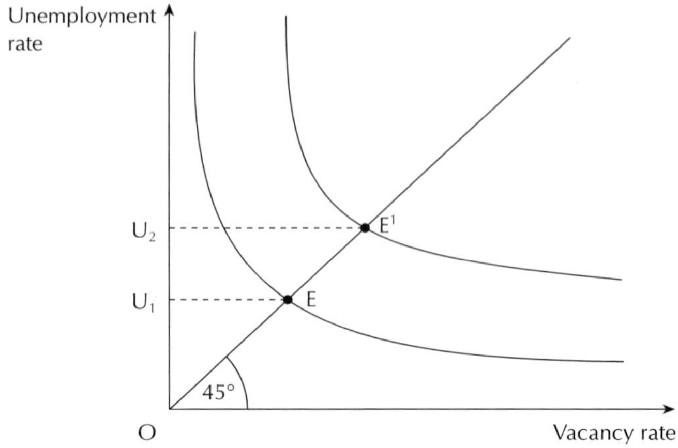

Figure 10.5 The U-V curve.

often referred to as the *Phillips' curve*. The natural rate, or NAIRU, can be identified by observing the unemployment rates at which inflation accelerates.

Further evidence on the natural rate of unemployment is provided by the *unemployment-vacancy curve* (U-V curve). As the name implies, the U-V curve depicts the relationship between the vacancy rate and the unemployment rate (Figure 10.5). When the labour market is relatively tight, unemployment is low and unfilled vacancies high; the opposite is true when the labour market is slack. Thus the U-V curve is downward sloping and convex to the origin.

Theoretically, the 45° line OE represents equilibrium in the labour market since unemployment equals vacancies. As discussed earlier, the measures of vacancies are very unreliable, and therefore it is not generally possible to identify the equilibrium U. However, shifts in the U-V curve outwards clearly represent increases in the equilibrium or natural rate of unemployment from, say, U_1 to U_2.

The U-V curve shifted outwards for many advanced economies in the mid- to late-1970s. The outward shift implied a greater natural rate of unemployment in the 1990s.

In summary, the natural rate of unemployment appears to have increased in most OECD economies. However, it has increased most in European countries and least in Japan and the United States.

The reasons for these differences between countries are still a matter of debate among economists. Among the reasons for economies experiencing shifts in the natural rate are increased generosity of unemployment benefits, an increase in mismatch resulting from structural change and labour market regulations. These suggest the need for further labour market reform.

LONG-TERM UNEMPLOYMENT AND HYSTERESIS

The problem of the long-term unemployed, currently defined as those unemployed for 52 weeks and over, is one which only became evident after the late 1970s. The issue of long-term unemployment is important not only for its own sake, but because it provides an explanation of the increase in the natural rate.

It is important to emphasise the dynamics of the relationship between the unemployment rate and the *long-term unemployment proportion*, the proportion of total unemployed who have been out of work for a lengthy period. A significant increase in the unemployment rate is associated with increases in the long-term unemployment proportion, but with a lag, and with the long-term proportion remaining high for some time. Once generated, long-term unemployment appears difficult to eliminate. The long-term unemployed find it difficult to find work and, indeed, some may be virtually unemployable. They are then no longer part of the effective labour supply and the 'natural rate' increases. Thus the 'natural rate' is not a constant but depends on the past history of unemployment.

Crucial to the understanding of long-term unemployment is the observed negative relation between duration of unemployment and the probability of obtaining employment. A lower exit rate from unemployment for those who have been unemployed for a significant period of time has traditionally been taken to result from two factors: *state* (or duration) *dependence* and the *heterogeneity effect*.

State dependence refers to the negative impact of duration *per se* on the probability of leaving the unemployment pool. This may arise for a number of reasons, including the 'scarring' effects of long periods of unemployment on motivation, confidence and skill acquisition, the deterioration of human capital and the 'stigma' effect which arises from firms using a worker's duration of unemployment as a measure of worker quality.

The heterogeneity effect refers to the fact that those individuals with the set of characteristics which gives them a higher probability of exiting into employment, irrespective of the duration of unemployment, will tend to leave unemployment sooner. The remaining pool is then made up of individuals with characteristics seen by employers as less desirable from an employment viewpoint. Whether or not the negative relationship between unemployment duration and employment probabilities is due to state dependence or heterogeneity is not too important here. What matters is that the long-term unemployed differ in some systematic way from the short-term unemployed.

Some economists have suggested an additional rationale for the negative relationship between duration of unemployment and re-employment probabilities, commonly referred to as *insider/outsider theory*. Insider 'rights' arise because of the costs of replacing existing workers with lower-cost workers. Such costs include redundancy payments, hiring and firing costs, retraining costs and costs which may occur through union resistance to dismissals. Workers may not lose their membership rights shortly after being displaced but may do so after some period of time has elapsed. It would be expected that, as the number of long-term unemployed increases, the nature of the processes which govern wage bargaining will also change. Hence the duration of unemployment affects labour market outcomes not only through its impact on human capital, but also through the diminution of insider power.

To summarise the above discussion, a standard account of unemployment is that observed unemployment is made up of a natural rate component and a cyclical component. Movements in the observed unemployment rate, according to this approach, may reflect either movements in the natural rate resulting from shifts in underlying structural factors and/or aggregate demand shocks which have only temporary effects.

A hysteresis account of unemployment suggests, however, that, in addition to the variables which impact on the natural rate, the natural rate may itself be conditioned by trends in the history of observed unemployment. Under the hysteresis alternative, increases in the unemployment rate feed on themselves to shift the equilibrium rate of unemployment. Hence policy should be geared to tackling increases in unemployment when it first occurs, before it has time to affect movements in the natural rate. Put in another form, one-off policy-induced contractions may have long-lasting effects.

NEW KEYNESIAN THEORIES

Earlier we categorised demand-deficient unemployment as being either Classical, caused by too high real wages, or Keynesian, caused by a deficiency of effective demand. In either case, if wages and prices were flexible, then unemployment could be only temporary. The traditional Keynesian analysis, although appearing to provide a good description of reality, has always sat uneasily with traditional economic theory. On the other hand, while the Classical assumptions of optimisation by firms and workers, together with flexible prices, are very much part of the conventional tools of economic analysis, it seems difficult to reconcile the conclusions of Classical economics with observed high and persistent unemployment.

New Keynesian theories attempt to explain wage and price rigidities as the result of rational decision making by firms and workers. They attempt to overcome the traditional Keynesian dilemma: either economic agents do not act rationally and adjust to what would be better outcomes by changing wages and prices, or economic agents choose not to adjust because they are rational and therefore unemployment is voluntary.

New Keynesian theories consist of those which seek to explain *nominal* price and wage *rigidity* and those which seek to explain *real* price and wage *rigidity*. Nominal rigidity relates to factors making it costly to make nominal price or wage adjustments. Real rigidity relates to factors which hinder adjustment of *relative* wages or prices.

Business cycles involve increases in labour demand during recoveries and decreases in labour demand during recessions, implying corresponding changes in wage rates. However, what we observe in most economies are contracts, explicit or implicit, between workers and employees, which maintain nominal wages over quite long periods. In some advanced economies there are added 'contractual' arrangements imposed by law by which employers must maintain certain minimum wages and conditions, to be discussed later in this chapter. Just why workers and employers find it beneficial to enter into such contracts is the subject of a huge literature. Suffice to say that workers and employers find wage contracts advantageous because frequent wage negotiations are costly in terms of research and possible industrial action. Contracts lower the frequency of costly negotiations.

A further rationale for infrequent adjustments in wages is given by *implicit contract theory*, a theory of real wage rigidity. The essential premise is that workers are risk-averse with respect to income. Both unemployment and lower wages reduce income, but employers cannot guarantee both employment and constant wages. It is assumed that workers choose wage stability.

Price adjustment costs refer to the costs to firms of frequent adjustment of goods prices. While some producers, such as farmers, are price takers in that their goods are sold on perfectly competitive markets, a large sector of the economy is made up of price makers selling goods in monopolistic or imperfectly competitive markets. Adjusting prices is not costless. For instance, new catalogues or menus need to be printed (hence the term *menu costs* sometimes used to describe these theories).

Another source of rigid goods prices is the use of *mark-up pricing* by firms. Under mark-up pricing, the price is set equal to the average variable cost plus a percentage, the mark-up, to cover fixed costs and profits. This method of pricing has been shown to be a prevalent pricing practice by firms and, under certain conditions, can be shown to be consistent with profit maximisation. It has been argued that it is efficient in the sense that it is a moderately costless method for management, and fair in the sense that firms only increase prices to consumers in response to cost increases.

Whatever the reasons for firms pursuing mark-up pricing, the result is that, in the short run, prices will not adjust in response to changes to demand, since input costs, particularly for labour, are fixed by contracts. In the long run, costs will also adjust due to changes in demand and the mark-up price will also adjust accordingly.

Real wage rigidities are explained by *efficiency wage* theories. There are four essential strands to these theories, but each hypothesises that worker effort, or the marginal productivity of labour, increases with the real wage.

The four strands can be summarised as shirking, turnover costs, selection and sociological models.

Shirking models are based on the premise that, in the absence of a costly monitoring process, workers will tend to shirk – that is, not give their full effort. By paying higher wages than workers could receive elsewhere, employers increase the costs of being fired and thus provide incentives not to shirk.

Turnover costs relate to the costs of firing workers plus the recruitment, other hiring costs and training of new workers. These costs make it profitable for firms to reduce labour turnover. By paying higher wages, a firm can reduce the loss of workers to other firms and hence reduce turnover costs.

Firms seek to select higher quality workers in preference to low quality workers. *Selection procedures* are often costly and employers have imperfect information about potential workers. If a firm pays low wages it will certainly not attract high quality workers. However, although it cannot guarantee hiring high quality workers, its chances will increase with higher wages. It follows, therefore, that firms which pay higher wages increase the probability of hiring better quality workers and hence increase average productivity of labour. *Sociological* theories of efficiency wages emphasise the importance of 'fairness' in the workplace. Increased wages improve morale and labour productivity.

Whatever the strand of efficiency theory, the important implications are the same. As a firm raises the wage rate, the money cost per unit of labour increases, but the productivity of labour also increases so the cost per unit of labour in *efficiency units* declines. Eventually a wage rate will be reached where the extra cost of increasing the wage by one unit will be just equal to the reduced cost due to improved productivity. This is the *efficiency wage.*

Suppose demand for a firm's output falls. The firm has no incentive to cut wages below the efficiency wage, since the costs per unit of output would increase. Instead it is optimal for the firm to reduce its workforce. It is also unprofitable to replace highly paid workers with unemployed workers willing to accept lower wages, since productivity would fall and the cost per unit of output rise.

The insider–outsider model was mentioned above in the context of long-term unemployment. It is based on the premise that frictions and imperfections in labour markets act to segment the labour market in terms of employment opportunities. Costs such as firing, hiring, retraining and possibly organised disruption create a costs 'wedge' between those in employment, the *insiders*, and the unemployed, *outsiders*. Insiders can use the existence of these costs of turning an outsider into an insider to achieve a higher bargained wage than the wage offers of the unemployed. In turn, insiders can influence the cost of replacing insiders by outsiders. By negotiating with employers about minimum entry standards (credentialism), increased redundancy payments, last-in/first-out firing policies and other conditions, insider power can be enhanced.

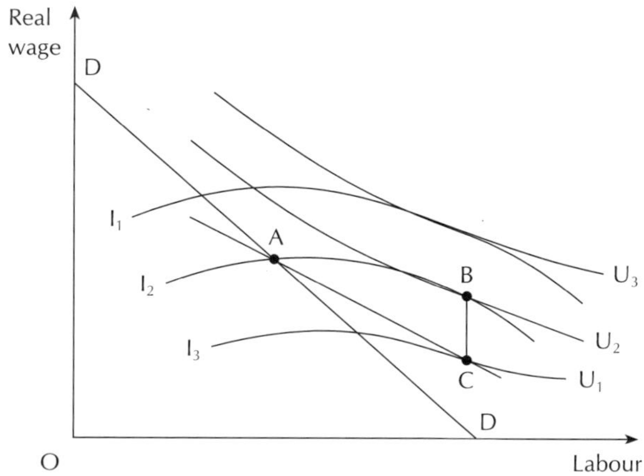

Figure 10.6 Unions' and firms' bargaining decisions.

UNIONS AND LABOUR MARKET FLEXIBILITY

The argument that unions cause unemployment is hardly new. By maintaining wages above the competitive equilibrium, 'Classical' unemployment is created. The size of the *union mark-up*, the percentage by which wages of union members exceed those of non-union members, has been estimated to be about 15 per cent for the United States and 13 per cent for the United Kingdom and Australia. More recently, however, the behaviour of unions has attracted the attention of new Keynesian economists. The main conclusion of this analysis is that where unions set wages and employers set employment, socially superior solutions can be achieved by bargaining over both employment and wages.

In Figure 10.6, consider the demand for labour curve DD. I_1, I_2 and I_3 represent different combinations of wages and employment yielding the same profit. Lower curves represent higher profit. Note that since the demand for labour is derived from profit maximisation by the firm, it must correspond to the peaks of each isoprofit curve. U_1, U_2 and U_3 show the 'utility' union members receive from different contributions of wages and employment. Higher utility curves represent higher utility.

Suppose the union sets the wage at A, then the demand curve shows the respective employment set by the firm for the given wage. Clearly, there are *Pareto superior* outcomes to A. Consider, for instance, the point B. The firm is indifferent between A and B, but union members are better off (on a higher indifference curve). Alternatively, at C union members are indifferent between A and C but the firm is better off (on a higher profit curve). All points on the line BC are Pareto superior to A. Unions can extract some of the monopoly rents from firms in the form of either wages or employment or both. Importantly, employment is always higher, although wages may be lower or higher.

It is convenient to distinguish between the numerical flexibility and functional flexibility of labour markets. *Numerical flexibility* refers to how easily the quantity of labour inputs can be varied, whereas *functional flexibility* refers to how easily the tasks performed by workers can be altered.

In the Classical model, numerical flexibility is achieved by relative wage adjustments. In industries and occupations where demand, relative to available supply, is high, wages should increase relative to those elsewhere, and vice versa. As employers and employees respond to the signals and incentives given by these wage changes, demand and supply would adjust and numerical flexibility would be achieved. Critics of centralised wage determination argue that setting minimum award wages for the various occupations and industries, and imposing the same minimums on all firms within an industry, severely impedes such adjustment. Inflexibility also arises because any relative wage changes that occur tend to be cancelled out through flow-on effects – that is, by workers in other industries receiving similar increases.

The above criticism is based on the premise that, in the absence of centrally determined wages, the labour market would respond to wage changes. However, the New Keynesian theories discussed above point to the labour market being characterised by rigidities.

It was shown above that where a monopoly union sets the wage and firms set employment, the resulting wage/employment is sub-optimal. There are Pareto superior solutions through bargaining and agreement over both wages and employment. Developments in New Keynesian theory provide further key premises for *prices and incomes agreements* between governments, business and unions. New Keynesian theory does so in two ways.

First, it emphasises the frictions and imperfections in labour markets which act to segment the market in terms of employment opportunities. Such frictions may generate involuntary unemployment. Against such a background, prices and incomes policies may work to increase the power of outsiders *vis-à-vis* insiders by reducing the influence of market imperfections and/or limiting the use of insider power.

The second element of New Keynesian theory which has important implications for prices and incomes type strategies is the focus on the persistence of involuntary unemployment following an adverse employment shock – that is, hysteresis. Corporatist policies increase the power of outsiders by encompassing them into the institutional structure. The cost to insiders will be reduced rents from the restriction of their power. The gain to the community at large is that high unemployment may persist for a shorter period of time.

NEW CLASSICAL ECONOMICS

New Classical economics consists of three basic elements. First, all markets clear; second, there is imperfect information; and third, expectations are rational. Although New Keynesians also assume rational expectations, discussion of this hypothesis has been delayed until now because it is such an essential element of New Classical economics. Historically, it developed out of consideration of Friedman's 'fooling' model, discussed above. To recap, if firms or workers wrongly perceive a general change in prices to be a real change, then shifts in aggregate demand can have real effects on output and unemployment. Friedman argued that workers were 'behind' in their expectations of price changes and took time to catch on – that is, they had been fooled. Thus inaccurate expectations can generate business cycles.

The premise that economic agents can persistently be fooled does not fit very well with the usual assumptions made in economics about rational behaviour. If workers kept making the same mistakes, surely they would catch on and adjust their behaviour accordingly. More formally, rational expectations are based on the premise that individuals form expectations about the behaviour of prices and other economic variables in such a way that all relevant information is considered. It follows that any differences between expected and actual prices must be random errors. If errors contain any systematic pattern, then this pattern could be used to improve estimated prices.

Robert Lucas, the American economist largely responsible for the development of New Classical economics, put together the rational expectations hypothesis with the other assumption of Classical economics, namely *market clearing*. However, although expectations may be rational, *imperfect information* also plays a crucial role. Economic agents can make quite large mistakes in expectations due to imperfect information, but as long as these errors are random, expectations are still rational.

To explore the New Classical model, it is necessary to make further use of the aggregate supply function, introduced in Chapter 9 but explored here in greater detail. This function is also sometimes called the Lucas supply function and suggests that the economy deviates from the natural rate of unemployment or output according to the extent to which expectations are met. Recall that:

$$Y = Y_F + \sigma(P - P^f)$$

where Y is actual output, Y_F is the natural or full employment output, P is the price level, P^f is the expected price level and σ is a positive constant. This is shown in Figure 10.7.

The vertical LRAS is the usual aggregate supply curve at the natural rate. The initial price level is given by P_0. If actual price rises are fully anticipated then $P = P^f$ and, since there has been no real change, output will remain at Y_F and the price level rises to P_1. If, however, the price level rises by more than the anticipated price then $P > P^f$ and supply will increase along $SRAS_0$. As the actual price rise is gradually perceived to be a general price rise and not a real price rise, the economy returns to Y_F but at the higher price P_1. At P_1 there is a new Lucas supply curve $SRAS_1$.

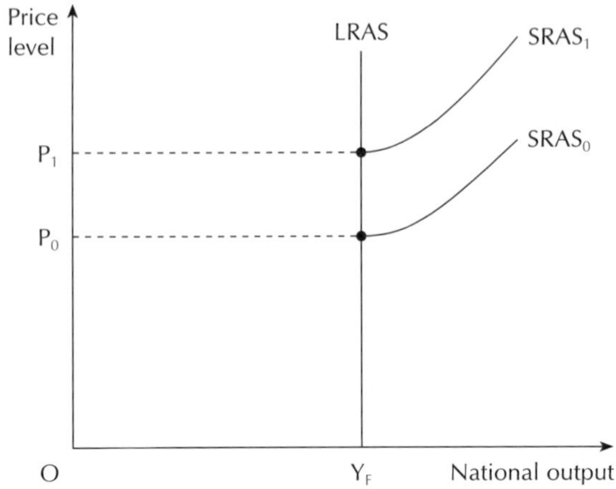

Figure 10.7 The Lucas aggregate supply curve.

The logic underlying a Lucas aggregate supply curve relates to the assumption of *imperfect information* by both firms and workers. For a firm to increase output, its price must rise above marginal cost. Whereas a firm may have good information about the price of its own output, it will only have somewhat imperfect knowledge of prices charged in other markets, including those for its own inputs. If there is a general increase in prices, a firm will observe an increase in its own price but will only gain information on other prices slowly.

Firms will do the best they can with the available information to avoid errors in estimating the general increase in prices. That is, they will make a rational expectation of the price level P^f. It was noted above that rational expectations can be very inaccurate, and therefore quite substantial real effects can be generated. The extent of these real effects depends on the general level of uncertainty, which prevents firms from distinguishing their own price rises from general price rises.

Clearly, the above analysis suggests that only shocks – events that are unanticipated – could be responsible for unemployment. However, somewhat more controversially, it also implies that much aggregate demand management is ineffective. The *policy ineffectiveness proposition* can be argued as follows. Suppose that when the economy is in recession the government's standard response is to increase aggregate demand by increasing the money supply. This is known as a *feedback rule*. The public will know that this is the common response of governments to recessions and will correctly anticipate a rise in the price level. Since the actual price level is equal to the expected price level, according to the Lucas supply curve, output will remain the same. It follows that only policy responses which are unanticipated – in other words, random shocks – can have any real effects. Clearly, random behaviour is not a particularly sound basis for economic policy.

If you find the above analysis to be somewhat unconvincing, then you would not be alone. Forecasts of inflation are readily available in the media and it is difficult to believe that previous recessions experienced by advanced economies were due to individuals being so wrong in their expectations of the price level. Further, experience shows that in fact monetary policy does have substantial real effects. Some economists therefore argue that a relatively smooth, and therefore anticipated, monetary rule may be more appropriate for controlling inflation.

REAL BUSINESS CYCLE THEORY

The real business cycle model was developed by New Classical macroeconomists dissatisfied with the plausibility of the Lucas theory of imperfect information. The business cycle is assumed to arise from real shocks rather than monetary shocks – that is, shifts in the aggregate supply curve rather than the aggregate demand curve. Rather than considering deviations in output from its natural rate due to deviations in the actual price level from the expected price level, as in the Lucas model, the natural rate itself changes. Changes in output result from shifts in the aggregate supply curve as a result of shifts in labour demand or labour supply.

Consider first a shift in labour demand due to, say, a technology shock or an oil price shock. This is shown in Figure 10.8. The shock causes a fall in labour productivity resulting in a shift in the labour demand curve from N_0^D to N_1^D. The real wage falls from $(W/P)_0$ to $(W/P)_1$ and employment

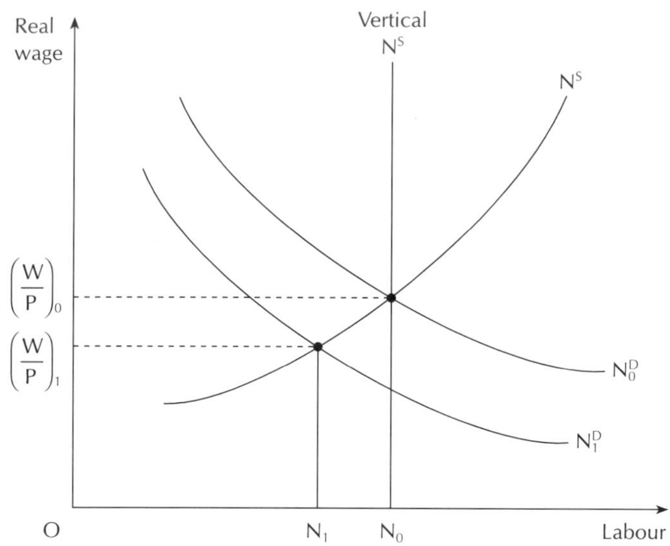

Figure 10.8 Effects of an adverse supply shock on labour demand and employment.

falls from N_0 to N_1. Real business cycle models are always in equilibrium and, therefore, the fall in employment must be voluntary, with workers choosing to work less at the lower wage with the possible anticipation of higher wages in the future. Note that if the supply of labour curve was vertical, the real wage would fall but there would be no reduction in employment.

A second explanation of business cycles is through shifts in the supply of labour. Consider, for example, an increase in interest rates. This makes it more attractive to work more, save now and consume more in the future. Thus the supply of labour curve shifts to the right, the real wage falls and employment rises.

Although most economists are willing to concede that shifts in labour demand and supply do occur and have significant effects on employment, they are rather sceptical about the potential of such shifts to create peaks and troughs in the business cycle of the order which is actually observed.

Summary

1. This chapter examined the macroeconomic theoretical implications of labour market arrangements.

2. Although the unemployment rate is the focus of much policy debate, examination of the concept and measurement of unemployment shows that the structure and duration of unemployment are important. Not all unemployment is the province of macroeconomics, and some components are better addressed by structural policy.

3. There are two major explanations of unemployment, namely Keynesian and Classical. Modern macroeconomic explanations of unemployment follow from these two views.

4. In the Classical model, unemployment arises through real wages being too high, thus resulting in excess supply of labour. If prices and wages were flexible, then real wages would fall to restore equilibrium.

5. The Keynesian view is that in a recession firms are unlikely to expand output in the face of falling prices, rising real wages and excess supply of goods. Therefore 'effective' demand for labour is less than 'notional' demand.

6. The natural, full employment or non-accelerating inflationary rate of unemployment is the rate of unemployment when the supply of labour is equal to the demand for labour.

7. The hysteresis view of the labour market suggests that the natural rate may itself be determined by trends in the history of unemployment. Thus policy-induced contractions in the economy may have long-lasting effects.

8. There is a clear link between long-term unemployment and hysteresis. As the duration of unemployment increases, the probability of finding employment

decreases. To the extent that the long-term unemployed are removed from the effective labour supply, the natural rate of unemployment increases as the proportion who are long-term unemployed increases.

9. New Keynesian theories attempt to explain wage and price rigidities as the result of rational decision making by firms and workers. The most important strands of New Keynesian economics are wage contracts, price adjustment costs, efficiency wages, insiders versus outsiders and unions.

10. New Classical economics takes the Classical model of the labour market, but adds to it the assumptions of imperfect information and rational expectations. This provides a rationale for the SRAS and LRAS curves of Chapter 9. The implications of the model are that only policy responses which are unexpected affect unemployment.

11. Real business cycle theories assume that business cycles arise from shifts in the labour demand and labour supply curves – that is, real shocks rather than monetary shocks.

12. Most economists are willing to include elements of both New Keynesian and New Classical theories as explanations of unemployment.

Further reading

Cuthbertson, K. and Taylor, M. (1987) *Macroeconomic Systems*, Oxford: Basil Blackwell, chapters 3 and 4.

Scarth, W. (1988) *Macroeconomics: An Introduction to Advanced Methods*, Toronto: Harcourt Brace Jovanovich, chapters 5 and 10.

11

Determinants of economic growth

Much of the preceding macroeconomic theory has been set within the time frame of the business cycle. The open economy models developed so far enable us to better understand short-run fluctuations in national output, employment and inflation and the role that fiscal, monetary and wages policies may play in influencing these variables over the course of any particular business cycle. Yet business cycles fluctuate around a *trend* rate of growth in real GDP, as depicted earlier in Chapter 2. The purpose of this chapter is to focus on the major influences on that trend rate of output growth.

Economic growth is simply defined as the percentage rate of increase in real aggregate output of an economy over time. What output growth means for an open economy can be interpreted through the tradable/non-tradable framework, outlined earlier in Chapter 4. Recall from that model that macroeconomic activity in a small open economy producing and consuming tradable and nontradable goods and services is captured by a supply side (the production possibilities frontier) and a demand side. As economic growth concerns the behaviour of the supply side of the economy, in the dependent economy framework growth implies an outward-shifting production frontier, as shown in Figure 11.1. If the economy was becoming even more open as a result of globalisation, there would be more output of tradable goods and services in relation to nontradables. This is conveyed by the shape of the higher production frontier in the diagram.

At the most fundamental level, certain institutional arrangements governing the way economic transactions are conducted throughout the economy and between residents and foreigners are necessary prerequisites for sustained economic growth. Nobel laureate and economic historian Douglass North, for instance, has proposed that economic growth in Europe was mainly conditional on the early establishment of a well-functioning legal system and clearly defined property rights.

The American economist Mancur Olson also highlighted the importance of institutional factors which govern economic exchange, but stressed

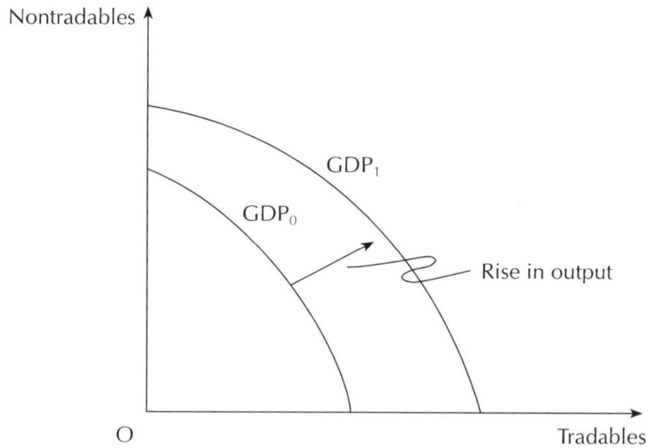

Figure 11.1 Economic growth in the tradables/nontradables framework.

institutional aspects which may slow the growth process in the most stable economies. Olson's argument is that special-interest groups successfully work through the political process to impede the effective operations of goods, services and factor markets. Layers of restrictions on economic production and exchange are then built up for the purpose of protecting special-interest groups. Such regulations stymie economic dynamism and retard the growth process.

Conventional growth analysis suggests it is also necessary to concentrate on the role of the main factor inputs to production in the economy to fully appreciate the main causes of long-term economic performance. These factor inputs are the domestic labour force, the economy's capital stock and the pace of technological advance. Before developing a framework for interpreting the relationship between factor inputs and the process of economic growth, let us first consider some general features of the growth record of advanced economies over recent decades.

RELATIVE GROWTH PERFORMANCE

One notable characteristic of the growth of GDP in advanced economies has been a change over time in the composition of domestic production, classified according to whether it is provided by the agricultural, industrial or services sector. In general, the relative importance of agricultural output diminished markedly in developed economies over the course of recent centuries, whereas the relative importance of the provision of services rose. Since the nineteenth century, for instance, the size of the agricultural sector in the United Kingdom, the United States, Japan and many other advanced economies has also shrunk dramatically as a source of employment.

Table 11.1 Relative income levels – select economies.

Country	*GNP per capita, 1998 (US$)*	*Average annual growth of GNP per capita (per cent), 1965–98*	*Average annual growth of GNP (per cent), 1965–98*
Argentina	8 030	0.4	1.9
Australia	20 640	1.7	3.2
Austria	26 830	2.6	2.9
Belgium	25 380	2.3	2.5
Brazil	4 630	2.2	4.3
Canada	19 170	1.8	3.1
China	750	6.8	8.6
Hong Kong (SAR)	23 660	5.5	7.4
Denmark	33 040	1.9	2.2
Finland	24 280	2.4	2.8
France	24 210	2.1	2.6
Germany	26 570	n.a.	n.a.
India	440	2.7	4.9
Indonesia	640	4.7	6.8
Ireland	18 710	3.0	3.8
Italy	20 090	2.5	2.7
Japan	32 350	3.5	4.3
Korea, Republic of	8 600	6.6	8.1
Malaysia	3 670	4.1	6.8
Mexico	3 840	1.5	3.9
Netherlands	24 780	1.9	2.6
New Zealand	14 600	0.7	1.7
Nigeria	300	0.0	3.0
Norway	34 310	3.0	3.5
Russian Federation	2 260	n.a.	n.a.
Saudi Arabia	6 910	0.5	5.4
Singapore	30 170	6.4	8.4
South Africa	3 310	0.1	2.4
Spain	14 100	2.3	3.0
Sweden	25 580	1.4	1.7
Switzerland	39 980	1.2	1.6
Thailand	2 160	5.0	7.3
United Kingdom	21 410	1.9	2.1
United States	29 240	1.6	2.6

Source Adapted from World Bank, *2000 World Development Indicators*, 2000 (tables 1.1, 1.4).

At the same time, the relative share of services in GDP (which include the provision of education, health, business and public services) has substantially offset declines in the relative share of agricultural output in GDP. The size of the manufacturing sectors of advanced economies has also diminished significantly over recent decades.

When making international comparisons of economic growth and welfare, it is obviously necessary to compare each nation's output performance on a *per capita* basis. China, for instance, has a much larger GDP than Belgium, but the average mainland Chinese is not nearly as well off as the average Belgian, if comparisons are made on the basis of income per head. Table 11.1 includes data on the relative income levels of selected OECD and East Asian economies.

A key ratio often used to examine an economy's growth behaviour and level of development is the *capital-output ratio*. The capital-output ratio is derived by simply dividing the value of the capital stock by the value of aggregate output over a given year. In developed economies, the capital-output ratio has remained fairly steady, in the vicinity of 4.0, over recent years. This ratio suggests that for the economy as a whole, it is necessary to have about four units of real capital to generate one unit of output each year.

Apparently small differences in annual average growth rates between nations can have quite a significant impact on relative living standards over longer periods. Take the often cited example of the United Kingdom versus the United States. In 1870, real GDP per capita was 20 per cent higher in the United Kingdom than in the United States. However, the situation has since reversed dramatically, with the average American having a real income more than 35 per cent higher than the average Briton. More surprisingly, perhaps, this huge difference in relative living standards arose even though the annual average growth rate was only about half a percentage point higher in the United States (at around 1.8 per cent) than in the United Kingdom (at around 1.3 per cent) over more than a century.

How this turnaround could happen even though growth rates did not seem that dissimilar is explained by the arithmetic phenomenon of compounding. The effect of compounding is illustrated using a simple numerical example, as shown in Table 11.2. In this example, it is assumed that two economies have the same initial value of output, valued in year one at 100 units. However, one economy grows continuously at 5 per cent per annum, whereas the other grows continuously at 7 per cent.

What this arithmetic reveals is that even over periods as short as a decade, the real values of each economy's output can quickly diverge, due to relatively small differences in growth rates. In the above example, growth at 5 per cent compounded through increases output by close to two thirds

Table 11.2 The effect of compounding.

	At 5 per cent	*At 7 per cent*
At year 1	100	100
After 5 years	128	140
After 10 years	163	197

of the original amount after a decade. In the other case, growth of 7 per cent compounded through almost doubles output in a decade. The faster growing economy is substantially better off than the slower one after only ten years.

Lest the figures chosen for the above example seem a little removed from reality, it is worth noting from Table 11.1 that many East Asian countries such as Hong Kong, Indonesia, Malaysia, Singapore, South Korea and Thailand actually recorded growth rates in the order of 7 per cent or more in the decades preceding the so-called 'Asian crisis'. In contrast, the average growth rate in OECD economies has only been between 3 and 4 per cent. If such trends were to return, the arithmetic of compounding dictates that living standards in OECD economies, measured in terms of income per capita, would eventually fall below those of the East Asian economies.

Concern about being left behind in the economic growth stakes has therefore stimulated policy discussion in many economies about the best means of improving growth. To understand the causes of economic growth, it is necessary to examine more closely how economists account for changes in output over time.

THE MACROECONOMIC PRODUCTION FUNCTION

A well-known framework for accounting for the main sources of output change in capitalist economies was developed by the American Nobel laureate Robert Solow. The starting point for the analysis of economic growth in this framework is a macroeconomic production function.

A macroeconomic production function simply relates the main inputs to the production process (which we recall are labour, capital and technology) to the generation of output, or the aggregate supply side of the economy. Recall that a macroeconomic production function underlay the long-run aggregate supply curve of the earlier AD-AS analysis which was used to model the dynamic effects of macroeconomic policy on equilibrium output and the domestic price level. Here, however, we abstract from the behaviour of the domestic price level and essentially examine the implications for GDP of changes in the quantities of real factor inputs over time.

The macroeconomic production function can be respecified in broader terms as:

$$Y = T \cdot f(K, L) \tag{11.1}$$

where T represents technology or multifactor productivity, K is the capital stock (defined to include land and buildings) and L is the labour force, usually measured in terms of number of hours worked. This formula simply suggests that given quantities of the main physical factor inputs, capital and labour, as well as improvements in technology, combine to produce aggregate output in the economy.

MACROECONOMIC GROWTH ACCOUNTING

The contribution which capital, labour and technical change make to changes in output over time can also be analysed by deriving what is known as the *growth accounting equation*. If the macroeconomic production function is characterised by constant returns to scale, then multiplying the quantities of all inputs to aggregate production by some percentage multiplies national output to the same extent. For instance, increasing the quantity of all inputs by 10 per cent will raise aggregate output by 10 per cent. Using this assumption, it is possible to express any change in GDP over time as:

$$\Delta Y = \Delta T\ f(K, L) + MP_K \Delta K + MP_L \Delta L \tag{11.2}$$

where MP_K and MP_L are the marginal products of capital and labour. Recall from Chapter 5 that the MP_K represents the addition to output from using an extra unit of capital. Similarly, the MP_L is the addition to output by employing one more worker. If Equation (11.2) above is divided by Equation (11.1), then it follows that:

$$\frac{\Delta Y}{Y} = \frac{\Delta T}{T} + \frac{MP_K}{Y}\Delta K + \frac{MP_L}{Y}\Delta L \tag{11.3}$$

The most common type of macroeconomic production function is known as the Cobb–Douglas production function. It is specified as:

$$Y = T \cdot K^{\gamma} L^{\beta} \tag{11.4}$$

where γ and β are weights signifying the contributions of capital and labour to production. If the economy exhibits constant returns to scale, then it follows that $\gamma + \beta = 1$ and hence that $\beta = (1 - \gamma)$. The value of the parameters γ and β in the Cobb–Douglas production function also indicate the relative shares of national income which accrue to capital and labour in the economy, assuming that all goods and factor markets are competitive.

Using a Cobb–Douglas production function, Equation (11.3) above can be further simplified to:

$$\hat{Y} = \hat{T} + \gamma\hat{K} + (1 - \gamma)\hat{L} \tag{11.5}$$

where the 'hats' above the variables again indicate the percentage growth in the variables over time. Hence, Equation (11.5) shows that economic growth essentially depends on improvements in technology and the rate of increase in the supplies of capital and labour as inputs to production, each weighted by income shares.

The national accounts of many OECD nations actually measure the relative income share of capital and labour, that is, the values of γ and $(1 - \gamma)$. The share of capital (γ) is approximated by the measure of gross operating surplus and can be around 0.25, in which case the share of labour $(1 - \gamma)$ measured as wages and salaries would be around 0.75. Note that according to the above growth accounting equation, the workforce would need to increase by around 1.3 per cent per year to produce an overall 1.0 per cent rise in annual real GDP. This is because, from the equation, $(0.75 \times \hat{L})$ only equals 1.0 per cent if $\hat{L}$, labour force growth, equals 1.3 per cent.

MULTIFACTOR PRODUCTIVITY

Empirical studies have shown that in OECD economies it is usually the extent of technical change which accounts for much of the growth in national output over time. The technical change term, T, is also often referred to as *multifactor productivity* (MFP). In effect, MFP explains growth in output that is not explained by growth in the main tangible factor inputs of capital and labour. Because MFP can be derived empirically as a remainder (by simply taking away the values of the contribution of labour and capital to total output growth), it is sometimes referred to as the 'Solow residual', after its discoverer.

In this traditional growth accounting approach, technical change, as captured in the MFP term, is considered to be exogenous. This way of thinking about technical change is also reflected in what is called *real business cycle* (RBC) theory, which has been mentioned in earlier chapters. RBC theory treats random fluctuations in MFP as the main source of fluctuations in aggregate output. RBC theorists argue that business cycles should be explained with reference to the same basic factors which explain long-run growth. Hence, RBC theory represents an aggregate supply-side approach to examining fluctuations in the business cycle. This contrasts with the aggregate demand-side emphasis of Keynesian approaches to the business cycle.

At this stage, RBC theory is not widely accepted as an explanation of business cycles, however. A major criticism of the approach is that it requires frequent technical regress to explain recessions. Yet, it is difficult to imagine how technology can actually go backwards on a fairly regular basis and on an economy-wide scale.

The measure of MFP in the context of traditional growth theory is quite broad in scope. Apart from straight technological advance arising from new inventions, it includes a range of other key influences, such as improved management expertise, the effect of government regulations and, very importantly, education of the workforce. Empirical estimates of the sources of economic growth imply that improved levels of education and training play a very major role in economic development. Hence, *human capital* (H), the educational and skill level of the workforce, is sometimes separately identified as an input to aggregate production, such that the general form of the macroeconomic production function then becomes:

$$Y = T \cdot f(K, H, L)$$

If human capital is included as a distinct input to aggregate production, this more narrowly defines MFP and hence reduces the size of its contribution to growth. Separate identification of the contribution of human capital has not yet become the standard practice of statistical agencies, however, as human capital is in practice very difficult to quantify with any precision.

FACTORS INFLUENCING GROWTH

The standard growth accounting equation, Equation (11.5), highlights and identifies the three main sources of growth. Let us now consider important features of each of these sources, beginning with the contribution of the labour force.

Most advanced economies have experienced a relatively high rate of population increase since the Second World War through natural increase and immigration. Those immigrants who do not enter the workforce also affect an economy's growth performance by influencing the size of the denominator of the GDP per capita measure. Post-war immigration rates have been high for instance, for the United Kingdom, the United States, Canada, Australia and New Zealand. Through immigration, an economy's labour force has been substantially larger than it would be if it relied solely on its natural rate of population increase.

The participation of women in the workforces of advanced economies has also increased markedly over recent decades. The majority of women of working age are now employed, whereas just twenty years ago, in some economies only around half of women of working age participated in the paid labour force, with the remainder performing domestic duties.

The next major source of output growth to describe is the contribution of the economy's physical capital stock to production. An economy's capital stock needs to expand continually over time through domestic and foreign investment in order to sustain the productivity of its workforce. Recall that in an open economy with a capital account surplus, total saving available for capital accumulation is made up of both domestic and foreign components. International capital movements thereby enable a nation's capital stock to be larger than it would be if it relied only on domestic saving. If real capital accumulates at a faster rate, this suggests that higher rates of growth in domestic output and income are possible.

Economies with higher investment shares of GDP tend to grow the fastest. In most economies, domestic investment is mainly undertaken by the private sector, although public sector investment is also significant. Private sector investment has averaged between 20 and 25 per cent of total national expenditure in OECD economies since 1950. However, the quality of the investment spending is important, as well as the quantity. For instance, at times there may be too much private investment in dwellings and office buildings and not enough investment in business equipment, machinery and information technology.

Public sector investment as a share of national expenditure has generally declined in OECD economies over more recent decades. Public sector investment, often referred to as spending on an economy's *infrastructure*, includes the provision by public sector authorities of services such as electric power, telecommunications, water supply, sewerage, garbage collection, roads, railways, ports and airports.

Some recent empirical studies suggest that a falling share of public infrastructure expenditure, particularly on highways, bridges and airports, may adversely affect overall productivity in these economies. However, it should be recognised that public investment usually complements private investment. Building more bridges and paving more footpaths will not, of itself, boost overall productivity in the economy in the long run if such spending is not accompanied by higher private investment.

The source of growth about which least is known is the role of technical change and the true nature of MFP. In essence, MFP as conventionally measured, inclusive of human capital improvements, captures all those influences on economic growth which are not embodied in new physical capital accumulation and higher workforce participation. For this reason, the size of MFP is sometimes referred to as a 'measure of our ignorance' about the growth process.

One key influence on MFP growth is the degree of research and development (R&D) activity of firms, as well as the research activity undertaken by scientists and academics at publicly funded institutions, such as universities. The actual impact of improvements in technology on aggregate output are hard to pinpoint, however. For instance, it is obvious that the computer and internet revolutions of the 1980s and 1990s greatly assisted in the economy, but by just how much is difficult to say.

Institutional arrangements governing workplace relations between employees and employers also affect the economy's overall efficiency and productivity. For example, an economy characterised by high levels of industrial disputation and strike activity is unlikely to grow as fast as an economy characterised by relatively harmonious employee–management relations.

THE DYNAMICS OF ECONOMIC GROWTH

In modeling short-run national income determination, macroeconomic analysis stresses the importance of investment flows on the aggregate demand side of the economy, yet presumes an invariant capital stock on the supply side. For instance, in the earlier aggregate demand–aggregate supply analysis, higher investment increases aggregate demand, but has no effect on short- or even long-run aggregate supply. On the other hand, so-called *neoclassical growth theory* models national output and income generation as a continuously smooth process, whose path inevitably leads to a long-run stationary or steady state. However, to better understand how domestic saving and productivity jointly determine the pattern of output growth over shorter periods, we use discrete time analysis in what follows.

First assume the following basic relations:

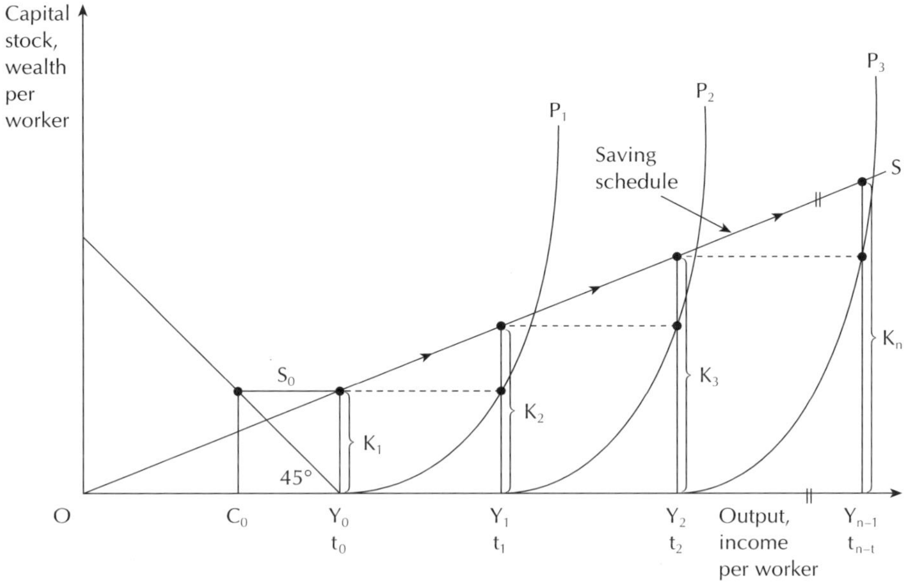

Figure 11.2 Capital accumulation and income generation.

$$C_0 + S_0 = Y_0 \tag{11.6}$$

$$S_t = aY_t = I_t \qquad 0 < a < 1 \tag{11.7}$$

$$K_t = K_{t-1} + I_t \tag{11.8}$$

$$Y_t = T_t \cdot P(K_{t-1}) \qquad \text{for } t > 0,\ MP_K > 0 \tag{11.9}$$

$$r_t = MP_K \tag{11.10}$$

where C_0, S_0 and Y_0 are the initial levels of consumption, saving and income per worker, a is the propensity to save out of income, I_t is investment per worker, K_t is the capital stock per worker, T_t is total-factor productivity, r_t is the interest rate and MP_K is the marginal product of capital. All variables are expressed in real terms.

With reference to Figure 11.2, initial consumption is C_0 out of initial income of Y_0, as shown on the horizontal axis. This yields saving of S_0, which through the 45° line, determines the size of the capital stock for use between t_0 and t_1. With capital stock per worker of K_1, the volume of aggregate output and income per worker is measured as the distance between Y_0 and Y_1. The saving schedule, S, depicts incremental saving during this time, which, as additional investment, augments the original capital stock thereby creating a higher level of real capital for use next period.

This framework abstracts from capital consumption although depreciation can easily be incorporated into Figure 11.2. Note, however, that the net saving schedule would then become progressively flatter over time as an increasing proportion of saving would have to be put aside to maintain the capital stock. In the long run, when depreciation completely exhausts domestic saving, the saving schedule becomes horizontal.[1]

The distance between Y_1 and Y_2 measures output per worker between t_1 and t_2. The stock of capital, K_2, for use between t_1 and t_2 is therefore comprised of the inherited stock plus the extra saving and investment over this time. Cumulative output per worker is the distance from the origin, and positive period-to-period output growth is reflected in the distance between any Y_t and Y_{t+1} exceeding that between any Y_{t-1} and Y_t. Figure 11.2 therefore shows that output growth per worker stems from the economy's saving rate, as well as the curvature of the period-specific capital productivity curve, each of which incorporates the latest technological advances and the many other factors affecting multifactor productivity.

The set of capital productivity curves ($P_1, P_2 \ldots P_n$) also satisfy the condition that the marginal product of capital would approach zero if the size of the capital stock approached infinity. As suggested in Equation (11.10), the slope of any production curve at the point of intersection above any Y_t reflects both the marginal productivity of capital and the real domestic interest rate. Hence, the more productive capital is, the flatter is the production curve and the higher is the domestic rate of return on capital.

HIGHER SAVING VERSUS PRODUCTIVITY

It is evident from Figure 11.2 that the rate of saving and productivity together determine macroeconomic performance over short, as well as longer, time spans. A question therefore arises as to which source of growth should be given the higher policy priority – increasing national saving or improving productivity? Figure 11.3 extends the geometry to show that a targeted rise in output per worker, measured by the distance between Y_3 and Y_3^*, can be achieved by either raising the rate of saving (shifting S to S*) over the previous interval or, instead, by improving the overall productivity of the inherited capital stock, K_3 (shifting P_3 to P_3^*).

The slope of the ray joining the start of the capital productivity curve P_3 and the production point itself reflects the economy's capital-output ratio. The flatter the slope of this ray, the smaller is the capital-output ratio and the greater the rise in productivity and income per worker, for unchanged saving behaviour. This suggests that higher output may be attained more easily through improved productivity rather than higher saving, because saving over any interval will only be a relatively small proportion of the pre-existing capital stock in advanced economies. Furthermore, higher productivity generates higher output more quickly than higher saving since the latter will only work to raise output and income per worker after a lag.

The importance of productivity growth in determining output and income in advanced economies stems from the fact that multifactor productivity gains imply more efficient use of the entire capital stock. Accordingly, this implies that economic measures in advanced economies aimed at raising

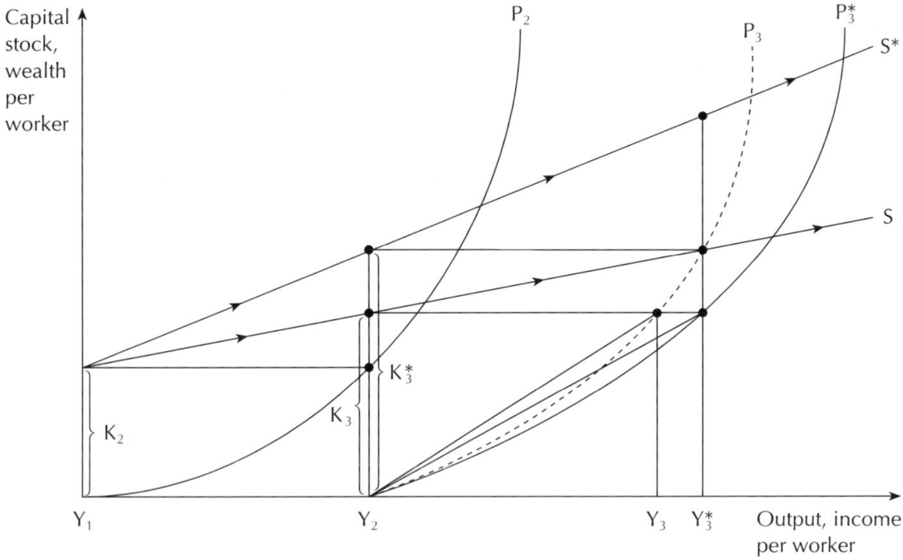

Figure 11.3 Higher saving versus productivity improvement.

multifactor productivity such as structural policies that strengthen competition between firms, warrant a higher priority as a means to higher national income, than attempts to boost national saving.

The discrete time geometric framework outlined above presents a useful way of conveying how the arrows of causality between saving and economic growth run both ways. It shows that both the rate of accumulation and the productivity of new and pre-existing capital play a role in determining an economy's short- and long-run pattern of output and income growth. In this way, the model helps explain the apparent paradox that advanced low-saving economies, such as the United States, the United Kingdom, Australia and Canada, can persistently sustain higher long-term growth rates than high-saving nations, such as Japan, due to better productivity performance.

Unlike standard Keynesian macroeconomic models of short-run income determination that neglect the capital stock altogether, the above geometry also makes clear that the ever-changing size and productivity of an economy's capital stock helps explain short-run output variation. However, technical regress is not proposed as the primary cause of cyclical downswings, as real business cycle theory suggests. Other factors also obviously contribute to business cycle fluctuations, such as discrepancies that arise between saving and production decisions made by firms and households *ex ante* and output and accumulation outcomes *ex post*.

Yet in the above framework, there are no within-period coordination failures and agents fulfil the expectations they have at the beginning of each period by the end of that period. Expectations and their formation also obviously remain an important link between the macroeconomics of the short and longer runs. Nonetheless, the framework bridges a gap between standard short-run analysis, which ignores the dynamics of saving, investment, productivity and wealth, and the long run when factor inputs change.

POLICIES TO INCREASE GROWTH

What policy measures can governments implement to improve an economy's long-run growth performance? Since economic growth, by definition, means increasing aggregate output or supply, most policy proposals are ultimately directed at increasing the contributions made to aggregate production by labour, capital or technical change. Note that here economic policy is aiming to shift the LRAS curve of our earlier AD–AS analysis rightward over time. This contrasts with the activist use of fiscal and monetary policy to shift the AD schedule for the purpose of managing the business cycle over shorter periods.

In the 1980s a group of American economists proposed a set of economic policies which were intended to shift the macroeconomic policy focus away from aggregate demand management toward the supply side. This gave rise to a body of thought known as *supply-side economics*. Foremost among the proposals of the supply-siders were policies aimed at promoting greater overall efficiency throughout the economy, by means of deregulating government controls over business and lowering taxes to improve work incentives.

The ideas of the supply-siders directly or indirectly influenced policy-makers in OECD economies, especially the notion that excessive government regulation and control of economic activity was retarding economic growth. The *structural reform* agenda put in place in the 1980s can be seen as a policy awakening to the macroeconomic importance of the supply side. Financial deregulation, less protection of domestic industry by means of tariffs and quotas on imports, privatisation of government assets and the internationalisation of economies' capital markets were the first steps. These were followed in some economies by further policy initiatives to make labour markers more flexible, improve air, rail and water transport efficiency, and encourage greater competition in post and telecommunications.

The benefits of economic growth seem fairly obvious. Higher income per capita allows higher consumption levels and hence an improved standard of living. As a macroeconomic policy objective, however, striving for higher growth rates is not without its critics. Conservationists in particular argue that higher economic growth rates tend to increase pollution, which poses a threat to the environment and the ecological system. In reply, however, proponents of growth would suggest that the best way to control pollution is not to stop economic growth as such, but to address pollution at its source. This may be achieved, for instance, through clearer definitions of property rights over air, land and water space or by governments imposing specific taxes at the individual enterprise level.

For open economies, factors of production continually flow across political boundaries. Policies aimed at increasing the scale of international resource flows by allowing freer trade in goods, services and assets are generally growth enhancing. As mentioned in the above discussion, higher immigration rates, for instance, can raise the contribution of the labour force to growth. Additionally, allowing free international capital movements to enlarge the size of the domestic capital stock can raise the contribution of capital to growth. Finally, allowing multinational corporations to freely establish production and distribution operations in the domestic economy can accelerate technical advance through the transfer of knowledge about new products and processes. These strictly international contributions to growth in an open economy are treated more explicitly in the next chapter.

Summary

1. Economic growth is simply the percentage change in an economy's output over time. International comparisons of nations' economic welfare are made on the basis of GDP per capita.
2. Rankings of GDP per capita can change quite dramatically over longer periods of time because of the impact of compounding, even when differences in growth rates seem quite small.
3. To understand why economic growth occurs, it is necessary to consider the role of the aggregate inputs to production (technology, capital and labour). The relation between factor inputs and economy-wide output is captured in a macroeconomic production function.
4. With a Cobb–Douglas macroeconomic production function, constant returns to scale and competitive conditions, the growth accounting approach suggests that aggregate output growth is explained by the degree of technical change as well as growth in capital and labour inputs, weighted by their relative shares of national income.
5. Multifactor productivity (MFP) is another term for technical change. MFP is usually defined broadly to capture all influences on an economy's overall efficiency, including levels of management expertise, government regulation, education and work skills.
6. Human capital, the knowledge base of the workforce, can in theory be separately identified as an input to macroeconomic production.
7. Saving improves economic growth, but growth also induces saving. Both the rate of saving and the productivity of capital influence the pattern of output and income growth through time.
8. Supply-side economics proposes that aggregate output can be raised by reducing unnecessary government regulation of business and by lowering taxes as a means of improving the incentive to work.

9. Structural reform policies also represent a supply-side response aimed at improving an economy's growth performance.

10. Structural reforms have involved deregulation of financial markets, encouraging greater international trade in goods and services, making labour markets more flexible and improving the efficiency of public transport and telecommunications.

Note

1. This of course corresponds to the relationship between saving and depreciation in the steady state of neoclassical growth theory.

Further reading

Lucas, R. (1988) 'On the mechanics of economic development', *Journal of Monetary Economics*, **22**, 3–42.

Romer, P. (1994) 'The origins of endogenous growth', *Journal of Economic Perspectives*, **8** (1), 3–22.

Solow, R. (1994) 'Perspectives on growth theory', *Journal of Economic Perspectives*, **8** (1), 45–54.

12

Economic growth in open economies

Earlier chapters of this book have mainly examined the international macroeconomic implications of globally integrated goods, services and financial asset markets. However, cross-border movements of capital, labour and technology, the main inputs to economy-wide production, also profoundly affect an open economy's performance.

To further understand why, this chapter extends the growth theory of the previous chapter to include foreign investment flows. It examines the macroeconomic implications of capital movements between small economies and between two large economies such as the United States and Japan. It then focuses on foreign direct investment and addresses some of the major points which have surfaced in policy discussion about the significance of current account imbalances, international capital flows and foreign debt levels, before using national balance sheet analysis to put international investment positions into macroeconomic perspective.

CAPITAL MOVEMENTS AND GROWTH

1. The small economy

The growth geometry used in the previous chapter can be extended to model accumulation and growth in small open economies facing an exogenous world interest rate. The key difference here is that in an open economy, capital accumulation is not constrained by the domestic saving rate. Foreign saving can be borrowed to finance the acquisition of more real capital, enabling the capital stock to exceed domestic saving to the extent of any international capital account surplus, or be less than domestic saving to the extent of any international capital account deficit.

The pattern of output and income per worker that emerges for an economy experiencing a capital account surplus and international investment is shown in Figure 12.1. In this figure, the initial capital stock of K_2 yields output of

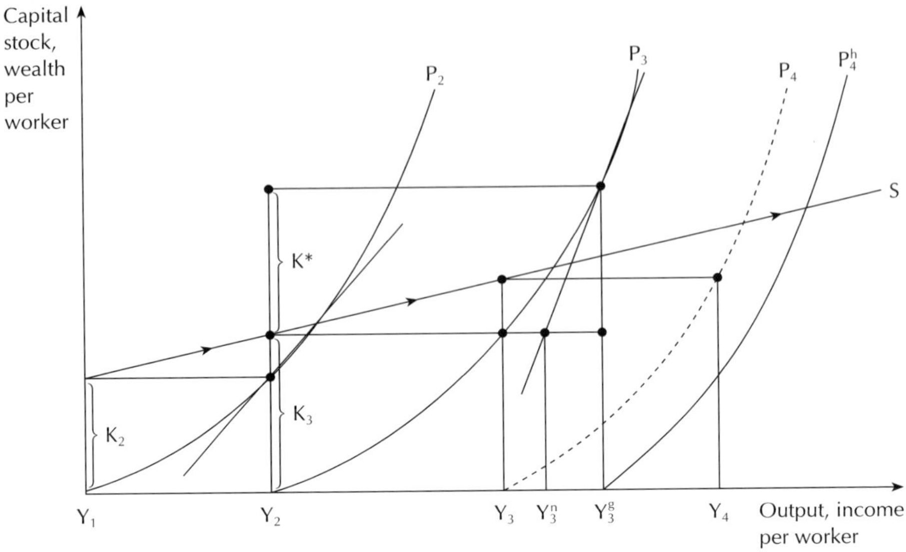

Figure 12.1 Income growth with foreign capital inflow.

Y_2. The marginal product of capital is reflected in the slope of the capital productivity curve P_2, which in equilibrium for a closed economy, is equal to the slope of the tangent reflecting the real domestic interest rate. Under these circumstances, domestic saving and investment over the first interval shown would enlarge the capital stock from K_2 to K_3, for use at the beginning of the next period.

However, in an open economy, the capital stock can grow by more than K_3 if foreign saving is borrowed at the world interest rate to acquire imported capital equipment. Foreign investment can therefore increase to the point where the productivity of capital, captured at any point by the slope of the P_3 schedule, equals the world interest rate. The world interest rate sets the slope of the tangent for a small open economy. The lower the world interest rate, the steeper is the tangent line. In the figure, the given world interest rate and tangent to P_3 implies foreign inward investment of K*.

With extra capital in place, national output and income of the open economy can then exceed the aggregate output and income that domestic saving alone would permit. Hence, by drawing on capital accumulated in the rest of the world, higher aggregate output of Y_3^g can be produced in the open economy, compared to Y_3 produced in an autarky economy employing the smaller capital stock, K_3.

Note, however, that for an open economy which draws on foreign saving, national income per worker will not rise by as much as national output per worker because the interest paid to foreign lenders for the use of borrowed funds has to be deducted from the value of national production. The difference between output and interest payments abroad therefore yields a national income of Y_3^n in the first interval. Nevertheless, the volume of

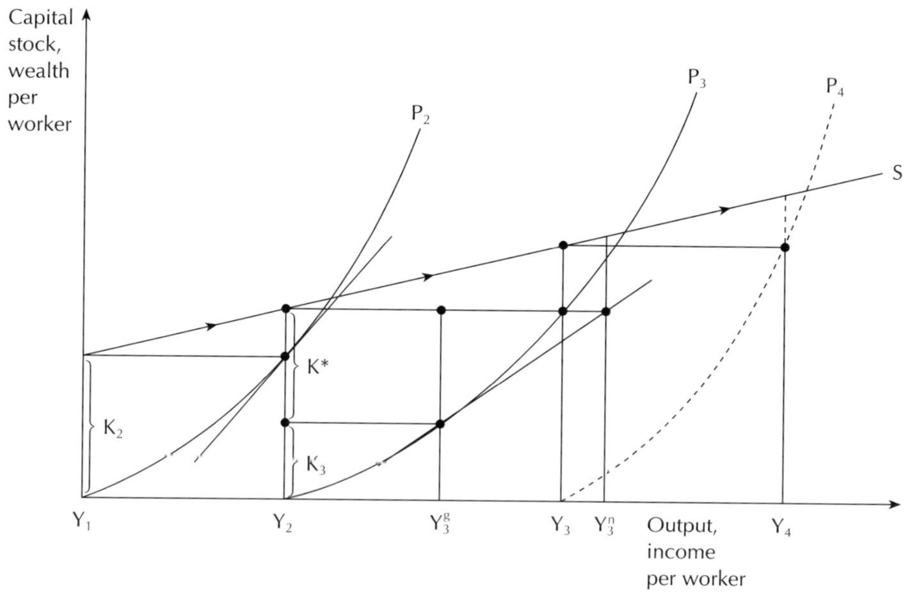

Figure 12.2 Income growth with capital outflow abroad.

national income remains higher than autarky national output and income, demonstrating that external borrowing to augment domestic capital accumulation is growth enhancing.

It also follows that national income can grow by more than otherwise if there is outward foreign investment – lending abroad and capital exporting by the home economy. Indeed, an open economy can quite easily switch from experiencing inward foreign investment to experiencing outward foreign investment if the productivity of capital in use domestically falls below the world interest rate. Under these circumstances, part of domestic saving can then be loaned abroad at the world interest rate to fund capital accumulation in the rest of the world, as depicted in Figure 12.2.

In this case, national income may exceed output by the difference between Y_3^g and Y_3^n. Under these circumstances, only K_3 of domestic saving is used for domestic production. The remainder is used for production abroad and generates additional national income, shown for the home economy as the distance between Y_3^g and Y_3^n. Note again, however, that with free capital movements, national income for the open economy can be higher, at Y_3^n than it would be if domestic saving had been solely used to fund domestic capital accumulation. Reliance on domestic saving alone would yield national output and income of Y_3. In short, the framework shows that capital account imbalances can enhance national income growth under quite plausible assumptions, irrespective of whether these imbalances appear as external deficits or surpluses.

If there are restrictions on international borrowing, lending and real capital movements, this would prevent cross-border flows of saving being channelled to their most productive use and hence allow different rates of return on capital to persist indefinitely. Such restrictions on international capital movements would impose identifiable economic welfare costs on economies that adopted them. This welfare cost is actually measurable as the difference between the national income that arises with full international capital mobility and the national income that arises without it.

In summary, the open economy analogue of the growth framework of the previous chapter demonstrates the macroeconomic gains from international capital flows. It also shows how external account imbalances arise, as the difference between an economy's own saving and investment, and how foreign capital flows can play a key role in raising national income for both borrower and lender countries.

2. Two large economies

Let us now consider the case where economies or regions are large enough to influence the international rate of return on capital. For instance, the macroeconomic effects of international capital movements can be examined for two regions, as shown in Figure 12.3. This diagram again highlights the contribution of real international investment flows. It reveals how such flows simultaneously bestow macroeconomic benefits on an economy or geographical region which hosts foreign investment and on the economy or region from which the international investment is sourced.

The figure depicts the combined real capital stock of the two economies, one a net importer of capital, the other a net exporter. For the sake of exposition, we will call the capital importer the United States and the

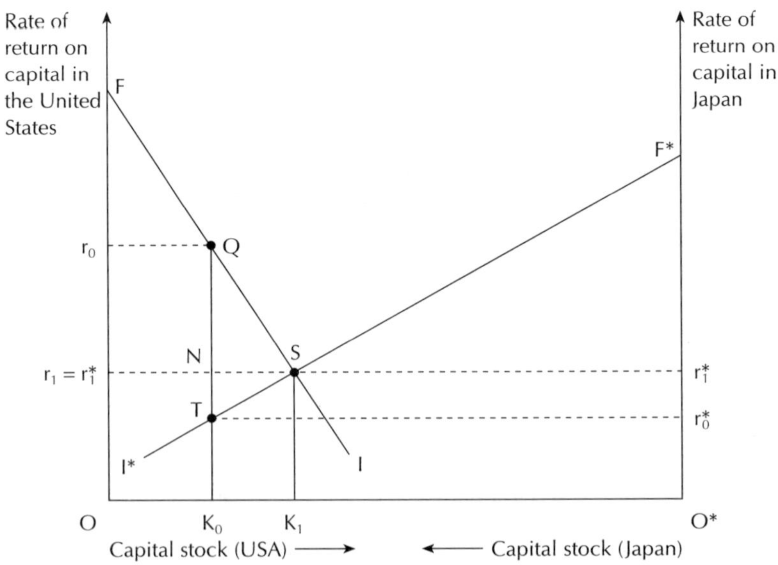

Figure 12.3 National income gains from foreign investment.

capital exporter Japan. The combined capital stock of the United States and Japan is OO*, the length of the bottom axis of the figure. Of the total capital stock, OK_0 is initially located in the United States and the remainder is located in Japan. Note that values on the horizontal axis are read from left to right for the United States and from right to left for Japan.

The FI and F*I* schedules reflect the respective marginal products of real capital in the United States and in Japan. For instance, the marginal product of real capital in the United States is r_0 when its capital stock is OK_0. It is r_0^* in Japan when its capital stock is O^*K_0.

In the absence of international capital movements, the total area under the FI schedule (area OK_0QF) is the value of the United States' output or GDP. Of this, OK_0Qr_0 is the income of the owners of capital, whereas the rest (r_0QF) is the income of the other main factor of production, labour. In Japan, under capital autarky conditions, the return on capital is lower than in the United States ($r_0^* < r_0$). Japan's GDP is $O^*K_0TF^*$ of which $O^*K_0Tr_0^*$ is the share of national income accruing to owners of capital, whereas the remainder of national income is ($TF^*r_0^*$) earned by workers.

Now assume that international capital inflows to the United States are permitted as a result of the abolition of domestic barriers which had prevented foreign investment flows between the two economies. At the same time, barriers to the export of capital from Japan are also abolished, allowing capital to move to where it can earn the highest return. Since the real return on the United States' capital as measured by its marginal product is higher than the corresponding return in Japan ($r_0 > r_0^*$), real capital will flow into the United States from Japan.

This trade in real capital continues until there is equality between the two rates of return on capital ($r_1 = r_1^*$). At that point, the United States' real capital stock is OK_1, higher than the original capital stock of OK_0. GDP for the United States is also now higher at area OK_1SF. Out of this amount however, area K_0K_1SN is paid to Japanese investors for the use of their capital. The same rectangular measure represents the sum of income paid abroad, which must then be subtracted from US GDP to give US national income.

The overall net gain in the United States' national income is the triangular amount NSQ in Figure 12.3. In Japan, national income rises in net terms by NST as the income received from the investment in Japan is added to Japan's GDP (now area $O^*K_1SF^*$). From the perspective of the two regions as a whole, the international movement of capital therefore benefits both the host economy and the economy transferring capital abroad. In short, by altering the international allocation of physical capital, foreign investment flows can raise combined income.

It is also important to note that the above analysis could be done all over again by allowing greater international labour mobility, instead of international capital mobility. Hence, it can be adapted to examine the real macroeconomic effects of the immigration of skilled labour from abroad. For instance, if the domestic and foreign physical capital stocks were held constant, but labour was allowed to migrate internationally to earn the highest rate of return, there would be similar macroeconomic welfare gains. The economy paying relatively high real wages because the return to labour was high would experience immigration, an inflow of workers, whereas the rest of the world would experience emigration. This assumes, however, that the human capital of migrating workers is at least at the same skill level as that of workers at home.

FOREIGN DIRECT INVESTMENT

The preceding analysis of the macroeconomic effects of foreign investment made no distinction between *direct* and *portfolio* foreign investment. As defined in Figure 12.4, direct foreign investment implies that foreigners can exert significant influence over the management of a domestically located enterprise in which their capital has been invested. Ever increasing flows of foreign direct investment are another indicator of rising global economic integration at the firm and industry levels. Direct foreign investment is usually a smaller share of total foreign investment flows than portfolio investment for advanced economies and occurs through the establishment of subsidiaries of multinational corporations (MNCs). The operations of Ford in the United Kingdom provide a good example.

Table 12.1 lists the top 25 non-financial MNCs in the world, valued according to the size of their assets measured in US$ billion. The range of global industries in which these MNCs have specialised is quite wide, and includes oil, motor vehicle and electronics production.

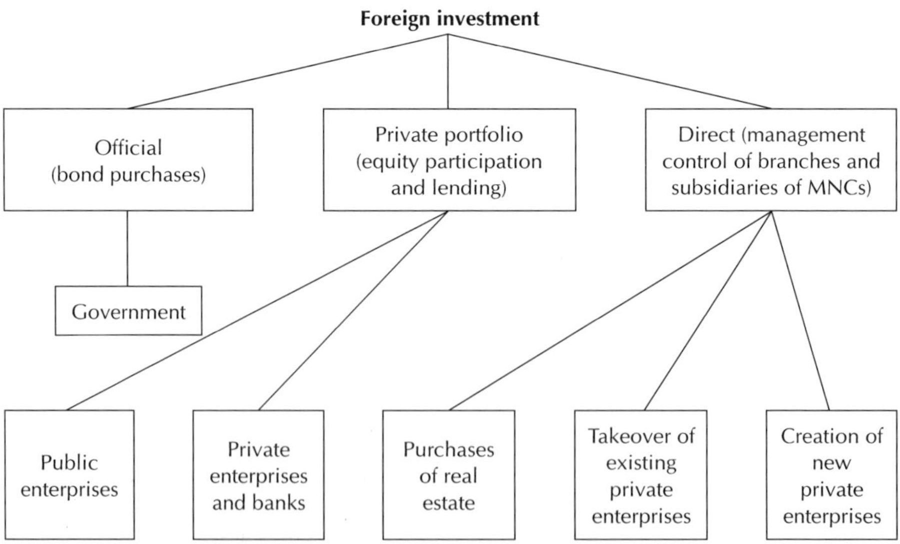

Figure 12.4 The nature of foreign investment.

Table 12.1 The 25 largest MNCs in the world, 1998 (ranked by foreign assets).

Rank	*Company*	*Industry*[a]	*Country*	*Foreign assets (US$ billion)*	*Total assets (US$ billion)*	*Foreign sales (US$ billion)*	*Percentage of total sales*	*Percentage foreign employment of total*
1	General Electric	Electronics	United States	128.6	335.9	28.7	28.6	44.4
2	General Motors	Motor vehicles	United States	73.1	246.7	49.9	32.1	n.a.
3	Royal Dutch/Shell Group[b]	Petroleum exploration, refining and distribution	Netherlands/United Kingdom	67.0	110.0	50.0	53.2	59.8
4	Ford Motor Company	Motor vehicles	United States	n.a.	237.5	43.8	30.3	49.6
5	Exxon Corporation[c]	Petroleum exploration, refining and distribution	United States	50.1	70.0	92.7	80.3	n.a.
6	Toyota	Motor vehicles	Japan	44.9	131.5	55.2	54.7	61.6
7	IBM	Computers	United States	43.6	86.1	46.4	56.8	51.5
8	BP AMOCO	Petroleum exploration, refining and distribution	United Kingdom	40.5	54.9	48.6	71.2	79.8
9	DaimlerChrysler	Motor vehicles	Germany	36.7	159.7	125.4	81.1	47.2
10	Nestlé SA	Food/beverages	Switzerland	35.6	41.1	51.2	98.5	97.3
11	Volkswagen Group	Motor vehicles	Germany	n.a.	70.1	52.3	65.2	47.8
12	Unilever	Food/beverages	Netherlands/United Kingdom	32.9	35.8	39.4	87.8	90.8
13	Suez Lyonnaise Des Eaux	Diversified/utility	France	n.a.	84.6	12.9	37.0	62.9
14	Wal-Mart Stores	Retailing	United States	30.2	50.0	19.4	14.1	n.a.
15	ABB	Electrical equipment	Switzerland	n.a.	32.9	23.1	83.4	94.8

Table 12.1 Continued.

Rank	*Company*	*Industry*[a]	*Country assets (US$ billion)*	*Foreign (US$ billion)*	*Total assets (US$ billion)*	*Foreign sales of total*	*Percentage employment of sales*	*Percentage foreign total*
16	Mobil Corporation[c]	Petroleum exploration, refining and distribution	United States	n.a.	42.8	29.7	55.5	53.3
17	Diageo Plc	Beverages	United Kingdom	27.9	46.3	10.5	84.7	84.9
18	Honda Motor Co Ltd	Motor vehicles	Japan	26.3	41.8	29.7	57.4	n.a.
19	Siemens AG	Electronics	Germany	n.a.	66.8	45.7	69.2	53.4
20	Sony Corporation	Electronics	Japan	n.a.	52.5	40.7	71.9	59.2
21	Renault SA	Motor vehicles	France	23.6	43.2	25.4	63.8	67.1
22	News Corporation	Media/publishing	Australia	22.9	33.6	10.5	89.7	n.a.
23	BMW AG	Motor vehicles	Germany	22.9	35.7	26.8	71.1	44.3
24	Mitsubishi Corporation	Diversified	Japan	21.7	74.9	43.5	37.5	31.5
25	Nissan Motor Co Ltd	Motor vehicles	Japan	21.6	57.2	25.8	47.4	n.a.

Source Adapted from United Nations Conference on Trade and Development, *World Investment Report 2000: Cross-border Mergers and Acquisitions and Development, Overview* (table 1).

Notes

a. Industry classification for companies follows the United States Standard Industrial Classification as used by the United States Securities and Exchange Commission (SEC).

b. Foreign assets, sales and employment refer to those outside Europe.

c. Mergers between Exxon and Mobil into ExxonMobil and Hoechst AG and Rhone-Poulenc SA into Aventis are not documented yet as they took place in 1999.

n.a. Data on foreign assets, foreign sales and foreign employment were not made available for the purpose of the study. In case of non-availability, they are estimated using secondary sources of information or on the basis of the ratios of foreign to total assets, foreign to total sales and foreign to total employment.

The list includes non-financial MNCs only. In some companies, foreign investors may hold a minority share of more than 10 per cent.

www.unctad.org/en/pub/ps1wir00.en.htm

The role of direct foreign investment and MNCs has been subject to considerable academic and political debate this century, stretching back to claims by Vladimir Lenin, the founder of the former Soviet Union, that foreign investment was inherently exploitative of host countries and represented the final stage of global capitalism. This hostile view of direct foreign investment and MNCs contrasts markedly to the attitudes of contemporary governments in the developed and developing world, including China.

Governments of all ideological persuasions are actively vying to attract ever greater shares of direct foreign investment these days. The reason is that although the domestic operations of MNCs are effectively foreign owned and controlled, MNCs can directly and indirectly generate productivity benefits through the transfer of technology and through product development. Domestic employees of MNCs are also exposed to international management practices and the presence of MNCs improves the level of competition in some domestic markets.

Greater internationalisation of economies' financial markets has rendered certain offshore borrowers (for example, governments and their instrumentalities) more prone to downgrading by the major international credit-rating agencies, such as the New York based agencies Moody's and Standard and Poors. If the nation's creditworthiness is diminished through downgrading, however, this really only makes it harder for domestic borrowers to continue borrowing at previous world interest rates since an additional risk premium may then be added to the interest rates charged by the foreign lenders. Of itself, however, a downgrading of creditworthiness makes foreign borrowing self-limiting.

3. Lessons from foreign investment theory

At the macroeconomic level, total foreign investment in all forms, net of investment abroad by domestic enterprises, is reflected in the capital-account surpluses that match the current-account deficits of host nations. What is generally not appreciated is that the more foreign investment an economy attracts, the higher its current-account deficit and foreign liabilities are likely to be.

With direct investment, MNCs often take real investment and funding decisions together. Thus, increased imports of capital goods recorded on the nation's trade account may be matched simultaneously by financial capital inflow from abroad recorded on the nation's international capital account to directly fund their purchase. However, MNCs sometimes fund the accumulation of capital through domestic borrowings.

Foreign capital inflow in aggregate, irrespective of its form, improves the nation's economic welfare to the extent that it frees an economy from the constraint of its own saving level. The amount of additional economic activity in a range of domestic activities would not be as great and overall GDP growth would be lower without the benefit of foreign investment.

By investing their excess saving in another economy, through equity participation, loans to resident firms, and purchases of real assets from residents, foreigners can finance much more domestic investment expenditure. Moreover, the pool of funds available for investment is also supplemented when real domestic assets, like property, are bought by foreigners. Hence, for a given positive savings level, greater foreign investment permits greater accumulation of real physical capital, which assists the future productive potential of the economy. Whenever the return on real capital in the host economy exceeds the rental cost of foreign capital, income per head should be higher because extra capital generates greater national output.

Consistent with the theoretical framework in Figure 12.3, a sufficient condition for this to be true is that the marginal productivity of the foreign-financed real capital used in the host economy be greater than the cost of the foreign funds used to finance its acquisition. Under such circumstances, capital account surpluses allow a higher living standard than otherwise. Similarly, when foreigners are paid a higher return on funds loaned abroad than they would earn at home, they too are made better off by running capital account deficits.

Concerns about rising foreign investment may be related to the nature of the investment activities which foreign funds finance, specifically whether foreign investment is directed toward expanding tradable or nontradable activities. However, even if foreign investment is funding nontradable activity, it should be noted that some nontradable industry sectors (for example, transport and business services) are inputs to tradable activities, so that foreign investment in such areas may ultimately improve the overall competitiveness of tradable industries.

Second, although foreign investment may directly finance the creation of new assets which would not otherwise be created, as with construction of buildings, the creation of those assets may simply have been motivated by the prospect of a capital gain on sale of the asset to other foreigners with no undesirable consequences for the local economy.

4. Concerns about foreign debt

Over recent decades, the behaviour of many economies' external accounts has been a major issue of macroeconomic policy. Current account imbalances and international investment statistics remain newsworthy for the United States, Japan and many other economies because they have major macroeconomic and financial implications.

One popular concern about growth in the size of an economy's current account deficit is that it becomes symptomatic of the economy 'living beyond its means'. Relatedly, rising international indebtedness associated with persistent current account deficits may be judged as unacceptably high. The 'living beyond its means' idea can actually be based on the national accounting identity:

$$Y = C + I + G + (X - M)$$

When rearranged, this relationship yields the 'absorption' equation derived earlier in Chapter 2. That is:

$$X - M = Y - (C + I + G)$$

which shows that the trade imbalance for a given period equals the difference between national expenditure and national income. To finance the extra spending, an increase in the level of external liabilities to foreigners has to be recorded in the foreign investment statistics. It is therefore definitionally true that a current account deficit shows an excess of spending over income per period. However, further evidence is required to establish that this difference can actually be attributed to excessive consumption expenditure, which is what living beyond one's means suggests in everyday parlance.

Consistent with the earlier analysis of saving, investment and the external accounts from Chapter 5, a trade deficit is persistently matched by foreign funds financing extra domestic investment activity. If the return on the additional domestic investment financed by borrowing overseas is greater than the servicing costs of the foreign borrowing, then the macroeconomic welfare rises to the extent that real income grows faster than otherwise. In effect, this just restates the major lesson of the theory of foreign investment outlined above.

At the microeconomic level, households cannot increase their private spending at a rate in excess of their income, without ultimately facing a showdown with their creditors. However, such an analogy falls down for the economy as a whole, since the economy is comprised of households and firms. Domestic firms produce the goods and services recorded as the production measure of GDP. In advanced economies, domestic firms also often account for the overwhelming share of overseas borrowings to finance, among other things, additional domestic investment spending, which of course increases the economy's longer-run productivity.

In advanced economies, calls for increased saving by households as a means of reducing current account deficits neglect that any sharp rise in saving at given income levels means that consumption has to be lower. In turn, this implies lower living standards for the households making the sacrifice. Although increased domestic saving would reduce interest and dividend payments transferred abroad by the next generation, the opportunity cost to the present generation in terms of present forgone consumption should also be recognised.

The notion that leaving bequests to future generations (who are likely to be richer than the present generation anyway, thanks to continual technology improvement) essentially neglects that consumption is really supposed to be the end goal of economic activity. One could quite justifiably ask: why less for us now and more for them later? After all, as the Cambridge Keynesian economist Joan Robinson once rather cynically asked, 'What has posterity ever done for us?'.

Any economy's external balance can change whenever its domestic saving or investment pattern changes or whenever saving or investment patterns change abroad. For instance, it is conceivable that if saving and investment prospects in the United States stayed exactly the same, but saving increased relatively faster abroad than domestic investment opportunities increased abroad, then the United States' external account balance would widen commensurately as some of the additional foreign saving was invested there. Under such circumstances, any further widening of the United States external imbalance would be due entirely to exogenous factors. Moreover, this could be a welcome result to the extent that additional international investment ultimately means a higher rate of domestic capital accumulation.

5. External debt and financial crises

In emerging economies with poorly developed financial systems, the absolute value of an economy's external debt may, however, be interpreted negatively, as a sign that the economy is on the verge of international insolvency. In this context, it is important to distinguish between sovereign, or official, debt and private debt, and consider whether there is any official underwriting of private sector debt (as often occurs in less-developed debtor countries with rudimentary capital markets). Governments of less-developed economies that have borrowed funds directly to finance public consumption expenditure sometimes find it an easier option, politically, to default rather than make unpopular decisions to cut back public expenditure or raise taxes in order to repay foreign debt commitments.

Escalating external debt is also more risky for emerging economies with under-developed financial sectors if it precipitates *capital flight*, defined as a sudden outflow of foreign capital. In practice, capital flight involves the liquidation by foreigners of financial instruments denominated in the local currency. Consequently, when it happens on a truly large scale, a significant proportion of the existing stock of foreign debt disappears and is accompanied by sharp exchange rate depreciations. Although depreciations improve competitiveness, which potentially reduces domestic expenditure on tradable goods and raises tradable production, problems experienced by the financial sector tend to stall domestic activity and generate recessions.

The adverse consequences of this exposure to international investment swings became starkly evident for many East Asian economies during their 1997–8 financial crisis. Although financial crises had earlier occurred in Latin America in the 1980s, the sharp reversal in 1997–8 of international capital inflows to previously fast-growing Asian economies easily represents the most significant international adjustment so far in this relatively new era of globally integrated capital markets.

This switch of foreign investment in conjunction with the flight of domestic investors' funds abroad caused very large depreciations against the United States dollar of the Indonesian rupiah, the Thai baht, the

Malaysian ringgit, the Philippines peso and the South Korean won. This sudden reversal of short-term international capital flows to the East Asian economies has prompted calls to limit the scale of such flows. Specifically, tighter restrictions should be put in place by the affected economies to limit the quantum of foreign funds that are borrowed and lent across their borders.

What this interpretation of events tends to ignore, however, is that without earlier capital inflow from abroad, Asian economies would be on a considerably lower plateau of economic development. Thanks in large part to globalisation, average income increased four-fold in Malaysia, Indonesia and Thailand over the three decades from 1965 to 1995 and a remarkable seven-fold in South Korea. These growth rates were significantly above historical averages recorded in times predating the present era of globalisation and were unparalleled by any other group of economies elsewhere in the world during the twentieth century.

Exchange rate management policies gave international investors a misplaced sense of exchange rate stability because many East Asian central banks had for some years successfully limited exchange rate variation, although there had been substantial once-only changes in previous decades. Weak prudential supervision of financial institutions in these economies was also a major contributing factor to financial crises.

Domestic banks had often been established with insufficient capitalisation, and incompletely reformed financial systems were prone to rapidly expanding bank credit and high levels of unhedged foreign debt. Similarly, provision of economic information on the nature of government–business relations and the size of external debt exposure and non-performing loans was limited, evidence of a general lack of transparency in financial dealings.

NATIONAL BALANCE SHEET ANALYSIS

Instead of focusing on the impact of foreign investment on GDP, a flow measure of macroeconomic welfare, it is also possible to examine changes in the net foreign investment position strictly in terms of macroeconomic stock measures.

As outlined earlier in Chapter 2, national wealth is just the excess of residents' total assets over the nation's external liabilities. National wealth may be estimated by constructing a national balance sheet. One side should include all national assets that potentially may be sold to foreigners; the other side should include outstanding claims on those assets by both residents and non-residents. All domestic assets and total claims to domestic assets should be valued at market prices.

National balance sheets including macroeconomic stock measures should be an integral part of national accounting. They are tied directly to aggregate flows through the national capital account, which records saving and investment aggregates, these in turn having been derived from the income and product accounts. While total domestic investment equals domestic saving plus net capital inflow, national wealth equals tangible assets less foreign liabilities.

As complements to the flow national income measures, national balance sheets complete the full System of National Accounts (SNA), as recommended by the United Nations. Although not yet routinely published by statistical agencies, they should include all assets and liabilities which have market values and can be expressed in dollar terms. For a globally integrated economy, market values should ideally reflect the prices bid for domestic assets if offered for sale on international goods, services and financial markets.

In practice, the tangible capital stock and the value of dwellings of the domestic private and public sectors can be recorded on the assets side of the national ledger, along with the economy's investment abroad, which represents residents' claims to foreign assets. Claims on domestic assets can be subdivided between foreign claims (gross external debt of the private and public sectors, and foreign-equity investment) and residents' claims. The total value of residents' assets less foreign claims to those assets is equivalent to national wealth.

In the following balance sheet, the private sector capital stock is the sum of the business capital and dwelling capital series at market prices. Included within business capital are non-dwelling construction (offices, factories, civil engineering, hotels) and equipment (office equipment, industrial machinery, vehicles, aircraft, ships). Dwelling capital data covers houses, flats and home units.

Some economists may argue that consumer durables (mainly passenger motor vehicles and household contents) should not be recorded in estimates of national assets since by national accounting convention these form part of measured consumption, which reduces the domestic pool of loanable funds available for investment. However, consumer durables should be included on the basis that these items are conceptually more akin to investment goods because they yield a stream of benefits through time, rather than ordinary consumption items (such as food, clothing, entertainment and petrol). Furthermore, consumer durables may, if necessary, be sold second-hand to extinguish liabilities.

The public capital stock and public housing stock series recorded as separate asset items are valued at replacement cost as market values do not exist. Gross foreign investment data measures foreign ownership of domestically issued bonds, equities, other debt instruments, dwellings and land. Valued at market prices, gross foreign investment represents total foreign claims on assets located in the host economy. Investment abroad is added to private and public sector capital asset items. 'Official' foreign investment includes the foreign assets of governments, whereas 'non-official' foreign investment includes the assets of private and public trading enterprises.

A hypothetical balance sheet, showing the value of stock changes, is shown in Table 12.2. In this example, expressed in relation to total assets, the economy's external debt is less than 10 per cent, which is relatively low

Table 12.2 National balance sheet.

National balance sheet ($US billion)					
Assets	*2000*	*2005*	*Claims on assets*	*2000*	*2005*
Private sector			Gross external debt		
Capital stock	215	430	Non-official	15	85
Dwellings	330	545	Official	10	25
Consumer durables	45	60			
	590	1035		25	110
Public sector			Foreign equity	35	60
Capital stock	175	220			
Dwellings	10	15	Foreign investment	60	170
	185	235			
Investment abroad					
Non-official	10	45			
Official	10	20	National wealth	735	1185
	20	65			
Total assets	795	1335			

Note The private sector capital stock at market prices is defined as the sum of equipment, non-dwelling construction and inventories.

in a gearing sense. The rise in the value of private sector assets dwarfed rises in gross external debt and foreign equity claims on real tangible assets domiciled in the economy.

This approach can put an economy's external liabilities and foreign debt in better national-accounting perspective. In the example, there is a rise in the external-debt component of liabilities, but it is also evident that real national asset values grew by substantially more than total external liabilities. Hence, the economy became better off in terms of the value of its real national wealth. Clearly, as a production unit, the economy geared up in a financial sense, but because the macroeconomic value of its assets far exceeded the rise in its external liabilities, higher economy-wide leverage can be favourable.

CONCLUSION

Discussion of the behaviour of an economy's external accounts often centres on current account balances, and ignores the matching capital account balances which can allow real investment and hence national output growth to be higher than otherwise. Similarly, a focus on the rise in external liabilities, reflecting a higher degree of economic integration with the rest of the world, can enable higher national wealth.

Many countries experienced large current account imbalances in earlier times without suffering adverse macroeconomic consequences. For instance, world capital flows and hence the external imbalances of many nations were also quite large from the late eighteenth century until the First World War, during the so-called golden era of free trade. Canada, for instance, ran a current account deficit of some 13 per cent of GDP between 1910 and 1913. More recently, Singapore had current account deficits reaching over 20 per cent of GDP in the early 1970s.

In open economies, large external imbalances can be acceptable on the grounds that the distribution of international investment opportunities does not necessarily coincide with the distribution of world saving. This is provided the financial systems that channel international saving are sound and that they closely monitor borrowing and lending risks.

International capital flows in effect act like a vehicle carrying an economy from one stage of development to another. To get to the destination of higher national income, funds need to flow through the financial system, which plays a similar role to a highway. This vehicle–highway–destination analogy is a useful device for thinking about how best to minimise occasional crises, or accidents, that occur on the way to higher economic growth.

One crisis minimisation option is to tax the use of vehicles. In this vein, a so called 'Tobin tax', originally proposed by James Tobin (1978), would apply to currency conversions related to short-term international capital flows. This tax would be difficult to implement worldwide, however, and avoidance problems would surface. Alternatively, the best way to minimise accidents while simultaneously allowing maximum travel is to upgrade the highway to make travel safer, as well as providing more advisory signs along the way.

In effect, this will only be achieved through major redesign of the practices governing the way in which many financial institutions operate in emerging economies. This could include more private sector involvement in preventing and resolving crises ('bail ins'), greater financial market disclosure, tighter capital adequacy and supervision rules. In the wake of the Asian financial crisis, further financial globalisation is not likely to proceed as quickly again in many emerging countries until these financial reforms are firmly in place and recognised as such by the international investors, including major multinational banks.

Summary

1. This chapter has examined international factors that influence economic growth in open economies.

2. The theory of foreign investment highlights the macroeconomic benefits of international capital movements. It demonstrates that there are mutual national

income gains as a consequence of real foreign investment flows which allow the domestic capital stock to be higher.

3. Multinational corporations (MNCs) are a vehicle for direct foreign investment in many advanced and emerging economies. MNCs usually generate important productivity benefits through technology transfer and product development.

4. Current account deficits and rising foreign debt levels in advanced economies are not necessarily problematic, as they may simply signify welfare enhancing international trade in saving.

5. On the other hand, capital flight from emerging economies with large foreign debt levels can fracture fragile financial systems, reduce investment and cause recessions.

6. National balance sheets put foreign liabilities in perspective by setting them against the value of the economy's real assets.

Further reading

Goldsmith, R. (1985) *Comparative National Balance Sheets*, Chicago, IL: University of Chicago Press.

Makin, A. (2000) *Global Finance and the Macroeconomy*, London: Palgrave, chapters 4, 8 and 9.

United Nations (1988) *Transnational Corporations in World Development*, New York: United Nations.

Bibliography

Abel, A. (1990) 'Consumption and investment', in B. Friedman and F. Hahn (eds) *Handbook of Monetary Economics*, vol. 2, Amsterdam: North-Holland, chapter 14, pp. 726–78.

Agenor, P. and Montiel, P. (19) *Development Macroeconomics*, Princeton, NJ: Princeton University Press.

Ando, A. and Modigliani, F. (1963) 'The life cycle hypothesis of saving: aggregate implications and tests', *American Economic Review*, **53** (1), 55–84.

Argy, V. (1981) *The Postwar International Money Crisis: An Analysis*, London: George Allen and Unwin.

Argy, V. (1994) *International Macroeconomics: Theory and Policy*, London: Routledge.

Azariades, C. (1993) *Intertemporal Macroeconomics*, London: Blackwell.

Balassa, B. (1964) 'The purchasing power parity doctrine: a re-appraisal', *Journal of Political Economy*, **72** (6), 584–96.

Barro, R. (1989) 'The Ricardian approach to budget deficits', *Journal of Economic Perspectives*, **3**, 37–54.

Barro, R. (1995) *Economic Growth*, New York: McGraw Hill.

Barro, R. (1997) *Macroeconomics*, 5th edn, Cambridge, MA: MIT Press.

Bird, G. (1998) *International Macroeconomics*, 2nd edn, London: Palgrave.

Blanchard, O. and Fischer, S. (1989) *Lectures on Macroeconomics*, Cambridge, MA: MIT Press.

Branson, W. and Henderson, D. (1985) 'The specification and influence of asset markets', in R. Jones and P. Kenen (eds) *Handbook of International Economics*, vol. 2, Amsterdam: North-Holland.

Bryant, R. (1987) *International Financial Intermediation*, Washington, DC: Brookings Institution.

Burtless, G., Lawrence, R., Litan, R. and Shapiro, R. (eds) (1998) *Globaphobia: Confronting Fears About Open Trade*, Washington, DC: Brookings Institution.

Caves, R. (1982) *Multinational Enterprise and Economic Analysis*, Cambridge: Cambridge University Press.

Claassen, E. (1996) *Global Monetary Economics*, Oxford: Oxford University Press.

Clements, K. (1981) 'The monetary approach to exchange rate determination: a geometric analysis', *Weltwertschaftliches Archiv*, **117** (1), 20–25.

Connolly, M. (1978) 'The monetary approach to the open economy: the fundamental theory', in Putnam, B. and D. Wilford (eds) *The Monetary Approach to International Adjustment*, New York: Praeger.

Contractor, F. (1998) *Economic Transformation in Emerging Economies: The Role of Investment, Trade and Finance*, Amsterdam: Elsevier.

Corden, M. (1994) *Economic Policy, Exchange Rates and the International System*, Oxford: Oxford University Press.

Cuthbertson, K. and Talor, M. (1987) *Macroeconomic Systems*, Oxford: Basil Blackwell, chapters 3 and 4.

De Grauwe, P. (1989) *International Money: Post-War Trends and Theories*, Oxford: Oxford University Press.

Dornbusch, R. (1980) *Open Economy Macroeconomics*, New York: Basic Books.

Dornbusch, R. and Giovannini, A. (1990) 'Monetary policy in an open economy', in Friedman, B. and F. Hahn (eds) *Handbook of Monetary Economics*, vol. 2, Amsterdam: North-Holland, chapter 23, pp. 1231–303.

The Economist (1997) 'One world?', 18 October, p. 99.

Eichengreen, B. (1994) 'History of the international monetary system', in F. Van Der Ploeg, *The Handbook of International Macroeconomics*, Oxford: Basil Blackwell.

Eichengreen, B. (1996) *Globalising Capital: History of the International Monetary System*, Princeton, NJ: Princeton University Press.

Eisner, R. (1988) 'Extended accounts for national income and product', *Journal of Economic Literature*, **26**, 1611–84.

Feldstein, M. and Horioka, C. (1980) 'Domestic saving and international capital flows', *Economic Journal*, **90** (June), 314–29.

Fischer, S. (1990) 'Rules versus discretion in monetary policy', in Friedman, B. and F. Hahn (eds) *Handbook of Monetary Economics*, Amsterdam: North-Holland.

Fisher, I. (1930) *The Theory of Interest*, New York: Macmillan.

Fleming, J. (1962) 'Domestic and financial policy under fixed and under floating exchange rates', *IMF Staff Papers*, **9**, 369–79.

Frenkel, J. and Mussa, M. (1985) 'Asset markets, exchange rates and the balance of payments', in R. Jones and P. Kenen (eds) *Handbook of International Economics*, vol. 2, Amsterdam: North-Holland.

Frenkel, J. and Razin, A. (1987) *Fiscal Policies and the World Economy*, Cambridge, MA: MIT Press.

Friedman, B. and Hahn, F. (eds) (1990) *Handbook of Monetary Economics*, Amsterdam: North-Holland.

Friedman, M. (1953) 'The case for flexible exchange rates', in M. Friedman, *Essays in Positive Economics*, Chicago, IL: University of Chicago Press.

Friedman, M. (1957) *A Theory of the Consumption Function*, Princeton, NJ: Princeton University Press.

Gandolfo, G. (2001) *International Finance and Open Economy Macroeconomics*, Berlin: Springer-Verlag.

Gartner, M. (1993) *Macroeconomics under Flexible Exchange Rates*, London: Harvester Wheatsheaf.

Goldsmith, R. (1985) *Comparative National Balance Sheets*, Chicago, IL: University of Chicago Press.

Hayashi, F. (1982) 'Tobin's marginal q and average q: a Neo-Classical interpretation', *Econometrica*, **50** (1), 213–24.

International Monetary Fund (1977) *The Monetary Approach to the Balance of Payments*, Washington, DC: IMF.

International Monetary Fund (various dates) *World Economic Outlook*, Washington, DC: IMF.

International Monetary Fund (1993) *Balance of Payments Manual*, 5th edn, Washington, DC: IMF.

Isard, P. (1995) *Exchange Rate Economics*, New York: Cambridge University Press.

Juttner, J. and Hawtrey, K. (1997) *Financial Markets, Money and Risk*, 4th edn, Melbourne: Addison Wesley Longman.

Kenen, P. (1988) *Managing Exchange Rates*, Routledge, New York.
Kenen, P. (1995) (ed.) *Understanding Interdependence: The Macroeconomics of the Open Economy*, Princeton, NJ: Princeton University Press.
Keynes, J. M. (1936) *The General Theory of Employment, Interest and Money*, London: Macmillan.
Krueger, A. (1983) *Exchange Rate Determination*, Cambridge: Cambridge University Press.
Krugman, P. (1989) *Exchange Rate Instability*, Cambridge, MA: MIT Press.
Layton, A. and Makin, A. (1993) 'Estimates of the macroeconomic impact of foreign investment in Australia', *International Economic Journal*, **7** (4), 35–42.
Lucas, R. (1988) 'On the mechanics of economic development', *Journal of Monetary Economics*, **22,** 3–42.
Makin, A. (1988) 'Targeting Australia's current account: a new mercantilism?', *Economic Analysis and Policy*, **18** (2), 199–211.
Makin, A. (1989) 'Is the current account deficit sustainable?', *Australian Economic Review*, 2nd quarter, 29–33.
Makin, A. (1990) 'The real federal budget imbalance', *Economic Record*, **66** (194), 249–53.
Makin, A. (1994) 'Open economy measures of wealth and Hicksian national income', *Open Economies Review*, **5,** 361–9.
Makin, A. (1996) *Open Economy Macroeconomics*, Melbourne: Addison Wesley Longman.
Makin, A. (1998) 'A dependent economy model of public expenditure and the exchange rate', *International Review of Economics and Finance*, **7** (4), 453–63.
Makin, A. (1999) 'The great East Asian capital flow reversal: reasons, responses amd ramifications', *The World Economy*, **22** (3), 407–19.
Makin, A. (2000) *Global Finance and the Macroeconomy*, London: Palgrave.
Mankiw, G. and Romer, R. (eds) (1991) *The New Keynesian Economics*, vols I and II, Cambridge, MA: MIT Press.
Mankiw, G., Romer, D. and Weil, D. (1992) 'A contribution to the empirics of economic growth', *Quarterly Journal of Economics* **107,** 407–37.
Marston, R. (1995) *International Financial Integration*, New York: Cambridge University Press.
McKibbin, W. and Sachs, J. (1991) *Global Linkages: Macroeconomic Interdependence and Co-operation in the World Economy*, Washington, DC: Brooking Institution.
McKinnon, R. (1979) *Money in International Exchange*, Oxford: Oxford University Press.
Mill, J. S. (1848) *Principles of Political Economy*, London.
Modigliani, F. (1970) 'The life cycle hypothesis of saving and inter-country differences in the saving ratio', in W. Eltis, M. Scott and J. Wolfe (eds) *Growth and Trade*, Oxford: Clarendon Press.
Mundell, R. (1963) 'Capital mobility and stabilization policy under fixed and flexible exchange rates', *Canadian Journal of Economics and Political Science*, **29,** 475–85.
Newman, P., Milgate, M. and Eatwell, J. (1992) *The New Palgrave Dictionary of Money and Finance*, London: Macmillan.
Niehans, J. (1984) *International Monetary Economics*, Oxford: Philip Allan.
North, D. and Thomas, R. (1973) *The Rise of the Western World: A New Economic History*, Cambridge: Cambridge University Press.
Obstfeld, M. and Rogoff, K. (1996) *Foundations of International Macroeconomics*, Cambridge, MA: MIT Press.
Olson, M. (1982) *The Rise and Decline of Nations: Economic Growth, Stagflation and Social Rigidities*, New Haven, CT: Yale University Press.

Prachowny, M. (1984) *Macroeconomic Analysis for Small Open Economies*, Oxford: Oxford University Press.
Prachowny, M. (1994) *The Goals of Macroeconomic Policy*, London: Routledge.
Romer, D. (2000) *Advanced Macroeconomics*, New York: McGraw Hill.
Romer, P. (1994) 'The origins of endogenous growth', *Journal of Economic Perspectives*, **8** (1), 3–22.
Salter, W. (1959) 'Internal and external balance: the role of expenditure and price effects', *Economic Record*, **35** (71), 226–38.
Scarth, W. (1988) *Macroeconomics: An Introduction to Advanced Methods*, Toronto: Harcourt Brace Jovanovich.
Seater, J. (1993) 'Ricardian equivalence', *Journal of Economic Literature*, **31** (1), 142–90.
Solow, R. (1994) 'Perspectives on growth theory', *Journal of Economic Perspectives*, **8** (1), 45–54.
Solow, R. (2000) *Growth Theory: An Exposition*, Oxford: Oxford University Press.
Swan, T. (1960) 'Economic control in a dependent economy', *Economic Record*, **36** (73), 51–66.
Taylor, J. and Woodford, M. (eds) (1999) *Handbook of Macroeconomics*, Amsterdam: Elsevier.
Tinbergen, J. (1952) *On the Theory of Economic Policy*, Amsterdam: North-Holland.
Tobin, J. (1969) 'A general equilibrium approach to monetary theory', *Journal of Money, Credit and Banking*, **1** (1), 15–29.
Tobin, J. (1978) 'A proposal for international monetary reform', *Eastern Economic Journal*, **4**, 153–9.
Tobin, J. (1982) *Asset Accumulation and Economic Activity*, Chicago, IL: University of Chicago Press.
Tsiang, S. (1989) 'Loanable funds', in Eatwell, J., Milgate, M. and P. Newman (eds) *The New Palgrave Dictionary of Money*, London: Macmillan, pp. 190–4.
United Nations (1949) *International Capital Movements During the Inter-War Period*, New York: United Nations.
United Nations (1988) *Transnational Corporations in World Development*, New York: United Nations.
United Nations (1993) *A System of National Accounts*, prepared under the auspices of the Inter-Secretariat Working Group on National Accounts, Brussels: Office for Official Publications of the European Communities.
Van der Ploeg, F. (1994) *The Handbook of International Macroeconomics*, Oxford: Blackwell.
Van Horne, J. (1990) *Financial Market Rates and Flows*, 3rd edn, New York: Prentice Hall.
White, G., Walsh, M., Makin, A. and Valentine, T. (eds) (1994) *Should We Worry About the Foreign Debt?*, Sydney: Centre for Independent Studies.
Williamson, J. (1996) 'Globalisation, convergence and history', *Journal of Economic History*, **56** (2), 277–306.
World Bank (various dates) *Global Development Finance*, Washington, DC: World Bank.

Index